P9-DIA-107

Work and Integrity draws on The Carnegie Foundation for the Advancement of Teaching's Preparation for the Professions Program, a comparative study of professional education in medicine, nursing, law, engineering, and the preparation of the clergy. The results of this study are to be published by Jossey-Bass in a new Preparation for the Professions Series.

Forthcoming books in the series are:

Educating Clergy

Educating Engineers

Educating Lawyers

Educating Nurses

Educating Physicians

Work and Integrity

William M. Sullivan

Foreword by Lee S. Shulman

Work and Integrity

The Crisis and Promise of Professionalism in America

Second Edition

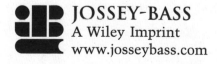

JOSSEY-BASS
A Wiley Imprint
www.josseybass.com

Published by Jossey-Bass
A Wiley Imprint
989 Market Street, San Francisco, CA 94103-1741   www.josseybass.com

Jossey-Bass books and products are available through most bookstores. To contact Jossey-Bass directly call our Customer Care Department within the U.S. at 800-956-7739, outside the U.S. at 317-572-3986 or fax 317-572-4002.

Jossey-Bass also publishes its books in a variety of electronic formats. Some content that appears in print may not be available in electronic books.

Library of Congress Cataloging-in-Publication Data

Sullivan, William M.
  Work and integrity : the crisis and promise of professionalism in America / William M. Sullivan.— 2nd ed.
     p. cm.
  Includes bibliographical references and index.
  ISBN 0-7879-7458-7
  1. Professional ethics—United States. 2. Professions—United States. 3. Professional socialization—United States. 4. Integrity. I. Title.
  BJ1725.S85 2004
  174—dc22
                              2004017940

Printed in the United States of America
SECOND EDITION
HB Printing   10 9 8 7 6 5 4 3 2 1

Contents

Foreword

What is the relationship signaled by the juxtaposition of *work* with *integrity*? Are they two elements in a zero-sum game where achievement of one precludes accomplishment of the other? Are they a matched pair, like love and marriage, or Abbott and Costello? Or is the relationship between the excellence of work and the integrity with which it is enacted a different matter entirely? This is a question that has arisen, in a number of forms, during the past several years in which my colleagues and I at The Carnegie Foundation for the Advancement of Teaching have been actively studying education in the professions. In his capacity as a senior scholar entrusted with the responsibility to look across our work on the professions and to ask the bigger cross-professional questions, William Sullivan has wrestled with this relationship from the very beginning of his appointment at the Foundation. Indeed, he has been asking that question for most of his career as philosopher, social scientist, and educator.

In a small conference room in a large public research university, I met with a group of senior students in mechanical engineering. I asked them to imagine that they meet a stranger who, upon learning that they are studying to be engineers, asks, "What's an engineer?" The students deliberated for a few moments and then responded: "An engineer is someone who uses mathematics and the sciences to mess with the world by designing and making things that other people will want to buy and use—and once you mess with the world, you are responsible for the mess you've made."

This group of novice professionals, still actively learning what they seek to profess, offered a definition of engineering that could well serve as a prototype for all professions. In their succinct definition, they captured aspects of the intellectual, practical, and moral dimensions of engineering work. The questions that animate the Carnegie Foundation's inquiries are questions about the educational genesis of professional work and about understanding the cognitive, the technical, and the ethical aspects and their integration in practice. To what extent was that idealistic definition exemplified in the educational practices of the professional school of engineering in which they studied?

Later that day, I was observing in a large lecture hall, where approximately 130 senior engineering students were gathered for a meeting of their senior design course. The instructor, a young assistant professor only four years beyond his Ph.D. from another prominent public doctoral university, had brought to class two obsolete pieces of modern technology—a six-year-old coffee maker and a six-month-old cell phone. He had taken each piece of technology apart and had arrayed its parts on tables in the front of the room. He had also photographed the assortment and was displaying the photo on a large screen in front of the hall. He invited the students to come and inspect the parts. He then asked them to consider two questions: "Now that these two artifacts are past their useful years, what will we do with their constituent parts? Even more important, how might they have been designed otherwise?" As the students had informed me earlier, they (or the members of their profession) had successfully messed with the world by designing technologies that people had bought and used. Now they were responsible for the mess they had made. In this engineering design course, we had observed quite vividly the effective integration of a pedagogy of engineering work with a pedagogy of engineering integrity. Moreover, we can see the seeds of a new "signature pedagogy" in this episode, as both students and faculty develop the habit of asking themselves, from the perspective of quality of environment and social responsibility, "How might this have been designed and manufactured otherwise?"

Another moral dimension of professional pedagogy deserves our attention. For those pedagogies that attempt to mirror the real complexities of practice in their teaching—as is the case in legal clinics, clinical medicine, or student teaching—we face a serious problem: How do we give to future professionals the indispensable opportunities to practice their work in realistic settings, without unduly subjecting clients to unacceptable levels of danger and exposure to harm? *Complications: A Surgeon's Notes on an Imperfect Science*, the lovely book of essays by Atul Gawande, offers many examples of the tension between opportunities to learn and dangers to the public that necessarily characterize the education of surgeons. As with many other professions, surgical education ultimately resorts to the time-honored triptych of "watch one, do one, teach one" as a teaching strategy. Many forms of professional preparation (though not law) can be characterized as processes in which students move through the stages of an academically controlled apprenticeship: from the academic study of texts and examples, to the observation of practice, to assistance with practice, to highly supervised and monitored practice, to increasingly autonomous practice. The moral challenge to the pedagogy is to guide the students through these increasingly responsible levels of practice, while sustaining the social contract with clients that guarantees zealous concern for their well-being and safety. Moreover, the ways in which educators manage those apprenticeships are simultaneously modeling for, and hence teaching, future practitioners about their own responsibilities to their clients, their communities, and the general society.

When we at the Carnegie Foundation decided to initiate a systematic and comparative study of education across the professions, we were confronted with the challenge of attracting two kinds of individuals to lead that effort. First, we would need top figures from each profession that we studied to design and conduct the investigations of each profession's instructional work. Second, we would need to designate right from the start several scholars whose roles would be crosscutting, comparative and synthetic, and whose challenge would be the integration of the individual studies. William Sullivan has played, and continues to inhabit, that role.

We knew that Bill Sullivan was fully capable of leading such an effort because his book *Work and Integrity* had dealt with the challenge of professionalism in contemporary society with such wisdom and eloquence. As we envisioned the series of books that will report what we have learned in our ongoing studies of preparation for the professions, we recognized the need for an opening volume, for a book that would set the stage for the set of investigations that would follow. When Sullivan offered to rewrite *Work and Integrity* in order to reflect what we had been learning in our studies, but in a manner continuous with his earlier book, we knew that we had the perfect way to introduce this body of work.

The integration of work and integrity can be problematic right from the beginning of professional education. Indeed, one of the general theories that drives education in the law is that thinking about justice and equity interferes with the development of the analytical reasoning needed by lawyers. In his classic *The Bramble Bush: Some Lectures on Law and Its Study*, a set of lectures delivered to law students in 1929, the eminent legal scholar and teacher Karl Llewellyn described the pedagogical challenges of the first year of law school:

> The first year . . . aims to drill into you the more essential techniques of handling cases. It lays a foundation simultaneously for law school and law practice. It aims, in the old phrase, to get you to "thinking like a lawyer." The hardest job of the first year is to lop off your common sense, to knock your ethics into temporary anesthesia. Your view of social policy, your sense of justice—to knock these out of you along with woozy thinking, along with ideas all fuzzed along their edges. You are to acquire ability to think precisely, to analyze coldly, to within a body of materials that is given, to see, and see only, and to manipulate, the machinery of the law. It is not easy thus to turn human beings into lawyers. Neither is it safe. For a mere legal machine is a social danger. Indeed, a mere legal machine is not

even a good lawyer. It lacks insight and judgment. It lacks the power to draw into hunching that body of intangibles that lie in social experience. None the less, it is an almost impossible process to achieve the technique without sacrificing some humanity first. Hence, as rapidly as we may, we shall cut under all the attributes of *homo*, through the *sapiens* we shall then duly endeavor to develop and thus regain the *homo* [p. 101].

Llewellyn may be overly sanguine about the capacity of most new professionals to turn integrity on and off like a light switch. Nevertheless, if learning the technical crafts associated with the learned professions—from medicine and accounting to engineering and architecture—generally entails a disconnect between work and integrity, then the challenge presented by Sullivan must be taken very seriously.

In the first edition of *Work and Integrity*, Bill Sullivan wrote a paragraph I have never forgotten. It is a constant reminder that the very idea of integrity is incomplete without the conflicts and tensions inherent in significant professional work.

Integrity is never a given, but always a quest that must be renewed and reshaped over time. It demands considerable individual self-awareness and self-command. Yet, it also depends for its realization upon the availability of actual social possibilities, since some situations clearly make it more likely that an individual can achieve integrity than others. . . . In fact, the qualities of integrity and the demands of professional life are in this way remarkably congruent. Integrity of vocation demands the balanced combination of individual autonomy with integration into shared purposes. Individual talent needs to blend with the best common standards of performance, while the individual must exercise personal judgment as to the proper application of these communal standards in a responsible way [p. 220].

Sullivan argues that integrity can only be achieved under conditions of competing imperatives. Unless you are torn between your lawyerly duties as a zealous advocate for your client and your communal responsibilities as an officer of the court, you cannot accomplish integrity. Unless you are confronted with the tensions inherent in the practice of any profession, the conditions for integrity are not present: "Integrity is never a given, but always a quest that must be renewed and reshaped over time."

Sullivan's lesson is being learned painfully in the accounting community. The past few years have not been kind to this profession. From Enron to Tyco, the public has felt betrayed by its public accountants, to the point where one of the world's largest accounting firms, Arthur Andersen, actually went under. Not surprisingly, the leaders of the profession have felt the need to confront these problems and to deal with them publicly. S. Scott Voynich became chair of the board of the American Institute of Certified Public Accountants (AICPA) in 2003 and chose to address these issues in his acceptance speech to the members of his profession.

> How can we make decisions that are right for a membership of immense diversity and for a public that relies on the work and integrity of CPAs? How do we balance our role as advocate for an honored profession with our role as advocate for the public interest? After much debate, and analysis, we have come to a surprisingly simple yet challenging conclusion: We must balance these roles, because that balance, that tension, is integral to the process. And this very balance brings us to one simple principle to guide our path into the future. . . . Our anchor for dealing with change comes from our core values. And of those values, integrity is the driving force. [O]ur value is not given to us because of our technical abilities; our value is attributed to us by the way we practice our profession and live by a code of ethics in all aspects of our daily lives. Integrity—by definition, a rigid adherence to a code of behavior—is key to our profession. We are expected to live by a code of ethics, which serves as the North Star for all of our activities.

The late John Gardner served as president of both the Carnegie Corporation and the Carnegie Foundation, was a member of

Lyndon Johnson's cabinet, and invented marvelous organizational instruments of communal integrity such as Common Cause and Independent Sector. He was once challenged to provide a succinct definition of democracy. He replied with a definition in nine words that eloquently captured the essential tensions and the social contract that ennoble a democratic society: "Liberty and duty. Freedom and responsibility. That's the deal."

I believe that the message of this superb book can be summarized with equal economy. I believe this is how Bill Sullivan would define the essence of profession and its social contract with the community: "Autonomy and obligation. Work and integrity. That's the deal."

In the Carnegie Foundation's studies of education in the professions, initiated by this lovely volume, we intend to demonstrate how the professionals, on whom we all depend for so much of the quality of our lives, can learn to balance those technical, intellectual, and moral equations. That's what professions do. That, indeed, is the deal.

Lee S. Shulman
Stanford, California
September, 2004

About the Author

William M. Sullivan is senior scholar at The Carnegie Foundation for the Advancement of Teaching. Since 1999 he has served as director and series editor for the Preparation for the Professions Program, whose studies compare education across the professions of law, engineering, the clergy, nursing, and medicine, drawing out common themes and identifying distinct practices in the various fields.

The author of the first edition of *Work and Integrity: The Crisis and Promise of Professionalism in America,* and coauthor of the best-selling *Habits of the Heart: Individualism and Commitment in American Life* as well as its sequel, *The Good Society,* Sullivan received his doctorate in philosophy from Fordham University and was professor of philosophy at La Salle University before joining the Carnegie Foundation. He has published extensively in social and political theory and ethics as well as education and the professions. He lives in San Francisco.

Work and Integrity

Introduction

The Crisis and Promise of Professionalism

On first impression, the professions make an odd fit with the contemporary world of work. An economy whose leading sectors have come to live by continuous and rapid innovation is now recasting the conditions of work in its image. The trends point toward a more enterprising, if also increasingly insecure, future in which workers will need to continuously upgrade their skills, repositioning and reinventing themselves in response to fast-changing markets. Some see these developments as increasing opportunity and have made a shibboleth of the individual's "competitiveness" and strategic "flexibility" in career. Workers, we are told, must surf the breaking waves of ever more tightly competitive markets in talent and skill. Experts agree that new technologies of information, research, and communication have set this economic vortex in motion.[1] But the demiurge most directly responsible is thought to be that highly educated portion of the workforce variously styled as knowledge workers, symbolic analysts, or the creative class.[2]

The Persistence of the Professions

Professionals such as engineers, academics, scientists, lawyers, and physicians have been central to the emergence of the high-technology, global economy. Yet the basic operating structures of the professions—corporate membership, controlled markets for their services, and monopolistic practices in training and recruitment—seem peculiar, if not antithetical to most extolled new patterns of work. So it is perhaps not surprising that professionalism rarely figures in popular description of the future of work. Professions such as law, medicine, and academe have established for themselves shelters from pure market competition, a privilege granted on the basis of specific expertise. Law and medicine, in particular, have long been prestigious occupations, and lawyers and doctors have long served as community leaders as well as experts in their specialized domains. But they have held such positions of honor on the basis of a social contract with the public they serve.

This contract is at the core of professionalism. Not only medicine and law but fields such as engineering, architecture, accounting, the clergy, nursing, and teaching operate within explicit legal regulation. In exchange, professions have received authority to control entry into their domains and key aspects of how they do their work. Where, then, do professions fit in a future depicted as a globalizing march toward a "frictionless capitalism" that is based upon information and communications technology?[3] What could be the role of professionalism in a future in which individuals are to shed one occupational identity for another as smoothly as they should migrate among disparate domains of activity? Are professions a doomed anachronism in this new economy of work?

Professionalism has become something of a contemporary preoccupation. The public's persistent worry about professionals, often somewhat misleadingly described as a concern about professional "ethics," is in fact a suspicion that professionals have broken faith with the public. Frequently, especially in popular journalism, the accusation is that professionals have abandoned the public; they have become self-protective and aloof from the significance of what they do. Lawyers have come to be the all-too-frequent butt of mean-spirited humor. Alarms are sounding in medicine, while the quality of America's schoolteachers has become a topic of anguish. The integrity of the accounting profession—and not only Arthur Andersen—has been put into question by the shame of Enron's last days. Such events are unnerving because they reveal how much the public depends upon a professional corps that attends to its public responsibilities. Perhaps it would not be a mistake to call the situation a low-intensity crisis of professionalism.

Recent events, however, prompt second thoughts about abandoning the professions. The collapse of the information-technology–led boom market of the late 1990s has been followed by revelations of the failure of markets to function well with less or no public regulation. These failures have rocked a number of key economic sectors, from the heart of the "new economy" in telecommunications through the energy and electricity industries to financial services and accounting. Because these were breakdowns not on the periphery but in core sectors of the emerging economy, they strongly suggest that the selling of self-correcting markets has been significantly overdone. It is surely also disturbing that much of the breakdown in public oversight was the responsibility of professionals.

The larger public seems instinctively to hold professionals accountable beyond the measure of profit and loss, presumably because the public believes that professionalism rests upon a fiduciary basis. Amid the general outcry over the revelations of fraud and malfeasance as the U.S. financial bubble burst after 2000, the sharpest outrage was directed at law and accounting firms. Quite correctly, both officials and the public at large saw the leading lawyers and accountants of those organizations as guilty of an insolent repudiation of public trust. They therefore judged these professionals corrupt and so more odious, if not more reprehensible, than mere business leaders of companies such as Enron and WorldCom. Like hypocrisy, indignation is premised upon moral expectation. The professions have persisted in part because of public need for this fiduciary role.

These expectations of high standards of competence coupled with public responsibility have been established in large measure through the professions' own efforts during the past century to establish secure social contracts with the public. The contract has been worked out gradually in statute and custom. In the process, professionalism has evolved as a social ideal.[4] Professionalism entails partnership between the public and functional groups, organized to advance social values in the interest of those they serve. This ideal has given legitimacy to the professions' peculiar occupational status. The professions demand long apprenticeship, carried out in formal educational institutions. This long preparation is in each field centered on mastery of complex skills and a body of knowledge that constitutes a kind of professional culture. Formed by distinctive occupational cultures, professionals have aspired, as organized bodies, to set standards and manage the organization of their own work. The markets for professional labor, as in health care, law, accounting, architecture, or scientific fields, are largely structured by qualifications the professions themselves have set, even when regulated by the state.

The professions have become responsible for key public values. They have in effect taken responsibility for domains of knowledge and skill that are essential to modern life. If individuals are to realize their potential in a modern society, then they must be able to rely upon certain public goods: health care, civil regulation and social justice, technological safety and environmental regulation, publicly available information that is reliable and comprehensible, and high-quality education.[5] It is this responsibility for public goods that sets off professionals from other knowledge workers. Although professionals are often engaged in generating or applying new ideas and advanced processes, and so are doing "creative" work, they are all directly pledged to an ethic of public service. In exchange for the privilege of setting standards for admission and authorizing practice, professions are legally obliged to maintain standards, even to discipline their own ranks, for the public welfare. That this is less honored than it needs to be is a major source of public disquiet about the professions.

These features of professional work also give the public at large an interest in the quality and reliability of professional performance. In business parlance, it makes the public stakeholders. Professions, in other words, are responsible for maintaining these public values.

From an economic viewpoint, such values as a functional legal system and a good health care system are public goods, meaning that they are values from which all benefit and that depend on everyone's cooperation, but to which no particular market actor has a strong incentive to contribute. The professions are publicly chartered to make it their primary concern to sustain such public goods. They are therefore in an important sense public occupations even when they work outside government or publicly supported institutions.

This kind of social partnership demands both accountability and responsibility on the part of the professions. It also calls for active participation and public concern on the part of citizens whom the professions serve. These are the stakeholders of the various professional enterprises in health, justice, education, and the rest. In this book, the ideal of social reciprocity is called *civic professionalism*. It has played an important role in the story of the professions' rise to prominence. But it has always been precarious and is today in real difficulty. One immediate question concerns the viability of professional organization of work in the contemporary economy. The future of professionalism as a civic ethic is also linked, however, to the condition of the polity. One may question how well professionalism can function in a time when interest and participation in civic affairs continue to decline, while the conditions of even much professional work tend increasingly to link skills less with public purposes than with market advantage.[6] The economic and civic questions intertwine.

So if the professions are not clearly obsolete in the new world of work, professional ideals are under severe strain. The causes are multiple and span the polity as well as the economy. For example, the legal profession's numbers have expanded vastly since the 1970s. In part, this represented gains from the political movements of the sixties, as women and minorities gained much fuller access to all professional fields than they had before. Simultaneously, however, public policy changed, relaxing controls on intraprofessional competition, declaring such controls to be monopolistic and therefore in restraint of trade. The result of the conjunction of an

increase in the supply of lawyers with a more competitive marketplace for legal services has been a desperate scramble for livelihood.

The old cleavage within the profession between the life and
income of partners at elite firms and the conditions of solo practice
has intensified, while firms themselves have become more inter-
nally competitive, adding to the general anxiety throughout the
profession. Lawyers now routinely report low satisfaction with their
choice of career. In areas like the law, the professional world, as
with American business, has become "leaner and meaner."[7] Other
fields such as school teaching have never recovered from the post-
1970 fall of public confidence in the schools, with the result that
over the past three decades teaching has experienced the largest
drop in status of any professional field. This in turn has made it difficult for teaching to attract and retain aspirants of high academic
achievement to the field.[8] Perhaps most notoriously, medicine is in
the midst of major ongoing reorganization, largely in reaction to
drastic changes in its regulatory and organizational context, a context that the profession is less and less able to control.[9]

The Professions in the New Economy

All professional fields have been feeling the effects of emergence of
the so-called new economy during the past three decades. The *new
economy* is itself, however, a vague (if currently popular) term. To
understand its impact on professional work, Robert Reich's efforts to
rethink "the future of success" can be a useful reference point.[10] Reich,
the former secretary of labor, has proposed that we think of employment in the sense of a long-term job that pays regular wages, rising
over time, and including a variety of health and retirement benefits,
as an artifact of the era of stable, mass-production industries that he
argues is now passing. This was the period from early in the twentieth century until the 1970s in which mass-production industries,
directed by expert managers, led the economy and set the standards
for work and life. Labor was also substantially organized, making it
possible to "set" wage rates generally throughout the economy.

The leading firms of the employment era were large corporations, which organized work in a bureaucratic manner—that is to say, like government bureaus or the military. Work meant grades of employees and standardized procedures—and secure, predictable careers. A major social consequence, Reich notes, was a society in which extremes of wealth and poverty began to converge toward a middle-class norm that for the first time included working people. The world of stable employment was celebrated as the embodiment of democratic equality. Those institutional developments came about, often through intense struggle, to ensure greater security and predictability for both business and its employees. As economic historian Karl Polanyi put it, this was a movement on the part of society to protect itself against the destructive instabilities of the market.[11] The rise of the modern professions was deeply implicated in this movement. By contrast, in the heyday of nineteenth-century laissez-faire few could plan and then count on a stable career path. The turbulent economy of those days threw up great fortunes and transformed the landscape. It also ruthlessly discarded failures and created shocking divergence in fortune between winners and losers. Nineteenth-century capitalism was immensely fertile in new technological breakthroughs, but for this very reason it was also ferociously competitive and highly volatile. Boom and bust, waste and penury were the norm.

For the generations since World War II, Americans have taken the more predictable managerial structure of work as "normal," allowing individuals to plan their lives so as to buy housing, educate children, and retire with dignity. No longer, says Reich.[12] The emerging forms of work in the new industries are far more entrepreneurial in character, more "contingent" upon the success—or failure—of the enterprise in market competition. They place a premium upon innovation, efficiency, and traveling light psychologically, with few loyalties or other encumbering ties except to economic ambition. It is this spirit that lies behind Bill Gates's reported remark, after frustrating meetings with officials of a French ministry, that you can't expect much of someone whose highest ambition is "to be a civil servant."

The emergence of new industries such as information technology and breakthroughs in other areas of transportation and engineering have created conditions that parallel the industrial era of the nineteenth century. Once again, only now on an increasingly global scale, economic changes are reshuffling the lives and fate of millions. The most profitable sectors of the economy are once again, like railroads and steel in the previous era, fast-changing, fast-growing, and extremely unstable. Political shifts since the 1970s have reintroduced features of the old laissez-faire, nineteenth-century American polity under the rubric of deregulation. The areas of business services and consulting, which employ many professionals in accounting and law, are also highly profitable, and they are larger now than in the last laissez-faire era.

The results of all this have been economically dynamic; Joseph Schumpeter's theory of economic progress through "creative destruction" has been much in vogue.[13] But the new conditions and the political policies that have favored them also brought on another era of polarization of wealth. This has confounded expectations and destabilized identities that were predicated on the way of life typical of the employment era. The sudden predominance of new and volatile, sharply competitive industries, which makes mature mass-production industries less attractive to investors, has also made it difficult for those caught up in rapid change to grasp the whole. It has proved hard to devise public policy that does more than try to either speed up or slow down the process.

Whether one takes these developments as a genuine revolution destined to reshape all work, as Reich seems at points to believe, or as a phenomenon likely to be confined to a few sectors of the economy, they have clearly had an effect on professional work. Analysts such as Derek Bok point to the great shift in compensation, and also prestige, within the professional ranks since the 1970s. Besides the general growth in the gap between the most successful earners and the majority that Reich emphasizes (which has been felt within fields such as law and academe), Bok calls attention to the relative decline in earnings and prestige among professions working in the public sector, especially education and government. For the professions most important to the new technological industries, such as science, engineering, medicine, and law, the major result has been the growth in income disparity *within* professional ranks. These developments have had influence outside these areas as well, directing the ambitions of those seeking wealth and prestige (or simply seeking to avoid penury and pay off student loans) into the profit-making arena and away from public service.[14] At just the moment that women and minorities were gaining access to the most prestigious professional careers, the rules of the game began to shift.

Steven Brint has documented similar developments across the range of economic sectors that employ professionals, concluding that there has been a long-term movement away from an earlier conception of professionalism as "social trusteeship." The drift is toward embracing a notion of the professional as a purveyor of expert services. In subsequent chapters, the term *technical professionalism* is employed to refer to this tendency. A redefinition of the professional as expert frees the most marketable members of a professional field to compete in an increasingly stratified and competitive marketplace for high-paying jobs, without being dogged by professions of social responsibility.[15] One might think of the rapid movement during the late 1990s on the part of leading legal and accounting firms to merge with one another and provide all-around business services. Here it was competitive advantage in the fast-paced and highly profitable area of business services that drove the process, over serious questions about the long-term public benefit of such an arrangement, as well as clashes between the regulatory processes of the two professions. Or think of the spread of commercial practices in higher education, where the most enterprising—and best positioned—institutions and faculty now market their discoveries and services more directly and aggressively than ever before.

Overall, generation of greater inequality within professional groups has placed considerable strain upon corporate organization of the professions. At the same time, the collegial form of professional work is also under attack from those eager to bring expensive professional services under managerial control. The continuing controversy between insurers and physicians working under managed care in the health field reveals the precarious situation of professionally controlled work.[16] Developments such as managed care may not represent something as definitive as the "death of the guild," in Elliott Krause's evocative phrase, but they point to the tenuous situation of professionalism in the contemporary scene. High-performance professional organizations are indeed attractive models, but they face heavy competition in the mind of the general public and policy makers.

The entrepreneur and entrepreneurial firm have made a major ideological comeback in the United States. Since the 1980s, the old American pursuit of the main chance has opened up with new vigor for the most educated portion of workers. Even before the new technological industries came onto the scene, a conjunction of developments—especially the climate of governmental deregulation, global expansion of American business and finance, demographic growth of the aging population served by Medicare, plus the growing financial and legal complexity of the 1980s—opened new kinds of opportunity for ambitious and well-positioned professionals. Even after the chastening collapse of the telecommunications and Internet boom, the volatile but lucrative markets of the new economy continue to hold the highly material imagination of venture capitalists and speculators.

Both as a model of work and as a lure for talent, the new economy threatens professionalism more than it supports it. One consequence of the trend is a siphoning off of enough "talent," lured by the charisma of the high-earning entrepreneurial expert, to dim the luster of the professional career, especially a career in the public sector. The new career options are open mainly to those with elite educational credentials, which means largely to those already from an affluent background. So it is perhaps not surprising that the idea of a fast-paced, entrepreneurial career has been particularly persuasive to college-educated young people, already highly attuned to the views of opinion leaders and "advanced" thinking.[17]

Overall, traditional professional work has lost some of its former mystique in favor of strategic marketing of skills by individual professionals. Should these trends continue, even though some educated workers will be among the socioeconomic elite, the future of professionalism as a distinct conception of work and ideal of life is far from bright. There is a real need, then, to better understand that conception and ideal.

Professions as Good Work

What, if anything, continues to set professional work apart? Is it really a distinctive way of viewing and organizing work? Despite the inroads of recent decades, professional work continues to maintain certain features that mark it as distinctive. These are observable, practical aspects of the way professionals go about their work. As we shall see, however, professional work carries intimations of a larger ideal of life—connections to professionalism as a public value. In becoming professionals, individuals are able to share in the benefits of a body of knowledge, skills, and attitudes, to develop themselves within and through a collective professional culture. Through the institutions of professional schools, apprenticeship, licensure, and a collegial workplace, a high level of formal education and craft skill has become embedded, as it were, in the practitioners. Professionals' greatest asset is this professional culture itself. It is this shared professional culture that enables individual teachers, lawyers, engineers, and physicians to customize their work to suit the needs of a variety of individual clients and situations. It also enables them to contribute to the maintenance of public goods in society. Not least, sharing in and contributing to a professional culture has done a great deal to sustain morale and *esprit de corps*.

The professions have been able to exert their considerable social influence on the basis of their claim to expert knowledge and skill. Law, medicine, engineering, and academe have all established "knowledge mandates," in the phrase of Terrence Halliday. The key point is that professional knowledge has enabled professional bodies to establish themselves and exert influence over the form of work and areas of social life.[18] Following Edward Shils, Halliday further distinguishes a spectrum among types of knowledge mandate. At one end lie those fields that base their claims on scientific knowledge, such as medicine and engineering and the scientific fields. At the other end of the spectrum, law and the clergy, as well as the humanities and social sciences in the academy, assert an expertise in understanding and criticizing the functioning of persons and society.

Medicine and engineering emphasize their claim to scientific understanding of natural processes—of what simply is—while law, theology, and many of the academic disciplines have gained influence because of their specialized expertise in dealing with the human world, especially questions of what might and should be. Moreover, Halliday contends, the more normative the knowledge mandate, the greater the field's potential social influence. Other factors, particularly how effectively a profession can mobilize its own members toward common action, also matter a good deal.[19] These considerations help us later understand the trajectory of professional influence and how the several fields have configured themselves over the course of the last century. As one might predict from Halliday's account, the narrowing of professional claims toward the purely cognitive or technical in recent decades has contributed to the weakening of professionalism that we note. But that is to get ahead of the story.

Legal, medical, and academic services rely upon highly credentialed workers. The conditions of work in these important sectors of the economy continue to put considerable discretion and initiative in the hands of practitioners. Strikingly, this has remained true whether the professionals are self-employed, partners in professional firms, or salaried employees. In most contexts in which professional services (which require both a high level of discretionary judgment and an advanced academic degree) remain the principal resources for organizational performance, considerable professional discretion has been preserved. So much is this the case that social scientists can generalize that "professions are the characteristic form of the organization of educated labor."[20] This helps explain the persistence of the ideals of professional work as a model to which many aspire, though as we have seen there is real debate about the long-term viability of that model.

In professionalized contexts, managers and financial exigency typically play a significantly less controlling role than in most organizations. Professionally organized work, in other words, is an important feature of the modern economy and can be empirically distinguished from both entrepreneurial and managerial or bureaucratic arrangements. Sociologist Eliot Freidson has characterized this distinctive professionally led organization of work "the third logic."[21] It stands out by contrast with both entrepreneurial and bureaucratic organizations. Entrepreneurial firms, such as many of those in the high-technology and business-services sectors, are market-driven. For such an organization, the consumer is in command while prices and profits define organizational purposes. This model, of course, exercised a destructive centrifugal pull on the major accounting firms caught up in the casinolike atmosphere of the nineties. In that sector, recent imposition of new federal regulation has introduced elements of the bureaucratic organization of work as a corrective. This is Freidson's second type. In bureaucratic structures, the aim is reliability and predictability, so that formal rules and standards of performance and evaluation by managerial superiors dominate the workplace.

"Professional markets," however, favor a collegial kind of organization. Professional work, even within a large, apparently bureaucratic structure such as a school, university, or medical center, thus affords a degree of shelter from consumers, managers, and intense competition. Subsequent chapters significantly qualify this statement in examining the changing conditions across the differing domains of professional work. But it is striking that such market shelters can continue, however anomalously, in an increasingly Darwinian economic environment. In strong professions, collegial relationships can enable practitioners to structure their work according to distinctly professional values. Recall that this organizational strength is grounded in claims to knowledge and skill that require discretionary judgment in their application. In such a context, peer review and a drive for excellence in the eyes of other practitioners and organizations become the key motivators of professional performance. The chief commitment in this third logic, according to Freidson, is thus to the intrinsic value of the work and to the belief that it importantly benefits others.[22] Viewed this way, professionalism acquires a concrete meaning as a specific type of work.

Most importantly, perhaps, such work presents a model of "good work . . . a commitment to a body of knowledge and skill both for its own sake and for the use to which it is put." Those who take part in such an enterprise become committed to "preserve, refine, and elaborate that knowledge and skill." That is, they typically find themselves within a context of peers who likewise seek to excel in doing such good work. The professional ethos leads them to seek to employ their capacities where they have application to worldly problems, "to perform it well for the benefit of others—to do Good Works."[23] The attractiveness of this way of life powerfully explains the persistence of professions. A significant degree of that attraction comes from professionals' reported investment in the intrinsic rewards of their work. Recent analysis suggests that these intrinsic rewards are linked to professionals' sense of their work as good in the ethical sense of contributing to the well-being of the society in which they work.[24]

Still, public understanding of professional work is burdened by some unhelpful stereotypes. The popular image of the self-employed lawyer or doctor in solo practice is not the norm in any profession. Professional work has always been organized in guildlike networks of practitioners. It has usually been significantly connected to large-scale organizations, especially in the fields of law, engineering, accounting, academe, nursing, teaching, and medicine. The venerable professions of the military and the clergy, for example, have been tied to the institutions of the state and the church. Within these fields, as in teaching, engineering, and the judiciary, careers have led from specialized schooling through a formal or informal

apprenticeship to a relatively secure position within a large organization. Professional work of that kind permits gradual advancement
through a hierarchy of responsibility and prestige. Such a professional life, for long time typically but not always exclusively a male
prerogative, yielded a career with a number of important goods. It
encouraged leadership and promised honor and esteem, at least
within a particular field and locale. The collegial networks of professional life have promoted continuing learning and the advance
of expertise. Professions have continued to provide the satisfactions
of an insiders' knowledge of how things work and, generally, security if not substantial financial reward.

Profession as Vocation

The great promise of a profession is the possibility of institutionalizing vocation in the modern economy. Professionals have traditionally been ascribed vocation as well as a career or job. Besides
earning a living and striving to distinguish themselves in their
domain of activity, professionals have been expected to carry out
their work as part of a larger collective project. Such a project, like
raising a family or serving one's country, is by necessity a long-term,
stable commitment. It shapes personal identity by binding the individual's voluntary efforts into a common life and purpose. Clearly,
not all work has this character, and not all workers desire such
work. But this sense of calling is a core feature of professionalism.
To carry this off successfully requires considerable individual discernment and capacity for initiative and judgment; although the
basic structures of professional work are institutionally constructed,
the specific forms of an individual's practice and career are very
much a personal accomplishment, involving a lifetime of creative
invention as well as labor.[25]

The idea of professional work as vocation has a specifically
American history. Bruce Kimball has traced the development of
"the true professional ideal" through three historical stages into
our own time.[26] Through a highly contingent process that looks

inevitable only in hindsight, Kimball shows how being a professional came to acquire the traits most often identified by social scientists today. That is, a profession is an occupation based upon formal knowledge and trained skill, organized in a collegial or guildlike way, and carried on in a spirit of service. Historically, Kimball shows that it was the combination of knowledge and service that came first.[27] The medieval university trained expert personnel— "doctors"—meaning those licensed to teach their subject, in three areas: theology, law, and medicine, with philosophy or preparatory studies as a fourth area, typically taught by masters of arts. In colonial America, a variation of that scheme continued in use as the ministry emerged as the "preeminent vocation." The minister enjoyed high intellectual and social prestige, and clergy were educated and credentialed in colleges such as Yale, Harvard, and what later became Princeton. The ministry helped define what theologians of the time called "dignified professions," continuing the medieval notion of profession as a religious calling to God's service.

In the new American republic, politics and law acquired enormous prestige through their central role in the new Revolutionary order. Calvinist Protestantism had long exalted the magistrate as the secular counterpart to the minister, equally the agent of God's intentions on earth. So as law and jurisprudence became a preeminent vocation alongside the clergy, the term *profession* could be extended and then reshaped into the adjective *professional*, which henceforth denoted a kind of occupation. The privileged or preeminent vocation was now marked by political and legal learning rather than theology. In a constitutional order informed by theories of social contract, "professional service" came to mean contractual relations between a "professional" and a "client." The legal profession early organized itself into voluntary associations of the kind Alexis de Tocqueville saw as distinctive of the American polity. Yet it was still to be informed by the earlier religious ethic of selfless service. These bodies of practitioners pledged themselves to both high standards of learning and an ethic of public service.

The beginning of the twentieth century saw a new configuration of prestige crystallizing around the natural and experimental sciences. The sciences were just then being institutionalized in the new American universities. Indeed, scientific expertise was beginning to shoulder aside legal and theological learning as the exemplary form of intellect. As a result, first the professor, as the expert within the new university system, and then the scientifically trained physician emerged with new claims on the term *professional*. These claims were based upon the growing mystique of scientific knowledge. In Kimball's account, it was the notion of the professional that finally emerged a century ago that became normative for Americans. The professional was learned (but especially scientifically trained in a university setting), was licensed and supported by a collegial organization of peers, and professed an ethic of service to clients and the public.[28]

These are, of course, ideal types or stages of an evolving true professional ideal. None ever fully described actual conditions. It is useful to recall this history, however. As we have seen, recent economic and political changes have put the question of the preeminent vocation once again in play. Today's market triumphalism would exalt economic enterprise to the position of commanding social value and highest individual virtue. But can the new economic scene really accommodate the idea of vocation? Or is the notion of a calling simply indigestible within our increasingly competitive, unequal, and market-driven society? To raise the question of vocation is to open up challenging questions about our current social and economic arrangements. What value should we place on the contributions of various social functions? If unregulated markets were really self-correcting, this would be a pointless question, since the labor market should settle, through the price mechanism, the true value of everyone's labor.[29] But outside of a market utopia, the social value of work remains a real and increasingly urgent problem, as does its corollary: the effect of a given form of work upon the well-being of those who perform it.

In American experience, freedom has always been a preeminent value. The most common understanding of freedom is that it means simply lack of external constraint, including the constraints of one's past. This idea continues to be invoked to give legitimacy to our notions of democratic rights and economic free enterprise. However, it is important to notice that this notion of freedom as lack of constraint is not only a negative definition (defining freedom as what it is not) but essentially private and individualistic in meaning. It is just this understanding of freedom that professionalism challenges, both as a model of work and as an ideal for living.

As a model of work, professionalism questions the belief that consumer demand offers always and everywhere the best guidance for the conduct of social functions. As an ideal of living, professionalism connects livelihood with vocation in institutionally stable ways. In holding up this notion of calling, professionalism immediately takes us beyond the simplistic idea that a market framework can solve the most important issues of social and political life. Among these issues is the question of what constitutes good work, for the society and for the individual. The question of how it might be possible to pursue one's work as a calling point toward professionalism as one solution to problems posed, but not answered, by the emerging economic order.

The Relevance of Professionalism in the Age of the "Terrific Deal"

The question of what good work means has become radical in today's ideological climate. For apologists for the unrestricted market, even the accelerated pace of work—with its ever-greater dominance in American lives—is offered as indirect vindication of personal freedom. This is not the freedom to be fulfilled in a calling; it is the liberty to get what we want. The connection is through the idea of enhanced consumer choice. Robert Reich has called attention to how today's more demanding and less secure conditions of work are actually the result of our new ability to pursue, as individuals, the "terrific deal" for us. "We are," says Reich, "on the way to getting exactly what we want instantly, from anywhere, at the best value for our money." Economically, this is a huge boon to everyone. But, he points out, "the balance between making a living and making a life is becoming harder to pull off because the logic of the new economy dictates that more attention be paid to work and less to personal life."

So the world of the terrific deal has a darker side. As Reich points out, "What it means for the rest of our lives—the parts that depend on firm relationships, continuity, and stability—is acutely problematic."[30] Of course, the forms of professional work and how professionals typically deliver their services are highly dependent upon just such things as firm relationships, continuity, and stability. This culture of the terrific deal is in several ways antithetical to the premises that underlie the hope for meaningful vocation. The driving force of this culture is the exhilarating promise of unlimited wealth and opportunity to realize infinite desires. Or at least, this is the vision of life trumpeted by many of the most successful and influential figures currently astride the world stage.

The new communications systems enable individuals with economic resources the freedom to search for greater individual satisfaction in consuming goods and experiences, but the same systems are also the platform for tightening the link between the consumer market and the labor market. To obtain the resources with which to hunt for "terrific" deals—that is, better deals than we now have—we all face more and more pressure to scramble for the consumers' fickle favor. We must be willing to make ourselves and our institutions into a better deal, relentlessly, all the time. In short, Reich concludes, "the rewards of the new economy are coming at the price of lives that are more frenzied, less secure, more economically divergent, more socially stratified. . . . As our earnings become less predictable, we leap at every chance to make hay while the sun shines. As the stakes rise . . . we'll do whatever we can to be in the winner's circle and to get our children safely there as well."[31] What appears at first to serve individual freedom thus turns out to be a paradoxical blessing. What attracts me as a consumer puts pressure on me as a worker. This deep contradiction looms over the promises of the new economy as a threat to personal integrity and life satisfaction. The economy of the terrific deal spreads alienation along with its plenty.

Embedded in the culture of the terrific deal is the notion of freedom as unlimited choice of experience. Beneath this view is a highly questionable, though currently widespread, understanding of human selfhood. It is the notion of the detached self, a spontaneous series of choices through which the self comes to be the sum of its experiences. Perhaps the most influential manifestation of this belief in a detached self is in the popular equation of identity with consumer preference, as though a person really were just a sort of running tally (surreptitiously maintained in cyberspace by "cookies") of clicks on a mouse, a "shopping cart" of choices and experiences.

Despite the ubiquity of this image of the self, it is a serious misunderstanding of identity and how people in fact develop. Here, perhaps, is the sharpest contrast between the premises of the better deal and the ideals of professionalism. Becoming oneself is more like apprenticeship than it is like choice in a market. What and who we come to admire, who we become involved with, what we learn to do, and the kind of activities we immerse ourselves in all gradually shape us, subtly shifting even our criteria of value and choice. Who we are is ultimately a moral question, bound up with the issue of whom we wish to be. It is also a question strongly shaped by the social and economic context in which the choosers are themselves formed. Recognizing this can lead to a deeper (because more realistic) understanding of what freedom really requires. It is this social dimension of choice and freedom that the currently ascendant celebration of markets downplays or ignores. But unlike a disappointing purchase (which most purchases are), the choices made in actual living have consequences. There is no "Escape. Undo." command to click on.

There is in the professional ideal an alternative set of goals—and a conception of freedom—promising a solution to the quandary posed by the culture of the terrific deal. That is, professionalism promises a satisfying sense of identity and personal achievement through contributing to values we hold in common. This idea of freedom as fulfillment in vocation is alive in popular understanding, though it is typically associated with exceptional callings and persons. Along with the idea of a religious sense of calling, it is widely understood that both in the arts and in science a contribution of value requires nothing less than the whole of a person's life and devotion. A profession, as a form of institutionalized vocation, makes it possible to engage upon serious life projects in the same spirit. The promise of professional work is that it can enable many people to achieve the freedom and fulfillment ascribed to the truly exceptional, the saints and geniuses of popular imagination.

A profession is a means of livelihood that is also a way of life. Professionalism seeks freedom in and through significant work, not by escaping from it. In professional work, the practitioner expresses freedom by directing the exercise of carefully developed knowledge and skill toward ends that refer beyond the self and the practitioner's private satisfaction. Concern for clients or patients and for the public values for which the profession stands is essential to genuine practice. The key point is that for a genuine professional the meaning of the work derives from both what it is and the ends toward which it is directed as much as or more than its significance comes from the return it affords. In this sense, it is always more than a job. In genuine professional work, the craft itself is a focus of attention. As Freidson put it, professional work is defined by a focus on the quality of the performance itself and the belief that it is of value to others. Or, as Lawrence Haworth has summarized the philosophy of professional work, among its key qualities are a certain objectivity and distance. These attitudes allow the physician, for example, to dwell in the present with the patient, focused on diagnosis and treatment, rather than on some extraneous outcome that has to be "sweatily anticipated."[32]

Far from diminishing individuality, this stance of objectivity actually frees the practitioner to affirm his or her distinctness as an individual—only in this case, Haworth argues, "the [kind of] self affirmed is defined by a distinctive manner of relating with matters beyond the self."[33] That is, the practitioner finds that the demands of the craft and the relationships within which the craft places him or her become challenges that, if well met, spur the growth of individual creativity and his or her sense of self-worth. Think, for instance, of the challenge faced by a teacher who discovers that a carefully prepared lesson is really not suited to the class and then improvises a more relevant way to deal with the subject. Or imagine the engineer who must work with clients and other specialists to redesign a product so that it not only works efficiently but can be more easily repaired. It is situations like these that draw out the practitioner's capacities. They thereby stimulate and enable growth of the person precisely in and through professional practice.

Finally, it is "affection for the subject matter," the particular domain of professional activity that motivates and consolidates love of craft into "a standing disposition" to serve. Haworth maintains that the liberating power of professional work lies in the fact that its significance, unlike work pursued primarily as a source of monetary gain, derives from its contribution to the larger social whole, seen as something "which itself has value that is both in jeopardy [and so needs the individual's contribution] and susceptible of enhancement [thereby calling out personal creativity and aspiration]"[34] Through the motivation such forms of work engender, Haworth argues, "a person may find a nearly total release of his own energies." The motivation is largely intrinsic to the work and the relationships it creates. Pursued as a life project, professional work is for practitioners a source of personal growth that is at the same time intrinsically "ethical . . . insofar as it is lived as within a larger life, so that they [practitioners] sense that their principal concerns are serious and that through the support the society lends to their pursuit of these concerns their personal dignity is acknowledged."[35]

The Challenge of Professional Reform: Renewing the Civic Partnership

American society needs the professions today. It needs them for what they do, certainly. But it also needs the professions as examples of ethical work. This ethical dimension—living "as within a larger life," as Lawrence Haworth has put it—is what is institutionalized in the professions' social contract. This is the essential, but jeopardized, civic dimension of professionalism. To become a professional is not only to join an occupation; it is to assume a civic identity. The core of professionalism is that by functioning as lawyer, engineer, doctor, accountant, architect, teacher, or nurse, an individual carries on a public undertaking and affirms public values. With this identity comes a certain public status and authority, as is granted by custom and the profession's social contract; but professionalism also means duties to the public. Chief among these duties is the demand that a professional work in such a way that the outcome of the work contributes to the public value for which the profession stands.

What has been missing, then, is not understanding or even appreciation of the value of professionalism so much as trust that professional groups are serious about their purposes. It is not that assertions of good faith on the part of the organized bar or medicine have been lacking in recent years. Rather, the public has seen these professions (in the other sense) as gestures that must be redeemed by concerted action. What has been missing is action in which the professions take public leadership in solving perceived public problems, including the problems of abuse of privilege and refusal of public accountability.

Emphasis upon the efficiency of markets, which in practice often means stimulating competition, threatens essential features of the professional-client relationship. This is true in many areas, such as health care, legal services, and education. As powerful third-party organizations pressure physicians into emphasizing economic efficiency at the expense of clinical judgment, the result is to recast the physician's practice as a profit center rather than a group of healers. Aided by new information technology, these trends inculcate a ceaseless search for the best "deal" in every area of life, recasting patients as consumers and narrowing professional roles to fit short-term encounters. These developments have helped to "empower" laypeople in ways that can help undercut the abuse of professional authority. In this way, they are to be welcomed. Yet these trends toward increased commercialization seriously risk reshaping relationships between professionals and clients for the worse, substituting a calculus of cost and benefit for ethical relations of care and trust. So in law the role of counselor becomes less possible in a context of truncated relationship, pushing the lawyer even further into the role of adversarial agent. In this climate, professionals find themselves unable to act as guardians of the values they profess unless they can reengage the public over the nature and value of what they do for the society at large.

Consequently, it is important to ask about all the professions, What connects knowledge and craft with the public good? Ethical codes and legal regulation play an indispensable part, to be sure. They are critical for upholding the institutional framework that supports all our lives. But as the professional failures exposed by the collapse of Enron and WorldCom and their ilk have made vividly clear, codes and laws are not in themselves enough. They cannot wholly take the place of the spirit or ethos that is essential to the identity of a profession. To be effective in the world, moral conviction needs a context in which the right way is accepted as typical and best practice as well.

Integrity of purpose is at once an aspect of individual responsibility and a source of human dignity. Its roots, however, extend beyond the individual into the social subsoil of personality, to the implicit judgment that others can prove trustworthy, that one can engage with them in common undertaking because, in the main, cooperation enhances the possibilities of living rather than undercutting it. At the other end, integrity and responsibility need knowledge and orientation. They depend upon institutions that are organized to recognize and promote the application of expertise toward the great common ends of social well-being and environmental sustainability. Among specialized institutional sectors, education (particularly higher education) is the one most directly charged with this task. Professional renewal has to begin in professional education, or it will have no lasting future.

The Challenge of Professional Education: Recovering the Formative Dimension

Among all occupations, the professions stand out for the central importance of education to the identity of their members. Formal and specialized education is the required portal to professional membership. Moreover, continuing education, officially credentialed and monitored, is typically required of professionals in many fields to maintain their license to practice. In addition, faculty from the professional schools are almost always conspicuously represented among the leading figures in every domain. It is within their formal education that not only physicians but engineers, lawyers, teachers, and the rest start the demanding process of acquiring the knowledge, skill, and perspective that make them able to perform according to the standards of their field. It is by their ability to function as professionals that novices achieve recognition from established practitioners in their domain. Finally, the public depends upon licensure and credentials to produce a certified level of competence among practitioners. It is no exaggeration to say that education remains a dominant feature of professional life, even long after leaving the formal phase of training.

The training has itself become professionalized. Professional education is today carried out mostly by specialized faculty who teach within institutions that either function within a university or college or have been constructed on an academic model. Professional schools are separately accredited and regulated by the professions they serve. At the same time, they are also subject to the standards and review common in the academy. In this sense, they are hybrid, bridge institutions with one foot in the academy, so to speak, and one in the world of practitioners. The task of these schools is thus complex. It is also very broad.

Within a limited period of time, professional schools are expected to equip their students with enough knowledge and skill to be able formally to enter the ranks of the profession for which they are training. In some cases—for engineering, teaching, and nursing, for example—this preparation typically goes on during the standard four years of undergraduate education. Law, medicine, and academic fields are all graduate education. But in every case, the organized profession insists that the school lay the groundwork for the aspirants' professional identity—that way of thinking and sense of self that shapes the student as a lawyer, engineer, physician, teacher, clergy, architect, and so forth, often marking the person for life.

Each distinct part of this education—including learning the theory, mastering practical skills, and achieving a new outlook upon work and identity—is finally about this effort to form a specific kind of worker, citizen, and person. Summarizing a large literature, historian Sheldon Rothblatt can state that "virtually all students of the subject agree that the study of the professions is more or less coterminous with the history of educational differentiation." He adds that "in some but by no means all countries, the evolution of higher education has meant the displacement of older socialization processes derived from guilds." The heritage accounts for the persistence, even within professional schools that are strongly academic in character, of some forms of master-apprentice teaching and learning. Such time-honored pedagogy aims to hone skills while shaping attitudes. The result is that even today the particular educational process of each professional field continues to mark all its students deeply, giving them a common outlook and common skills, whether the education be primarily by apprenticeship or science or some combination of both.[36]

Becoming a professional is a matter of learning how to appropriate a complex body of knowledge, skill, and lore—the living professional culture that distinguishes each field of professional endeavor. For example, in a sociological study of medical doctors Freidson characterized medical education as essentially a matter of forming in aspiring physicians a "clinical mentality," a particular habit of mind or disposition to look upon self and others, necessary to enable the "work of consultants who must intervene [with esoteric knowledge] in everyday practical affairs."[37] Something analogous could be said of every profession. This is the formative dimension of professional education.

Preparation for a profession is expected to elucidate and instill this understanding, along with imparting the foundation of professional knowledge and craft. At the same time, the pace of technological development, rapid change in the nation's demographic composition, and changes in service-delivery institutions are propelling new attention to how professional schools are preparing tomorrow's providers of professional services. There has never been a time when the quality of professional education was more important, or more subject to question, than the present. The collapse of major corporations and disruption of the nation's financial markets owing to a lack of integrity and accountability in the world of finance underscores how much the security of everyday life depends upon the way our professionals carry out their tasks. Indeed, as we have seen, professions are set apart from other occupations by their public pledge to deploy technical expertise and judgment not only skillfully but also for public-regarding ends and in a public-regarding way.

The story of the modern professions is one of the gradual assumption by the academy of greater and greater control over the shaping of future professionals. This has made it more difficult to achieve and monitor formative goals. Comparing professional education across Western nations over time reveals the current situation, different in each country, as the result of a long competition between practitioner-controlled and school-based forms of professional education. Even within the United States, the outcome has differed with the domain. Medical education, for example, has long been far more responsive to the concerns of practitioners than has education in the law. Medicine gives priority to clinical, apprenticelike forms of training, in contrast to the tendency for the legal academy to eschew responsibility for clinical and practical training.

Overall, however, the trend has been to divide professional education into specialized areas, separating the cognitive from the practical and ethical dimensions, in curriculum, faculty, and institutional locus. The result is ever-greater emphasis upon the intellectual training in which academics take pride, with the sometimes unintended result that intellectual training is largely separated from, and has generally eclipsed, the kind of moral formation that was the focus of professional apprenticeship organized by practitioners.[38] This poses the urgent curricular and pedagogical issue of how contemporary professional schools manage—or fail to manage—reintegration of the capacities for skillful practice and ethical identity with cognitive training of students in the formation of professional competence. We explore this issue in some detail in a later chapter. The outlines of the problem, however, are fairly clear.

In programs of professional education, three clusters of value stand out: the values of the academy, the values of professional practice, and the ethical-social values of professional identity. Of course, professional education is designed to foster development of the capacities needed to perform the profession. But concern for the needs of the profession is far from the only influence on the character of a professional school. Particularly powerful is the intellectual and institutional context of higher education. Being a *professor* of law or *professor* of medicine, that is, overlaps with yet is distinct from the role of the professional who is *only* a practicing lawyer or physician.

Professional education also attaches importance to a second set of values, which reflect more directly the concerns of practitioners. They include respect for the complexity and technical demands of practical skills and belief in the importance of practical experience. The differences between professional education based in the values of the academy and the values of practice are often reflected in organizational divisions within a professional school or program. For example, in legal education, academic courses are frequently the responsibility of distinct, and often more prestigious, faculty than those who teach in clinical or applied courses.

In part, the tensions among the clusters of value are rooted in the nature of professional work itself. They reflect common strains within all professional occupations. Professions require theoretically elaborated knowledge of the kind prized in the academy, but they also entail complex activities that integrate theory and practice, skills that academic life does not typically develop. A professional has to be knowledgeable but also able to make effective judgments in the face of uncertainty and, importantly, able to learn from such experience. Despite differences of emphasis, most professional schools recognize the value of these goals.[39] In professional practice, however, the claims of technical competence, both theoretical and practical, must be integrated within the normative ends of the particular professional domain. They constitute the third cluster of values in professional education.

This third set of values emphasizes the professional's integrity, sense of direction, and ability to assume responsibility for the quality of his or her own work and the standards associated with the field of practice. These values ground professional education in a broader conception of the purpose of the profession and the ideals to which it aspires, connecting training directly with the field's social contract. As we have seen, this blending of the normative and the technical is of the essence of good work, "something that allows the full expression of what is best in us . . . in activities that exhibit the highest sense of responsibility."[40] Professional education in a given field is likely to be characterized by a specific balance among the three sets of values, so that difference in the kinds of balance may be part of the distinctiveness of professional education in various fields, or in institutions within the same field. In every case, the coherence or lack of coherence among the three values clusters plays the key role in shaping the understanding and character of entrants into each professional field.

It is this third dimension of professional education that typically receives the least attention in the formal curriculum. Yet it is being taught constantly by a hidden curriculum of the daily routines and taken-for-granted attitudes of the school. It is to this powerfully socializing experience—through which students are shaped as apprentices to the practices of the professional school as a whole—that future practitioners owe a great deal of their own assumptions about what really matters for being a professional. As we shall see in later chapters, some areas of professional preparation have begun to recognize this powerful socializing force and are attempting to give the goals of teaching judgment and integrity, fusing competence and purpose, the focal position they deserve. Because it includes in principle all areas of professional preparation, this third cluster of values holds the greatest promise for integrating the whole educational experience, permeating its currently disparate parts with explicit concern for developing in students the capacity and disposition to perform in accordance with the best standards of a field in a way that serves the larger society.

Professional integrity in this sense is a core concern that implicitly links disparate fields of professional preparation such as law, engineering, education, and training for ministry. As such, professional integrity could become an explicitly common educational objective. Such a focus would give professional schools in one domain an interest in how other fields are grappling with the question of how best to balance and unify the three sets of values. Starting in 1999, the Carnegie Foundation for the Advancement of Teaching began a comparative study of preparation in law, engineering, and the clergy, complemented by a study of teacher preparation as well as medicine and nursing. The aim of these studies, which this volume introduces, is to understand better how these fields are working to enhance the integrative and formative aspects of how they prepare future practitioners.

The Aims of This Book

The chapters that follow are an exploration of the fortunes and prospects of professionalism. The term can mean a number of things and produce profoundly divergent outcomes. At its worst, professionalism can lock individuals into a narrow focus upon technical competence (and sometimes individual success) to the exclusion of all other considerations. At its best, however, professionalism is far more than that. By taking responsibility through one's work for ends of social importance, an individual's skills and aspirations acquire value for others. Professionalism thereby forms a crucial link between the individual's struggle for freedom in a fulfilling existence and the needs of the larger society, so that individual opportunity can serve the demands of interdependence.

The strategy of the following chapters is first to survey the contemporary complaint about the professions and professionalism, and then to distinguish among the varying and often conflicting ways in which the idea of professional work is currently viewed by scholars. These tasks occupy Chapter One.

The next several chapters, Two through Four, describe how the professions have developed from a limited kind of genteel occupation into a widely emulated and sought-after model of work. These chapters focus on the United States but cast some comparative glances across the Atlantic at how the modern professions have functioned differently in Britain and Europe. The coming of greater European integration and globalization, of course, has put all these matters into newly accelerated motion, notably the rise of the complex institutions of industrial and postindustrial society, especially the university; the common school of the professions; as well as the bureaucratic structures of business, government, health care, and education, the major homes of professional work.

The later chapters, Five through Eight, are topical. They take up key issues and controversies about professionalism that have surfaced in the course of the historical survey and from analysis of contemporary scholarly debates. Chapter Five proposes a revised model of what professionalism needs to become in order to reclaim its historic aim of humanizing modern work and improving the equity and quality of contemporary life. Here the theme of civic professionalism receives extended development, approached through the notion of practical reason as a common theme of professional practice.

Chapter Six introduces the conceptual framework and comparative questions that have motivated and directed the Carnegie Foundation's comparative studies of specific domains of professional education: in medicine, nursing, law, engineering, and preparation of the clergy. The chapter examines the teaching of the relations between theory and practice and between the technical and moral aspects of professional training. The related concern with what constitutes professional knowledge and competence occupies Chapter Seven, which continues the development of the idea of practical reason begun in Chapter Five.

Those issues inevitably lead to the question of how professional expertise is related to the ethical concerns of actual practice and public policy. This is the subject of Chapter Eight. Finally, we conclude with a reflection on how current trends in the professions and professional education appear in light of the historic mission of the professional enterprise to advance public values.

Throughout this study, the focus of attention is on how professionalism has been and is understood and articulated with reference to the changing forms of American economic and social life. The book's critical argument is that professionalism has proven an ambiguous good. The ambiguity stems in large measure from professionalism's loss of direction. This in turn has been due to weakening connections between the professions and the culture of civic democracy. The culture is itself in crisis, so that the problems of professionalism emerge as tied up with the difficulties inherent in keeping the ideals of democracy and public service alive within an ever more complex but incoherent economic and social environment.

Taken as a whole, this book makes the case that professional life can and needs to be restructured in ways that suffuse technical competence with civic awareness and purpose. Thanks in part to the challenges so unrelentingly posed by technological development and the increasingly global networks of communications, commerce, and international order, specialists find themselves more than ever having to come to grips with each other's specialties in order to pursue their own projects. They are also under heightened pressure to relate their expertise to the publics concerned and affected by unexpected change. In response to these challenges, new understandings of professionalism and forms of professional practice and training are emerging.

The unmet need is to ensure that these new forms of work and education recognize that there is no successful separation between the skills of problem solving and those of deliberation and judgment, no viable pursuit of technical excellence without participation in those civic enterprises through which esoteric knowledge and skill discover their human meaning. In these developments, we can glimpse the possibility of transforming for the better professional thinking and practice, along with the benefits such changes can bring.

Chapter One

Professionalism

Symbols of success are not everywhere. The briefcase has become one of the most recognizable emblems of status in modern society. Every weekday, ranks of these status symbols, gripped like the leather shields of an invading army, inundate metropolitan centers. In the same metropolises, and a host of suburban office parks, those human waves are almost always smartly dressed. Even if they tread softly in running shoes, the shoes are uniformly in good taste. The briefcases and their bearers may not turn many heads, but they still emanate an alluring scent of success.

In modern life, a briefcase is more than a substitute for a rucksack or paper bag. It is a sign of a certain status. A briefcase announces that its bearer holds an occupation sufficiently responsible that work is not confined to a production shift or opening hours. Carrying a briefcase advertises that its bearer commands an ample amount of the rarest form of credit: autonomy in work. The briefcase asserts that this person can be counted upon to do the job without direct supervision, out of the shop, and off hours. If asked to name this kind of highly valued, highly trusted work, most of us would likely say, "professional work." Those who do such work seem to occupy an important and enviable place in the world.

Professional is a loosely defined term. Originally, of course, it referred to the classic honorific occupations of medicine, the bar, and the clergy. These occupations certainly enjoy high status; when asked to rank the most desirable jobs, Americans have consistently placed medical doctor just below Supreme Court justice (the top-ranked job). Lawyers, clergy, dentists, college professors, and architects always appear among the top twenty ranks.[1] A profession is typically described as an occupation characterized by three features: specialized training in a field of codified knowledge usually acquired by formal education and apprenticeship, public recognition of a certain autonomy on the part of the community of practitioners to regulate their own standards of practice, and a commitment to provide service to the public that goes beyond the economic welfare of the practitioner.

Observers of modern society have repeatedly pointed out great changes in the world of work. As farming and then manufacturing has absorbed less of the American workforce, those occupations involving services and information have expanded enormously. In particular, jobs classified as "professional and managerial" have become increasingly numerous and important. The reasons are not hard to see. As American society has shifted from a rural, local base to an urban and technological pattern of life, expertise and coordination become increasingly essential. The complicated organization of the modern economy has made us all far more interdependent than in the past. Our livelihood, our health, our knowledge of the world, the whole quality of contemporary life depend upon the integrated meshing of a vast number of skills and capacities. It is this complex interdependence that has set the great waves of briefcases in motion across America.

Skilled professionals have become indispensable to modern society. They furnish the specific skills that are basic to the operation of complex modern institutions in the spheres of industry, government, education, health care, and the law. Professionals such as therapists and social service providers help negotiate that complexity as they aid many in seeking direction and assistance amid the often harsh accidents of life. Historian Harold Perkin has characterized British history during the last century as dominated by the professional organization and outlook.[2] Similar views have been put forward about modern society generally, and the United States in particular.[3] Because of their knowledge and the strategic importance of their functions, professionals are frequently beneficiaries of trust and high expectations on the part of the larger society. The professions depend upon a kind of social compact of reciprocal trust and good faith between the practitioners and the publics they serve. Where professional fields are licensed, this compact may be quite explicit, but it is always presumed. This is one reason malfeasance on the part of professionals can excite moral outrage.

Popular moral vocabulary has come to give special prominence to professionalism. It has emerged as a widely esteemed and sought-after virtue. Saying someone acts "professionally" is high praise in any situation, while the most damning epithet hurled at politicians, financiers, and athletes by their enemies is the charge of being "unprofessional." So seriously is it taken that even in the contemporary climate of moral relativism, when the substance of such formerly solid terms as "indecent" and "disrespectful" have been opened to question, few speak of professional behavior as existing only in the eye of the beholder. Examples of the importance of public concern about the moral health of the professions appear daily. When an underfunded New York hospital whose patients are poor in disproportionate numbers found its supply of medical interns was to be cut off because fewer interns chose to train among the poor, an anguished staff member remonstrated, "If everything was perfect, we wouldn't need them the way we do. . . . I thought they [physicians] took an oath."[4]

In the case of the traditional professions of the clergy, the bar, and medicine, clear standards affirm professional status. This is the effect of official licensing, specialized and accredited professional education, and codification of formalized expertise combined with jurisdiction over vital public activities. There is more ambiguity in the public mind about which other occupations are really professional. The picture is complicated by the increasing tendency of managers to seek professional status; witness the explosion of the master's of business administration degree.

There is, of course, a difference in status between the MBA-credentialed executive of a firm and the manager of a local McDonald's. But it is noteworthy that the latter is also likely to speak of managing as an important and specific sort of art—and to carry work home in a briefcase. In other words, modern management aspires toward a recognizably professional identity. Becoming professional is a key dimension of success for occupational groups as well as for individuals. The very dispute over just which occupations deserve to be called professions indicates the symbolic power of the designation *professional*. However, the aspiration to being professional connotes more than a claim to higher social status. Professional work also requires the practitioner to adhere to demanding standards of competence and public service. When professional groups fail (as they often do) to hold their own members accountable to these standards, charges of malpractice can in some fields be taken to court.

Calling or Career: Tensions Within Professionalism

Far more than the symbolic briefcase, then, professional work is freighted with social and individual value. By infusing occupations with a sense of calling, professions contribute to the wider civic order. The ethical spirit of civic life can be manifested and given content in professional work. Within this civic understanding of the professional vocation, each specific professional responsibility gets its point and value from the contribution it makes through shared commitment to the good society and the good life.

For a viable democratic society, a sense of collective purpose needs to operate in the public sphere, especially in politics, the law, and civic deliberation. But it must also be made effective in the everyday realms of work and living. The professions are important because they stand for, and in part actualize, the spirit of vocation. Professionalism promises to link performance of specific tasks with this larger civic spirit. By enabling workers to connect their activities and careers to the service of public ends, professionalism suggests how to organize the complex modern division of labor to ensure that specific functions are performed well and with a sense of responsibility for the good of the whole.

A professional career starts with formal education, often beyond the baccalaureate level. It typically continues through a substantial apprenticeship, either in a practice situation or as part of formal clinical education. In most established professions, the student's craft, knowledge, and character are tested and certified by formal licensing procedures regulated by law. The goal is to develop students into practitioners who can respond capably and self-confidently to demands for professional service. At the same time, professional work—particularly higher education—has long been held up as defining ideals of middle class aspiration.[5] In America, achieving economic well-being has been a significant and honorable aspect of a professional career. But it has always meant more than that as well. Professional licensing and grant of control over recruitment and training of practitioners are part of a social contract between the organized field and society. A profession is understood to offer a career, an opportunity for social and economic advancement, while professionalism demands the kind of dedication to purpose characteristic of a vocation or calling. Not infrequently, however, the two elements of career and calling pull against each other.

Authentic professionalism can impart a strong sense of identity because, beyond providing a livelihood, it is a way of life with public value. It is the kind of thing one can build a life around. For the person possessing the requisite capacities and sufficient commitment, a profession can be not only a career but a calling to useful work as well. Providing counsel and care, curing illness, bringing justice, teaching and the pursuit of knowledge, designing and building for convenience and safety—these are activities that generate more than jobs and satisfaction for individuals. By their nature, they create goods that at some time are essential for everyone, and important for society as a whole. They are activities that sustain public values.

The continuing appeal of professionalism, even amid so many complex tensions, shows that it articulates a hunger for something often missing or suppressed in contemporary work. Certainly, part of this something is a sense of dignity and public assurance that one's talents and work deserve recognition. Another aspect, though, is engagement through one's work with common purposes that give point and value to individual effort. Purposes such as competent performance, dignity, justice, and fellowship are in the end civic goods. They make possible a civil and meaningful public realm. They are also the promise of genuine professionalism. However, these are not goods that individuals can possess or enjoy alone, or even achieve entirely by their own efforts. We can see them as the goods of self-discovery, even a satisfying kind of self-fulfillment, though this self-fulfillment is not what often goes by that name. It comes, almost paradoxically, through a kind of transcendence and change of self, gaining a wider sense of identity through engagement with technical excellence while taking responsibility for shared ends.

Among all contemporary forms of work, professional occupations stand out as examples of good work, labor that "allows the full expression of what is best in us . . . activities that exhibit the highest sense of responsibility."[6] For work to be consistently valuable to society as well as personally rewarding, however, there has to be significant alignment between personal commitment and the purposes of the larger institution of which the worker is part. Here lies the key importance of the profession as a collective enterprise. We shall see that professions cannot long make available the conditions of good work, no matter how financially lucrative they may become for some practitioners, in the absence of collective commitment to the fiduciary responsibility they hold for social purposes. Without willingness to uphold the contract with society, professional work ceases to be good, for individual practitioners or for the public.

These functions are carried on in a commercial society in which professional skills, like others, are marketed. The labor market puts pressure on professionals to behave competitively toward their peers, and to accede to the demands of profit when they conflict with professional standards of excellence. Indeed, it is in part to temper such market pressures that professional organizations exist. Yet, for a profession as organized interest, the aim at self-aggrandizement has proven to be perhaps stronger than it is for the individual. As critics of the professions stridently point out, abuse of public trust is a discouragingly familiar aspect of professional history. The situation of professional life is further complicated by the fact that today most professionals are no longer the solo practitioners of popular image, but employees of large bureaucratic organizations. The purposes of these organizations, like the profit motive of the market, do not always support service according to high professional standards.

But what exactly do professional standards entail? In several domains, this has itself long been an arena of tension in which differing views compete. For example, consider the question of professional responsibility. In law, the attorney is expected to be a zealous advocate for the client's interests—an attitude reinforced by the American adversarial system of justice. Yet at the same time, attorneys are legally "officers of the court." They share with the judiciary a responsibility to the public for maintaining the legal system as a whole. Collectively, therefore, lawyers have an interest in mediating conflict and seeing that justice is done. Yet this responsibility strains against their training in adversarial ingenuity. Accountants are similarly caught between a legal obligation to enforce public standards in auditing and reporting financial accounts on the one hand and their obvious need to demonstrate loyalty to their clients' best interests on the other. We shall see in Chapter Two that over time professional standards have changed in several fields as the balance among their several responsibilities shifts in response to changing social contexts.

Professionals are enjoined both to be competent, in the technical sense of being effective lawyers, engineers, architects, or physicians, and also to conduct themselves with due regard for their public obligations. These obligations are partly defined by the written codes of their guild but even more strongly by the distinctive cultures that mark lawyers off from physicians and accountants from architects. In aiming at a balance between these two criteria—the technical and the moral—which should be emphasized? As between the ethics of the guild and public accountability, which should have priority? Practically speaking, who should have primary responsibility for achieving and maintaining this balance? Is it the proper role of professional societies and organizations, or of some form of public oversight?

As we shall see, these tensions are among the chief issues roiling professional life in many fields. They also help define the parameters of professional education, a critical matter we explore in detail in Chapter Six. There, it turns out that the balance in these matters depends heavily upon who has the upper hand in preparing future professionals. When the academic guild is in charge, professional training emphasizes the cognitive and technical. In a situation in which the practitioners themselves control education and licensing, performance and the culture of the guild tend to have much more importance as decisive standards of professional quality.

Finally, if today's most salient challenge to professionalism comes from the increasing dominance of market thinking within professional life and organization, there are also real differences in attitude toward market forces among the sectors of the professional workforce. Teachers, academics, social workers, and other professionals heavily involved in government and public institutions are less positive toward business values than professionals in fields such as accounting and engineering, which are deeply embedded in the corporate world.[7] This tension operates among fields at least as much as within them, as the example of accounting in the age of Enron shows.

Is Professionalism Obsolete? A Test Case

It is now a commonplace that the prestige of the traditional professions is under siege. Not just their performance but their claim to distinct expertise, the very core of professional legitimacy, has come under withering fire. Skepticism is leveled particularly at professional claims to serve the public interest. Lawyers now routinely expect denigration for their professional affiliation (even from other attorneys). Physicians are not only challenged by the proponents of "alternative medicine," but face patients armed with all kinds of medical knowledge obtained through the Internet. The prevalence of "emergency" teaching credentials in school classrooms calls into question the value of professional teacher training. The list goes on. Each of these challenges is distinct and relates to the particular circumstances of one or another professional field. However, these specific challenges circulate within a larger current of thought that is deeply skeptical of the value of the professional organization of work. It questions whether any value is really added to provision of expert services by the peculiar features of the professions—their guildlike structures of corporate monopoly over esoteric knowledge within an occupational domain, particularly over recruiting, training, and licensing personnel.

As a kind of thought experiment, imagine such an elimination of professional organization in provision of expert services. Social and individual needs would be met both more efficiently and effectively, according to this line of thinking, if "knowledge workers" could compete for jobs now monopolized by licensed professionals on the basis of whatever skills and credentials consumers and employers decided were useful. This would mean the end of the monopoly of profession-specific schools in which teachers from the profession are expected to serve as gatekeepers of the field as well as contributors to its base of knowledge. If this seems odd when applied to legal counsel or medicine or teaching, consider that it is typical in fields such as journalism and business, which sometimes claim the professional aura. In nineteenth-century laissez-faire America, that was the state of affairs in health care, engineering, school teaching, religious preaching, and much else.

Now, prophets proclaim the advent of a "frictionless capitalism," to be enabled by ever-improving information technology, which can render dependence upon professionals obsolete. In this once-and-future vision, consumers have virtually perfect access to the information now encumbered by professional monopolies and restrictions. The result is to be a true market in expert services—expertise upon demand. Thanks to the beneficent force of market competition, we can expect increased efficiency along with more personal freedom of choice.

But perhaps we do not need such a thought experiment. The advent of the so-called managed care revolution in health care seems to have set into motion just such a process within existing professional occupations. Medicine is being defined as an element in the health care industry. Physicians and other health care professionals are increasingly described as employees to be subjected to managerial scrutiny and discipline, for the sake of consistency of product and economic efficiency. Large insurance companies compete, at least in theory, to offer the best "package" of services to consumers. The final beneficiaries of such efficiency measures, we are told, will be patients, now redefined as consumers.

For critics of the professions supportive of these developments, physicians are really just highly specialized service providers who have walled themselves off through an elaborate occupational culture bolstered by state licensing and education requirements to monopolize medical knowledge. After all, critics can argue, top docs trade on their positions to dazzle a gullible and often desperate public and collect outrageous fees. What are professional protestations about independent standards, after all, but camouflage for special interests?

The authoritative model lurking in the background here is the ideology of deregulation currently in vogue. In this view, the only moral obligation of any enterprise is to maximize its economic well-being. By defining all public activities as self-interested, profit-oriented enterprises, this powerful trend works to strip away any moral understanding of the relationship between profession and society, or between professional and client, except that of commercial exchange. Advancing rationality, technological and economic, is simply rendering the claims of professionalism—for the indispensability of discretionary judgment, peer review, and accountability in the public interest—anachronistic. Or is it?

The "irrational exuberance" of the Roaring Nineties tested the inherent rationality of unregulated markets, both in the heartland of the "new economy" such as telecommunications and information technology and on Wall Street. The claims for a deregulated economy have been found severely wanting. Recent history gives painful yet potent indirect proof of our collective dependence upon professional integrity for the functioning of even that least sentimental domain of modern society. According to the textbooks, after all, the law of gravity in economic affairs is alleged to be self-interest. As the debacle of 2001 and 2002 illustrates all too clearly, however, the health of the investment economy depends paradoxically on regulators' willingness to resist the siren call of getting in on the main chance. As if in illustration, the story of the demise of the venerable and long-trusted auditing firm of Arthur Andersen stands as a sad emblem of professional failure and its consequences for the general welfare.

The long boom of the last decade saw the largest economic expansion in American history, outside of World War II. Nearly everyone benefited, not least American business, which became the envy of the world. By 2001, however, bursting of the overinflated stock market reduced aggregate wealth significantly. As a consequence, not only the holdings of investors but the retirement incomes of millions of workers were in real jeopardy. As part of the fallout, Enron—heralded as a model of the new economy in the recently deregulated energy industry—collapsed utterly. By 2002, the recently deregulated telecommunications industry had produced the wreckage of WorldCom, the largest bankruptcy in history. Then, as a sad coda, along with Enron, WorldCom, Global Crossing, and a line of other huge enterprises went their auditor, Arthur Andersen.

Joseph Stiglitz received the Nobel Prize in 2001 for pioneering economic analyses showing the inadequacy of market self-regulation because of imperfect information, therefore undermining the fantasies of the market utopians. He has recently presented a rare insider's view of the nineties boom. From his experience as head of the Council of Economic Advisors during the early Clinton years, Stiglitz argues that the real culprit was an ideological and untested faith that deregulation—not reformed regulation—was the general elixir of economic growth. The old regulatory system—policed by the Securities and Exchange Commission, which was set up in response to the financial debacle of the Great Depression—had underwritten the spectacularly successful postwar performance of the economy. However, that system was already becoming increasingly strained by the complexities of the more globally integrated and technologically speeded-up economy of the 1990s. New financial techniques were being developed in rapid succession, and "investors and regulators alike were having an increasingly difficult time assessing companies' balance sheets." Under such conditions, accurate information was bound to be difficult to arrive at, threatening the efficiency of the capital markets. At just this time, Stiglitz points out, when caution would have been the intelligent policy to ensure long-term economic stability, "the special interests, their power augmented by an unwavering faith in markets, remained dominant in policymaking and continued to chant the mantra of deregulation."[8] This was the larger business climate in which the Big Five accounting firms, including Arthur Andersen, found themselves.

"Where Were the Auditors?"

Accounting is a highly technical field, rooted in mathematical sophistication. To do audits of publicly traded companies, accountants must be certified, which requires passing stiff examinations. Beyond that, auditing requires considerable finesse within a fast-changing and complex economic environment. Accountants doing public audit work must handle vast amounts of sensitive financial information in a short time. They must also make critical decisions about how to treat data and how to deploy sophisticated mathematical measures. They unavoidably incur risks and must rely heavily on educated judgment. The special nature of this expertise is what enabled public accounting firms such as Arthur Andersen to become multibillion-dollar enterprises of international scope.

The Andersen firm began in 1912 as a start-up. Arthur Andersen, an accounting professor and later dean at Northwestern University's fledgling business school, encouraged the best of his students to join the firm, which specialized in auditing publicly held companies in the booming financial center of Chicago. From the start, Andersen sought to instill high standards of probity as the hallmark of both the nascent accounting profession and his firm, insisting that it was independence and probity that would give the profession and the firm public stature and significance. Throughout its history, the firm prided itself on choosing not only the brightest accounting talent but also those most evidently committed to a high-minded view of the profession. So seriously was this aim taken that even as a global organization with tens of thousands of professional employees, only partners, not human resources personnel, did the final interviewing and selecting of new hires into the firm.

Arthur Andersen was not alone. His major rival at Price Waterhouse, George May, an expatriate British-trained accountant, thought the same way.

Emphasizing the quasi-public role of accounting during this period of unregulated capitalism, May frequently stressed the "high ethical obligations" assumed by auditors at the Price Waterhouse firm, saying that "it is the assumption of such obligations that makes what might otherwise be a business, a profession. Of all the groups of professions which are closely allied with business, there is none in which the practitioner is under a greater ethical obligation to persons who are not his immediate clients."[9]

Like the lawyer who is supposed to balance serving a client with the role of officer of the court, the public accountant was to serve the particular interests of the client by auditing corporate accounts, while protecting the public interest in having sound financial information. The most visible manifestation of this were nearly legendary anecdotes of Arthur Andersen, George May, and their peers refusing to acquiesce to the demands of influential clients that they overlook accounting irregularities for the sake of profit. Another was the push toward GAAP (Generally Accepted Accounting Principles), which could give accountants a clear basis upon which to state their claim to independence. Accountants wanted to establish themselves as a profession, and their leaders knew that the key to this purpose was winning and keeping the public trust.

In 2001, the Securities Exchange Commission charged Enron with fraud for overstating earnings while concealing vast indebtedness. Enron's auditors at the Andersen firm were by that time, like the public accounting field as a whole, part of a domain that George May (or Arthur Andersen) would hardly have recognized. For decades before the crash, selling business consulting services had overshadowed auditing on Andersen's bottom line. Although auditing was a form of civic regulation in the public interest, rooted in a professional culture of rigor, and licensed and regulated, consulting was a freewheeling, innovative trade with few formal rules and little government oversight.

As consulting grew in the deregulated economic environment of the 1980s and 1990s, the clash between the flashy and vastly profitable consulting business and the traditional audit culture of the firm produced internal tensions.

By the booming nineties, auditing had become the subordinate player, seen by many consulting partners as simply providing "annuity clients" to be carefully cultivated over the years in the interest of selling them any number of highly profitable consulting services. Thanks to consulting, Andersen partners could expect not merely a comfortable living in a respected profession at a firm with a good name, but personal wealth. By the time the consulting business had spun off on its own as Accenture, Andersen was already mired in the accounting fraud of Enron and was soon to be joined by its other notorious clients: WorldCom, Global Crossing, Qwest, and more. By the time the federal indictment for obstruction of justice (the famous Andersen shredding of documents) came down in

2002, the compromised culture of the firm had left little of its old reputation intact.

Throughout the painful aftermath, the persistent cry on both Wall Street and Main Street has been, "Where were the auditors?" Markets are only as efficient in deploying resources as the information upon which they are based is accurate. In the American economy, share prices of publicly traded stocks are a key signal for investment. It was this share price that auditors were expected to certify as justified by company performance. Without effective regulation, however, competitive economic interest leads not to the utopia of the free marketers' dreams but to disastrous market failure. Real economies depend upon noneconomic values in order to function; good faith remains the necessary condition for all contracts, the very foundation of commerce. So when auditors began to act as enablers of corporate fraud, they abandoned their loyalty to the public value of accurate financial knowledge. Once the fraud came to light, the result was loss of faith on the part of investors, precipitating the ruin of hordes of massively overextended corporate behemoths. The response was much tighter federal regulations, in the form of the Sarbanes-Oxley Act of 2002, which among other measures insisted upon splitting most consulting activity from auditing firms. It has also largely removed self-regulation from the accounting profession.

But what is effective regulation? Since its establishment in the 1930s, the Securities and Exchange Commission has tussled with the organized accounting profession over the sufficiency of rules and enforcement to furnish effective regulation of capital markets. Regulators, spurred by political pressure, have at times pressed to remove professional discretion in auditing so as to ensure uniform results. The profession has countered with the claim that high-stakes auditing of publicly traded corporations requires fine judgment calls and thus trust in professional discretion.

In the wake of the Andersen disaster, the public mood has supported increased reliance upon official regulation more than trust in the profession's probity. Yet the viability of investor capitalism depends upon professional integrity in carrying out functions essential to the functioning of the system as a whole. Because of the complexity of accounting, there is in the end a need for professional good faith. Without professional honor, as recent events demonstrate, the arena within which pursuit of self-interest can produce socially positive results implodes. At its end, many in the Andersen firm still could not imagine collective responsibility for the failure. The firm and its professional leaders seemed to have lost their sense of professional purpose amid the heady atmosphere of this new economy from which so many of the old rules and constraints appeared to have melted away.

Looking back, it seems clear that there is indeed important value added in professional services by a professional commitment to the public interest beyond service to the particular client. It is also evident that professionalism in its honorific sense depends upon supportive institutions if it is to thrive. Healthy institutions make maintenance of high standards of competence and an orientation toward serving the public standard operating procedures. They also set the protective social context within which the goods of professionalism can be nurtured, understood, and passed on as a collective asset that defines a sense of common purpose within an occupation. When this larger institutional context is missing, or allowed to decay, the result is nearly textbook anomie: loss of morale and purpose that leaves individuals, and groups such as professional firms, highly vulnerable to the opportunistic path of least resistance. Such outcomes represent institutional failure as much as individual corruption. They also raise the difficult question of how the essential purposes of professional work can be sustained amid the conflicting pressures of the contemporary environment.

The Need for a Broader View: Understanding the Professions

This is a time of scrutiny for all the institutions of American society. It is also a time of widespread disaffection, alienation, and resentment aimed at virtually all established organizations. As we have seen, despite their history of good repute the professions are now no exception. But the prevalent tone of scrutiny and skepticism, encouraged through popular journalism—important as it is for understanding— cannot do much to address the problem of conserving the essential purposes and moral resources of professionalism.

Our need is for a broad view of how the various aspects and tensions of the professional enterprise hang together. In other words, we need a theoretical perspective to illuminate and try to explain events such as the self-undermining of accounting's public trust. But our purpose in doing so is ultimately practical. It is because we want to rescue and renew the positive potential of professionalism that it is important to assimilate the work of historians and social scientists, philosophers, and educational researchers on the problems of professional life and education. These efforts can amount to tools for understanding and thereby the means for deliberation about what is to be done.

Among students of the professions, there is general agreement about the story of the rise to prominence in America. In outline, this trajectory begins in a nineteenth-century United States in which all forms of closed groups were suspect as undemocratic. Out of this unpromising social context, the modern professions began to establish themselves in the decades after the Civil War. Even more than today, organizing work through professions was then an uncertain and disputed matter. In the United States, professions have always been dependent upon myriad complex relationships with other groups and forces beyond their occupational group. In this sense, they are inherently social, cultural, indeed civic and political entities and not simply categories of specialized labor. To grasp this complexity, we need a perspective enabling us to appreciate and learn from the critiques of professional pretension developed by social scientists, not so as to abandon the professional project but to reformulate its ideals and purposes to better fit the demands of civic engagement in a pluralistic society. For this we need to approach history and the social sciences to learn from them how to be wiser and more constructive participants in the complex context of contemporary professional work.

The traditional learned professions distantly echo, in culture and organizational form, those medieval guilds rooted in the universities.[10] In the medieval university, the bachelor of arts degree was the essential prerequisite of beginning study for the guilds of law and medicine as well as for the higher clergy. Part of the status and mystique of those guilds, like the clerical order itself, derived from possession of this prestigious cultural heritage, not the least fluency in the Latin language. Part of their prestige also stemmed from the fiduciary nature of their services. That is, priests, lawyers, and physicians (who could be the same person) possessed knowledge of the mysteries and complexities of this world and the next that were believed to be beyond what a typical layperson could pretend to. It was widely accepted that the work of the traditional learned professions required a significant domain of discretion in how they conducted their practice. Such work was accordingly thought to require a stronger sense of moral dedication than most occupations did.

Unexpectedly, aspects of this traditional professional culture were revised and acquired new currency from proponents of professionalism in the late nineteenth-century United States. The development of professionalized fields modified the laissez-faire pattern of American occupational life. Successful efforts to professionalize occupations, as happened in medicine and law, gave their members a degree of economic security as well as hope of collective mobility toward improved social and economic status. The key to this process became, as it had been in the Middle Ages, possession of educational credentials.[11] The cultural prestige represented by the venerable traditions of law, medicine, and divinity, along with the new model university focused on specialized scholarship and science, resonated sufficiently among the politically connected "better classes" to enable these fields to establish something resembling a guild monopoly. Thus the rise of the modern professions in America has been organically intertwined with the elaboration of a vast and decentralized system of higher education.[12]

In this process, once ill-defined means of training practitioners for the law, medicine, and the Protestant clergy moved from informal apprenticeship toward education in professional schools. These fields (together with a few others such as college teaching) were able to establish effective control over entry into the occupation and therefore over the training process and size of the labor force. Fields less successful in their efforts at professionalization (such as engineering, nursing, and teaching) never succeeded in gaining such power. They were correspondingly less able to bestow on their members "market shelter," leaving those members unable to escape economically precarious positions. There were many paths to entry into school teaching or engineering, but the portals to medicine, law, architecture, and the like narrowed and all finally came under the control of the guild itself. These increasingly self-contained occupational domains thereby became the model case of what it meant to be a profession.

These early efforts at establishing professional authority were bolstered, notes sociologist Steven Brint, by the emergence of an understanding of professionals as "trustees of the community." Ministers, lawyers, physicians, and teachers were a small fraction of the population of any community in those days; along with local businessmen, they often found themselves selected for leadership within community organizations. Business leaders brought resources of wealth and connections; professionals brought education and cultural links with a world beyond the local community. With little in the way of government institutions, professionals' involvement in such organizations as school boards, charity societies, libraries, and associations of all kinds formed a strong link in the public understanding between professional knowledge and service in the interest of the local community.[13]

This history is essential for understanding even why professions are characterized as they are. As we have already seen in the Introduction, the aspects of professions most often used to classify an occupation as a profession are actually the result of a particular history. In the main, Americans came to accept first the ministry, then law, and finally academic teaching and medicine as embodying a true professional ideal. That is, the professional came to be defined first of all as learned and formally educated, publicly licensed, and supported by a collegial organization of peers committed to an ethic of service to clients and the public.[14]

Security of career and socioeconomic mobility, in other words, were directly dependent upon the authority and prestige a given field was able to achieve. A number of historians have detailed how various professional groups sought "authority and honor," in Samuel Haber's phrase, within a highly competitive society deeply suspicious of claims of special privilege. Unlike Europe, where professions were often associated with a powerful national government or a superior social class, in the United States the professions had to struggle for status in a distinctly American way. They bargained for honor, guaranteed by legally enforced privileges, in exchange for service and community trusteeship. This social contract became the moral basis of professionalism in America, giving American professions a civic orientation. Professions evolved into entities much like such legally chartered corporations as universities and colleges, which were granted autonomy and special status for a public purpose.[15]

The first lesson from this history is that it took more than demonstration of functional skill to establish a strong professional niche in the modern labor market. Political connections, effective organization, and especially the ability to establish and mobilize cultural significance were all essential. Professions are thus historically emergent social groups who share common educational experiences and a resulting outlook on themselves and the world. They are, in Randall Collins's phrase, "consciousness communities" with a sense of boundaries and interest in defining situations in a way consistent with a distinct viewpoint.[16] Yet professions depend for their form and economic position upon a process of social negotiation with those outside the domain and ultimately upon political recognition and support.

One important implication is that a true professional ideal becomes socially real only through its embodiment in a social contract between the professional group and the larger public. A second

implication is the ambiguous position professions occupy in a democratic society. On the one hand, as groups able to control entry to a
domain, they manifest the proclivity of the traditional guild toward
monopolizing economic opportunity and social prestige for self-
aggrandizement. On the other hand, as organized around important
public values, professions can promote the *esprit de corps* necessary
to maintain and advance standards of practice.

Sociologists and historians are divided over the importance one
should give to one or the other tendency. A chronologically earlier
group of analysts focused upon the emergence of professionalism as
a paradigm of modern work, adding a generally positive assessment
of its significance as an alternative to competitive economic laissez-
faire on the one hand or bureaucratic organization on the other.[17]
A second set of analysts have taken a more critical stance, highlighting the tension between the professions' social and economic
privileges and their claims to public benevolence. Some among
these studies emphasize professionalism as primarily a "project of
collective mobility," stressing the economic dimensions of professionalization as a trend within the division of labor in liberal capitalism. (The studies by Larson and Krause, for example, stress these
aspects.) Another set of analysts also employ a strategic lens but
emphasize the nascent professions' use of devices for enhancing
cultural and social authority to define and control a specific area of
expertise.[18]

Another Test Case: The Rise and Decline of "Sovereign" Medicine

The case of American medicine illustrates the contrasting strengths
of these approaches. The more critical views are valuable for gaining
analytical insight, but it is the first approach, which includes appreciation of the social value of professionalism, that can help to address
the present situation constructively. Medicine's history illustrates the
ambiguities of professionalism as it has been institutionalized. On the
one hand, this history vindicates one claim for professionalizing

work: strong, guildlike organization can improve the standards of knowledge and skill, linking education and training closely to practice.[19] Unfortunately, the same history also underscores how easily privileges granted for public purposes can be appropriated for private advantage. However, the story also points toward an answer to the question of how professionalism can be renewed as a positive force. The answer is both strengthened accountability and a professional leadership attentive to public needs as well as attuned to practitioner wants, one concerned to improve standards and also to strengthen links between the profession and the public.

The most informed account of American medicine and what is called the health care industry in the twentieth century is still Paul Starr's *The Social Transformation of American Medicine*.[20] Its major points have recently been illustrated in Kenneth Ludmerer's detailed study of American medical education.[21] Starr presents the career of medicine as a long, ascending curve toward achieving the autonomy of a well-established "sovereign profession," followed by a time of internal conflict and descent. At the same time, Starr's account also calls attention to how much the history of medicine's professionalization has always intersected the shifting alliances among competing social interests in American politics.[22]

In Starr's narrative, American medicine successfully developed itself into a uniquely sovereign profession by tight organization and insistence that physicians, not third parties of any kind, control how medical services are provided and paid for. Remarkably, and unlike the story in most other industrial nations, American medicine harnessed scientific and technological advances to a model of practice in which the individual physician remained at the center. As private practitioners, doctors worked within a cartel administered by the local medical society and based in the community hospital, which the local physicians controlled. By early in the twentieth century, organized medicine achieved guildlike monopoly over its sphere of interest. Aided by the fledgling Carnegie Foundation for the Advancement of Teaching's famous Flexner Report, the American Medical Association was able to establish control over medical education and licensing throughout the country. This linked medical training and credentials to the university system, allying elite practitioners with academic teaching hospitals.

The decline in medicine's professional sovereignty began, paradoxically, with its greatest expansion during the burst of national enthusiasm for scientific progress that followed victory in World War II. In that era for the first time, organized medicine accepted government as a partner. The federal government became massively involved through support for both research and the growth of medical schools and teaching hospitals. By the 1960s, an increasingly prestigious and confident academic medical establishment became sympathetic to what emerged as the federal initiatives of Medicare and Medicaid. This led to a break in the medical ranks. Although willing to accept government funding for education and research, the AMA maintained fierce and longstanding opposition to any encroachment by "socialized medicine" upon the autonomy of practice. With the support of most practitioners, the organization opposed the federal initiatives.

In the long term, these developments transformed medical practice; they also increased the divergence between the elite of academic medicine and the practitioner base of the AMA, such that medicine could no longer speak with a single voice. By involving government as a third-party payer as well as dispenser of largesse for expansion, medicine had less room for autonomous maneuver. Expansion and technological developments together fueled a steady rise in health care expenditures, which now showed up in the federal budget and on corporate balance sheets as insurance costs. In this way the huge expansion of medicine during the postwar period, though initially greatly enhancing the wealth, power, and prestige of the profession, also fatally entangled medicine with economic and political developments that it was able to exploit temporarily but not finally control.

This is the context of the "health care crisis" that has enveloped all the health care professions during the past two decades. As Starr summarized the trajectory: "the underlying

tension between a medical care system geared toward expansion
and a society and state requiring some means of control over med-
ication expenditures . . . [forced] a redrawing of the 'contract'
between the medical profession and society, subjecting medical
care to the discipline of politics or markets, or reorganizing its basic
institutional structure."[23] At a more concrete level, as Ludmerer
notes, individual physicians found themselves increasingly in conflict as to where their fiduciary responsibilities lay: with the needs
of patients or with insurance companies, health care systems, and
investors.[24] After an unsuccessful effort by the Clinton administration to develop a form of joint federal-private insurer-provided
national health insurance system, the denouement has been the
takeover of much of health care by for-profit managed care, with a
high likelihood of some degree of government oversight and regulation, as yet to be determined. However it is finally decided, it
seems clear that physicians will never again be the primary force
determining how health care is delivered in the United States.

In this "redrawing" of "the contract between the medical profession and society," the stronger interests have prevailed, with the
public reduced to bystander status and medicine itself more passive
than active. Was this outcome inevitable? Here the differences
among various analysts' theoretical perspectives show up forcefully.
To those who view the professions as essentially "collective mobility projects" aiming at maximum autonomy, it may seem so. Krause
has described the reigning in of the powers of American medicine
as part of a general social tendency to subordinate professional
organizations more effectively to the control of state and business
(frequently acting together). This transformation is the final "death
of the guilds," a process Krause finds proceeding apace in all industrial nations.[25] From this perspective, professionalism—at least
when understood as primarily an ideological defense of guild powers—can mount only a losing rear-guard action against the
inevitable advance of the Darwinian efficiency of the market,
whose ends the modern state exists to serve.

For historians such as Harold Perkin, on the other hand, the situation is more complex and outside causes less wholly determinative. Perkin argues that the spread of the idea of professionalism and its public legitimacy are inexplicable unless it answers in some way to real social needs that have become ever more pressing as the postindustrial or knowledge society develops. "The whole point and purpose of professional society," writes Perkin, "is to apply knowledge and expertise to the production of enough sophisticated goods and services to meet the needs of every citizen . . . so that for the first time in human history the economy is capable of producing enough 'created assets' to give everyone . . . access to the full range of satisfactions once open only to the rich and powerful."[26] In this context the integrity of professional services becomes a key public good. Thus, realizing the potential of such a new kind of society depends on institutionalizing an understanding of society as a body politic rooted in an ethos of equity and cooperation among different functional interests. For Perkin, this was summed up in the "professional social ideal," a blending of social justice and economic efficiency that he finds at the core of twentieth-century social reform.[27]

These themes resonate with the early-twentieth-century formulations of professionalism as an ideology of civic reform. As Brint and others have described it, that period saw not just the rise of the guild power of medicine but also the efforts of professionals to draw a contract with the public in which professional social responsibility played a featured role. By contrast, the eclipse of that earlier civically oriented notion of professionalism by a conception of the professional as simply a technical expert has made professionalism less effective. The very success of the professions turned later-twentieth-century professional leadership inward toward building its own organizations and prestige. Claims to professional expertise displaced community trusteeship as the coin of legitimacy for most professional groups. This long-term development pushed toward "the transformation of professionalism from an ideology linking community and authority into an ideology linking markets and skills" so that "the cultural connection of professionals to pub-lic life" grew weaker even as the strength and reach of professional organizations expanded.[28]

An unexpected result of that shift has been to diminish the importance of the professional voice in public debate.[29] Or so the recent history of medicine seems to show. Devising a way beyond the present situation may require of medicine a return to the ear-lier ideals of civic professionalism. This would be to "go public" in a way that departs from much of the history of organized medicine. Such a new start, indeed, would require less-exclusive reliance upon the technical model of the physician as expert, in favor of a new conception. The new model of the physician would fuse some-thing of the old ideal of the professional as active trustee for the patient's and the community's health with a more cooperative rela-tionship to allied health fields and the public at large. The new type of professional leadership must be able to persuade the medical field to assume new responsibilities for and with the public.

Rethinking Professionalism: Toward a New Social Contract

There have been recent movements within medicine toward a renewed professionalism. Some of them began in academic medicine and medical education, where the focus was on cultivating a physi-cian identity over time that would be responsive to the concerns of a more patient-focused and socially orienting kind of practice. Other movements began to address the large issue of corporate leadership in the field and its relationship to practitioners and public. In the United Kingdom, for example, a strong movement for a new profes-sionalism emerged, spurred by serious malpractice scandals in the mid-1990s. At the same time, in the United States several founda-tions associated with internal medicine, the largest of the specialist bodies, issued a "Charter on Medical Professionalism."

The British understanding of the new professionalism, as described by Sir Donald Irvine, recent president of the General Medical Council, has three features: first, maintaining knowledge and skills needed for good patient care; second, fostering respect, communication, and patient-guided care, including promotion of access to quality health care for all; and third, accountability, both personally on the part of individual physicians and collectively through professional self-monitoring in cooperation with public regulation.[30] The British new professionalism emphasizes individual physician responsibility and the collective accountability of the profession. "In future as doctors," concludes Irvine, "we must take our professionalism—and with it professional regulation—as our basic professional asset . . . as a living thing, the contemporary embodiment of medical culture."[31]

The Charter on Medical Professionalism was produced by the American Board of Internal Medicine Foundation and the American College of Physicians-American Specialty of Internal Medicine Foundation of the United States, together with the European Federation of Internal Medicine. The Preamble to the charter sets out the notion that medicine's contract with society is based upon three things: first, placing the interests of patients as the highest priority; second, "setting and maintaining standards of [physician] competence and integrity"; third, "providing expert advice to society on matters of health." The charter emphasizes not only patient welfare but patient autonomy as well, suggesting more participatory relationships between doctors and patients. Finally, the charter's Preamble notes that the contract depends upon "public trust in physicians," which in turn rests upon "the integrity *of both individual physicians* and the *whole profession*" (my emphasis).[32] Distinguishing a living culture, in Irvine's words, from a merely inert concept of professionalism, these developments reach out to the public by beginning to open up professional practice, and especially professional self-government, to scrutiny and evaluation. The point of all this, however, is ultimately partnership for the greater good of the whole society.

The future of the professions may increasingly hinge on how professionalism is understood and practiced. It is once again a serious question whether or not a profession can secure public recognition of its claims to traditional professional prerogatives on the basis of the marketability of its technical skills alone. Or will public support and legal recognition for a profession increasingly require that it demonstrate significant contributions to advancing civic welfare? Historically, the legitimacy, authority, and legal privileges of the most prestigious professions have depended heavily on their claims (and finally their demonstration) of civic performance, especially social leadership in the public interest. As fields such as medicine come under the sway of large market-driven organizations, it is far from clear that these fields will be able to sustain their social importance without reengaging the public over the value of their work to the society at large. If the professions are to have a future, they may need to make their case from a civic understanding, rather than a wholly technical one, of what it is that professionals are about.

The entropy of professional legitimacy and the concomitant need to rethink the basis of its social contract are not unique to medicine. Law, the other old and highly successful field, has been experiencing its own sort of professional malaise. The experience of the legal profession too points to the need for renewed professionalism. Deborah Rhode, an astute inside observer and critic of the American legal profession, has directly linked the profession's current ills to failure to understand and practice professionalism in just the full, activist, civic sense under discussion in medicine.

Rhode makes a strong case that law has been losing public confidence largely because as a profession it fails to live up to its fiduciary responsibility to make the system of justice function well and equitably. "The central challenge for the legal profession," Rhode writes, "is how to strengthen a sense of ethical obligation and to inspire a richer sense of what it demands in practice."[33] However, Rhode argues that this is not easy, even with plenty of good will. Like medicine, the legal profession has evolved into what is in many ways a series of fragments rather than a unified professional field. This makes acting together as a profession a rare and difficult achievement. Rhode sums up the situation by saying: "Commercialism and incivility are increasing; collegiality and collective responsibility are in decline. The priority of profits and the resulting sweatshop schedules have squeezed out time for public service and family commitments. . . ."[34] The public is deliberately kept at arm's length and denied input into professional decision making and self-disciplining. The consequence, she emphasizes, is the paradox of a prominent and influential profession whose members feel powerless in the face of the profession's most crippling ills.

The upshot of this analysis is that the loss of morale among legal practitioners leaves the profession strangely unable to address and solve its own most pressing problems. The reason for this sense of powerlessness lies not in weakness of character on the part of individual lawyers. It stems from weak professional solidarity, manifested in the failure of the organized bar to take leadership in reform. This is an important lesson. Individual practitioners cannot long or effectively confront the deforming pressures that analysts such as Rhode catalogue without strong support from an organized profession that is trying to meet its public obligations. There is an important reminder here that professionalism is rooted in a professional social contract. Professions are collegial organizations that carry a grant of public privilege and responsibility in exchange for accountability to the public. In the absence of the exercise of professional responsibility at the level of collective organization, individual practitioners are simply not able to function effectively.

What is needed, then, is collective empowerment of practitioners, guided by accountability to the public. Taken together, the experience of medicine and law suggest that professionalism flourishes only if key players within a profession take leadership in enforcing high standards of practice, while inviting public response and involvement in the profession's efforts to clarify its mission and responsibilities. This is the practical import of civic professionalism today. It should be the goal of efforts to understand and criticize the professions' existing state and the implications of their histories. This effort is the substance of the chapters on the evolution of the professions that follow.

The approach of the next chapters also makes it easier to grasp both the limitations and the potential of the several types of profession for responding to the challenges of the present. The aim is to shed light on the crucial cultural dimension of the professional enterprise. Reconstructing the socioeconomic and political contexts that gave rise to the particular professional types makes it clear how and why the meaning of professional life remains a contested issue. Hence the qualities of autonomy, personal probity, and social leadership associated with professionalism derive from the early learned professions, which formed around themselves the aura of social responsibility and leadership. In a parallel way, the ascendancy of confidence in learned expertise, specialization, and the applicability of science and technology to human problems indicates the continuing currency of values that launched the later technologically oriented professions such as engineering.

Tracing the conflicts and innovations through which the several types of profession arose also indicates their close association with characteristic institutions and influential currents in American culture. The most constant tension, as we have seen, is between a technical emphasis stressing specialization—broadly linked to a utilitarian conception of society as a project for enhancing efficiency and individual satisfaction—and a sense of professional mission that insists upon the prominence of the ethical and civic dimensions of the enterprise. This conflict within professionalism has at times mirrored a wider conflict within American society, while at other times the direction taken by the culture of professionalism has held a leading part in the larger drama of cultural change.

This framework of analysis makes no pretense to neutrality in the ongoing contest of the identity and destiny of the professional enterprise. It seeks to reclaim and continue a tradition of civic professionalism. This is a tradition that, although acknowledging the genuine importance of technical proficiency in every field, views the professional enterprise as humanly engaged practices generating values of great significance for a modern society. The burden of the several chapters that follow is to show how the civic orientation in professionalism has been eclipsed by a more narrowly technical understanding, often to the detriment of professional life and the social compact that links professions to the larger society. The latter part of the book attempts to make constructive use of this analysis in order to discern and explore the possibilities a renewed civic professionalism holds out for American democracy. These conflicts have repeatedly been focused on the central issue of how professionals should be trained. Hence, professional education becomes an important theme in these later chapters, to diagnose past and present conflicts and to envision renewal.

Chapter Two

The Evolution of the Professions

From Professions of Office to the Organizational Professions

Today the professions appear to be a natural and established feature of American society, as of all developed nations. In fact, however, the professions' achievement of social importance was hardly an expected nor necessary feature of the development of the United States. Since its founding, American society has been especially agitated by conflicts that pit a belief in egalitarianism against an ideal of individual achievement. This conflict has led to dramatic swings, at one moment toward public recognition of the competence of certain specialized groups to regulate a whole occupational sphere, such as health care, while at other moments toward public opinion stripping occupational groups of any special prerogatives or privileges.

Since a professional career has always been a route to individual success, professions have been a focal point in the struggle to balance democratic openness to individual achievement with the need for the professions to be trusted to work for the benefit of others, in pursuit of agreed-upon, common ends. Professionals take part in commercial society as the owners of a special type of wealth-producing property or "capital" of a peculiarly intellectual sort: the skills and knowledge acquired through their specialized training and experience. This is sometimes referred to as "human," as opposed to physical, capital. Like physical capital, human capital can be traded in the market; like physical capital, its security and negotiability depend upon a structure of legal definitions and procedures.

The human capital of professionals, however, is peculiarly dependent upon public, legal acceptance of the value of services offered by the professional. The professional's services are often beyond the lay buyer's ability to understand or fully judge. There is thus an inescapable, reciprocal fiduciary relationship between the professional and client. That is, the professional (including the group of professionals providing a certain service) must persuade clients to accept the professional's definition and valuation of that service, even as the clients must acknowledge and trust the competence of the provider. In this way, professionalization is always the result of a two-way process of political accommodation. More than many other kinds of property, the human capital of professionals is visibly a social and political artifact. Hence it can only be secured so long as, in the main, the terms of reciprocity seem fair to the public or the profession can wield political power to uphold its privileged position.

In this sense, the professions live a precarious existence in a democratic society. Ideally, they operate within a social compact, one requiring that, in exchange for their elevated status and a regulated market for their services that ensures a good livelihood, professionals demonstrate civic responsibility and even community leadership. These capacities are rarely in abundant supply in any group, and their appearance, nurture, and uncertain functioning among professionals is a major part of the story of the rise of professionalism in the United States, a story unfolding within a larger struggle over the moral legitimacy of professional standing itself.

From the beginning of European settlement, the colonists of British North America seemed to prefer the risks of individual opportunity to the relatively secure but limited prospects of the European craft guilds and estates. For much of American history, an egalitarian can-do spirit of self-help and spontaneous mutual aid seemed sufficient to most needs. This is a nation that embraced the all-around individual who could learn whatever special skills might be needed to grasp an opportunity. At the same time, however, Americans also embraced the promise of the European Enlightenment: that everyday life could be significantly improved through application of trained reason to all areas of human affairs, including the realm of the arts and crafts as well as medical, legal, and academic scholarship. Thus, although the traditional professions were always distinguished by confidence in learning, in modern society the professions are supported by public confidence that application of rational reflection is a main engine of progress. In the American experience, however, it has rarely proved easy to reconcile this confidence in the value of trained expertise with the moral claims of a strong egalitarian populism.

By contrast, in Continental Europe the professions grew up under the tutelage of the established institutions of church and state. Like the United States, modern European nations developed on the basis of an expanding commercial system and new (or violently recast) national states. There too scientific scholarship and expertise were embraced by the leading groups in the population. Only in Europe were the state and its institutions (often encompassing both the academy and the church) felt to carry the collective purposes and values of the national spirit. The European nations, including Britain, gradually created a central core of national institutions to handle the complexity and conflicts set in motion by the industrial and democratic revolutions.

From the late eighteenth century onward, European states founded new institutions of learning or renovated old ones to train a new class of prestigious professionals: the pastor, the lawyer, the judge, the military officer, the professor, the civil servant. All were professionals of office. They drew their authority from the institutions they served and to which most of the educated ranks of society were connected, at least through education if not direct employment. Today, as civil servants in those societies, contemporary European professionals continue to identify themselves closely with the institutions they serve and the state-related university system that educates them. By contrast, in the United States *professional* designates independent status, different from business or wage labor but less tied to authoritative public institutions than its Continental relatives.[1] For most of its history, the United States has lacked the central core institutions of the European national state. Consequently, and momentously, the American professions are far more diversified,

competitive, and ambitious than their European (or Japanese) counterparts, less identified with the prestige and larger purposes of
public institutions, and more focused upon the rewards of commercial success.

The significant exception to the typical American pattern was
(in this way as in many others) New England. In the colonies settled by English Calvinist dissenters, deliberate and major efforts by
the colonists saw to it that the authority of church and state was
strong. Calvinism was in part a movement for communal renewal,
and when as in New England it had a fairly free hand to fashion
society in its terms, the result was a corporate polity with established
ecclesiastical, educational, and judicial institutions supported by
taxation. There two of the early modern professions of office found
a central place, as the minister and the magistrate, the theologian
and the jurist, became the chief figures shaping the direction of the
new society.[2]

The Calvinist emphasis upon law, both religious and civil,
ensured that learning, rational debate, and persuasion would play
major roles in ordering public life. Intellectuals could outrank men
of wealth in such a polity, and New England institutions encouraged identification of both men of intellect and men of property
with the order represented in church and state. From this development came the notion that a profession ought to have a "mission,"
a sacred trust to promote and act for the sake of declared common
purposes, in terms of which practitioners are to be held accountable
before the public as a whole.

The paradigm case of this understanding of the profession of
office in America was the New England Congregational minister.
Trained at a publicly sponsored school and a similarly sponsored
college such as Harvard or Yale, the minister was an elected and
publicly funded official of the town. As historian Donald Scott puts
it, "The minister conducted what was referred to as 'public wor-
ship,' performing the rituals and delivering the Word that ordered
the community as an organic whole. In this sense the minister
belonged to the town."[3]

With the coming of the Revolution, the chartered royal governments collapsed, while religious establishment fell into bad odor
in most of the new states (though not in Massachusetts). Tolerant,
multiethnic Pennsylvania, rather than hierarchical and established
Massachusetts, became the more typical pattern for the new republic. The great waves of egalitarian spirit and republican hopes that
the Revolution sent abroad eroded the earlier tendencies toward a
society controlled by local gentlemen. The vertical ties of personal
economic and political patronage that had held colonial society
together loosened in new and unexpected ways with the spread of
the horizontal bonds of commerce. Accelerated commerce weakened older dependencies and intensified the division of labor,
giving rise to new groups of economically independent, politically
enfranchised citizens.

Under the new conditions, the inherited conception of the common good, as a balanced and just ordering of a whole made up
of unequal parts, gave way to the dynamic image of networks of
exchange binding yet propelling independent individuals forward in
time and space. For many of the founding generation of American
leaders, notably Thomas Jefferson and John Adams, the experience
of revolution and nation building proved a sobering one. Directly
opposite to the unifying and centralizing tendencies then explosively
at work in European nation-states, the United States after independence expanded rapidly but with little central coordination, despite
the efforts of the Federalists. This pattern fostered dispersed loyalties
and narrow perspectives, but also a leveling spirit, especially along
the ever-expanding frontier in the West, as well as great commercial
vitality.[4] At first, the expectation was widespread that the new freedom and equality would spontaneously generate "civic virtue," an
ideal of public-spiritedness once confined to a ruling class. But in fact,
individual liberty tended more often to assertion of self-interest, now
released to compete in a free market of property and votes, than to
republican virtue.

In this emerging civil society of unfettered commercial exchange,
many looked to the state to underwrite faster development. But

concerned republicans such as Jefferson began looking for a way to ensure that leadership would reside in the hands of what he called a natural aristocracy: those of all stations who demonstrated capacity and virtue in assuming public responsibility. This was his more egalitarian alternative to the strategy of John Adams and Alexander Hamilton to solidify a powerful (and hopefully responsible) aristocracy of birth and wealth. It was to identify and train his natural aristocrats that Jefferson urged the establishment of education, including a state-supported university. Education would introduce those with promise of high achievement to the ideals of civic humanism and the techniques of science in order to counterbalance the blandishments of irresponsible wealth.[5] Something of the public spirit of the professions of office continued to cling to these proposals. Jefferson and the Federalists agreed at least on this: that the well-being of the republic required promotion of learning and intellect, infused with a spirit of public service, in order to develop an expanding class of responsible social leaders.

The Free Professions: Rise, Defeat, and Metamorphosis

In fact, the nascent civil society of nineteenth-century America was to prove far more fluid, and more allergic to institutionalization of either intellect or leadership, than even Jefferson imagined. During that time, the learned professions of law, medicine, and the ministry (largely including education) were forced to seek a new institutional form. This form was what has been called the commercial or free professions. In the early period, the free professions linked themselves with the wealthy gentlemen farmers and merchants of the eastern cities and towns. By means of gentry influence, professional licensing was established in many states, and the formation of professional bodies as separate, privileged occupational groups was under way. Through attendance at colleges serving the sons of the socially established, aspiring members of the bar, the clergy, and medicine joined the circle of this eastern gentry. They shared with much of this gentry a humanist education, a cosmopolitan culture and outlook linked to Europe, and they often married into prominent families.

The United States in the first decades of the nineteenth century, despite the tolerance of slavery and the slow engulfment of the Native American nations, was by world standards a comparatively open and egalitarian society. The atomizing effects of rapid economic and geographic mobility were to some degree offset by shared legal norms and an internalized morality that defined clear identities for men and women and subjected them to close scrutiny by their neighbors. Individuals were tightly bound into local communities and graded as respectable or not as they approximated notions of character, encompassing the virtues of hard work, honesty, loyalty, and fair play. This fluid, loosely articulated society sustained a boisterous public realm in which diverse interests could clash and struggle openly.

Centered on the mercantile towns and cities, a broadly democratic civic culture was supported by voluntary societies, educational organizations for working people, as well as merchants, newspapers, and political clubs. In this locally based society, professionally trained men were often conspicuous leaders.[6] Alexis de Tocqueville, visiting the nation during the 1830s and 1840s and no doubt noticing the public sway of figures such as Daniel Webster, Henry Clay, and John Calhoun, identified lawyers as playing the role of an American aristocracy, balancing the egalitarian passions of democracy with a conservative feeling for continuity and precedent.[7] However, in the struggle to control public opinion the nascent free professions suffered the enormous setback signaled by the election of Andrew Jackson.

Jackson combined egalitarian enthusiasm for economic independence with resentment against the gilded privilege of the eastern elites, to fuel a powerful political movement hostile to professional privilege in any form. Led by a vigorous President Jackson, a wave of populist sentiment overwhelmed the bastions of gentry strength and professional privilege, ending licensing of doctors and religious establishment, even in the New England states.

Jackson's first inaugural address proclaimed the theme. "Let us go on elevating our people," Jackson cried, "perfecting our institutions, until democracy shall reach such a point of perfection that we can acclaim with the truth that the voice of the people is the voice of God."[8]

Those events of the 1830s continue in a powerful way to affect our American present. When twenty-first-century politicians intone the phrase "traditional values," it is usually an idealized version of a Jacksonian persuasion they are invoking. Jacksonians opposed "the people" to "the interests" of privilege. Andrew Jackson himself defined his constituency as "the real people, the bone and sinew of the country . . . whose success depends upon their own industry and economy."[9] Denouncing privilege and celebrating the virtues of hard work created a bond of moral agreement among a quite diverse constituency. The people so described actually included southern, slave-owning planters along with western farmers and eastern mechanics and laborers. The people's enemy was not wealth as such; everyone aspired to that. It was, rather, those interests requiring grants of special legal privilege that were the object of anger and attack. This class included those with an interest in professional licensing and the credentials of learning.

Democrats, as Jackson interpreted the term, wanted to clear the land of all obstacles to economic opportunity. This is what linked together the otherwise disparate features of Jackson's presidency. The attack on the federally chartered Bank of the United States, forcible removal by the great "Indian Fighter" of all Native Americans living east of the Mississippi, and the delicensing of professions and institutions of learning were all successful efforts to clear the ground for the people's entrepreneurial energy. Would-be professionals frequently adapted by acting as free economic agents themselves, hanging out a shingle and plying the trade of their fancy. So successful were the Jacksonians in identifying individual economic opportunity with democracy that when institutionalized credentials and professions began their comeback at the end of the century, their advocates would justify them by reason of their usefulness, especially their

potential contribution to national economic progress. This was arguing the case for professions on terms Jacksonians would understand,
if not always accept.

Jacksonian America relied upon a simple, replicable, uniform
culture to stabilize and guide the disorientations attendant upon the
policy of *laissez-nous faire*. This common culture was based upon
the (Protestant) Bible, the family, enterprise, and the presumed
equality of all native-born white males, according to the same rules
of fair play. Modern populist passion has continued to draw strength
from latter-day versions of this moral system, somewhat broadened
over the intervening time. American populism has generally been
in favor of rural life and small, homogeneous communities, but it
has also strongly endorsed economic advance through market competition. It is hostile to inherited privilege and urban life, skeptical
of cosmopolitan culture, irreligion, intellectuals, artists, and moral
experimentation. This combination of themes reveals its origins in
a social environment where the household was the economic unit
and enterprise was small, unspecialized, and local in scope.

The center of the Jacksonian moral world was the figure of the
independent citizen, in which the lore (if not the full reality) of
Ben Franklin lived on. This figure continued to reappear at the
center of American aspirations as the successful breadwinner, hus-
band, and father who "knows best."[10]

Contemporaries could be quite blunt, and revealing, when
assessing the political significance of the independent citizen ideal.
Near midcentury, Martin Van Buren, Jackson's successor as president and leader of the Democratic party, wryly summed up the reasons for the continued success of the party of Jackson. Van Buren
found the key in a prevalent social cleavage. Very simply, Van
Buren said, Jacksonians spoke for the mass of "sweats" as against the
few educated "wits" of the nation. As long as there are more
"sweats, especially farmers and mechanics," any political party
(such as the opposition Whigs) perceived as the preserve of the
wits was bound to fail.[11] All this seemed confirmed when the Whig
party, led by gentlemen opponents of the Jacksonian Democrats

(and soon to be reborn as the Republicans), finally found in Abraham Lincoln a wit leader acceptable to many sweats.

"Honest Abe" Lincoln, the rail splitter from Illinois, seemed the perfect image of the self-made man from the West, a Ben Franklin for the times. Lincoln articulated the party's platform stands against the expansion of slavery and in favor of expanded property ownership. But Republican party propagandists were also proud to assure voters that Mr. Lincoln had risen to fortune as a legal professional, not only a defender of the people's rights but once the general counsel to that pioneering high-tech corporation called the Illinois Central Railroad. In fact Lincoln, Januslike, could assume both faces. Part of Lincoln did look to the homesteads and Main Streets of sweat equity, local entrepreneurship, and democratic fairness. The other Lincoln understood and functioned within the emerging industrial society of hierarchical, highly technical organizations that often worked closely with government, of which the Illinois Central was a harbinger. Lincoln himself anticipated the national trend in moving from sweat to wit while, like every successful politician after him, nurturing ties to both constituencies.

In his fateful role as president, however, Lincoln became the free professional in heroic proportions, the counselor to a bitterly divided nation who tried to shape American dispersion into a coherent national society. As the self-declared admirer of that earlier advocate of national unification, Henry Clay, Lincoln brought to the presidency a vision of national unity and greatness unseen since the era of the revolutionary gentry's ascendancy. Even during the height of the conflict over slavery and the Union, Lincoln worked methodically to develop and expand the nation into the West under federal aegis, chartering the transcontinental railroad, promoting the Homestead Act, and using the power of the national state to foster higher education through land-grant colleges. Significantly, during the early years of the Civil War that brought Lincoln to tragic greatness, his son was among the wits, studying at Harvard. Yet Lincoln's goal of a more just yet unified national society was to be realized only in part. In nineteenth-century America, the claims of enterprise, equality, and institutional authority seemed unable to find a stable point of balance.

The Free Professions and the Search for Professional Integrity

In *Democracy in America*, de Tocqueville interpreted the new democratic country he had visited during the Jacksonian era as a glimpse of the likely future of all modern nations. He saw America's historically unprecedented commitment to individual liberty and equality as embodying at once a great moral gain and a fundamental human dilemma. To de Tocqueville, the United States was the advance guard of a new kind of society, which he called "democratic," where individuals gained a novel degree of dignity and freedom to define themselves in ways of their own choosing. Previously, in Europe and other civilizations, people lived according to inherited codes, distinct from each other in hereditary groupings, bound into a stratified order. De Tocqueville termed this type of society "aristocratic." Since he was writing for the political enlightenment of public opinion in less-egalitarian Europe, de Tocqueville sought to warn his readers of what he saw as the difficulties inherent in a democratic type of society.[12]

Individual freedom was not a natural condition, as de Tocqueville saw it, but a collective achievement. It could only be maintained by people who understood that their individual well-being, because it was interdependent with the well-being of many others, required taking responsibility for maintaining the patterns of life that ensured their security and freedom. De Tocqueville gave famous expression to this notion by arguing that Americans combated the atomizing effects of individualism through a variety of civic institutions operating according to the principle of "self-interest rightly understood."[13] He also pointed out that freedom in a democratic society required stabilizing practices: vigorous religious morality; civic participation; and what he termed "the severity of the *mores* surrounding marriage," which he thought gave American women greater standing and freedom than their European counterparts while it helped domesticate their husbands.

There was a further, more troubling dimension to the paradox of democratic equality. De Tocqueville believed that in a commercial society individuals, now free from dependence upon social superiors, would define their liberty in mostly material terms, taking security and comfort as their defining life goals. But this "virtuous materialism," because it focused narrowly on the individual and a small circle of family and associates, undermined the very moral capacities that gave meaning to the idea of freedom. Unless the democratic individual were to understand that real fulfillment came not in comfort alone but through engagement with things of intrinsic significance and high value, democracy would slump into a dull materialism without spirit. As it was, the utilitarian cast of democratic life tended to undermine institutions of authority, allowing few cases for distinction other than raw power and ostentatious wealth. Such a society would become easy prey to would-be despots only too ready to allow the many their pleasures. In a word, the great promise of democracy, human dignity, and excellence for all would be lost.

The key problem, de Tocqueville thought, was that in an egalitarian society it was harder, not easier, to distinguish true freedom from its counterfeit. In de Tocqueville's time the powerful surge of romantic culture gave a new importance to the realm of the arts. For romantics, the idea of beauty, the "purposeless purposiveness" of things of recognizable intrinsic excellence, seemed the perfect refutation of the utilitarian tendency to see all values as mere instruments to satisfaction. In the aesthetic realm, the disinterested concern for quality and the integrity of objects and actions seemed to point out truths the world of commerce had forgotten. Beauty, for the romantic sensibility, served as an aesthetic analogue for moral and religious truths. De Tocqueville too found in the practice of the arts an important analogy for understanding the peculiar features of democratic society. His description of the paradox of artistic freedom in America would prove prescient regarding the key social problem facing the free professions of those days: the integrity of professional work and standards.

"Democratic peoples," wrote de Tocqueville, "habitually put use before beauty, and they want beauty itself to be useful."[14] The situation was quite different in those societies formed by a long tradition of aristocracy, such as de Tocqueville's France. In aristocratic societies, "the practice of almost all the arts becomes a privilege, and every profession a world apart into which all and sundry cannot enter." Within these "professional" worlds, a "corporate public opinion" and a "corporate pride" soon develop. Hence, no craftsman can pursue his fortune except by submitting to the standards of the guild. "Corporate interests count for more with him than either his own self-interest or even the purchaser's needs." The consequence, argued de Tocqueville, is that such a social context places the craftsman's emphasis on "doing things as well as possible, not as quickly or as cheaply as one can."[15]

The contrast with the typical arrangement in democratic society is dramatic. There every art and craft is open to all, since it is believed that all should be able to try—and quit—any field of endeavor. There is consequently little stability in any craft community, "the social link between them is broken, and each, left to himself, only tries to make as much money as easily as possible." Thus the only restraint and guidance the artist feels comes from the market, in the form of the customer's wishes. Furthermore, de Tocqueville continued, the market for the arts is itself differently organized in the two types of society.

In aristocratic conditions, because the patrons occupy a secure position or aspire to a way of life defined by long-established institutions and practices, customers "naturally like things very well made and lasting." This taste in turn "affects the way a people looks at the arts." That is, the practices and tastes of the larger society support and encourage the smaller community of artists in identification of their interests with the standards and reputation of their guild.

In democratic countries, as de Tocqueville saw things, the art-buying and appreciating public have few such inherited standards to guide their interaction with the often equally isolated artists. Lacking secure social standing grounded in considerations other than purchasing power, the customer in the democratic society typically wants not high quality but "a look of brilliance." Since democratic competition always produces a "crowd of citizens whose desires outstrip their means," the common interest of craftsman and customer alike is to make, buy, and sell the most products possible as cheaply as they can. There are few institutional supports for standards of excellence that could counter or qualify the activities of either producer or customer. The whole artistic enterprise tends to become *only* a market, directed not by aesthetic values as such but by the pursuit of maximum financial gain. Thus, de Tocqueville concluded, in both the fine and useful arts "quantity increases; quality goes down."[16]

What makes this analysis particularly striking is that de Tocqueville could have been describing the problems faced by responsible free professionals in nineteenth-century America. The root of the professional problem, like that of the arts, stemmed from the anomalous status of the professions in a utilitarian commercial society, a situation they shared with the arts, education, and religion. In the first place, a profession is "in business" for more than itself. In the case of the professions of office, this was inherent in becoming a public official. For the free professions, however, the situation was more ambiguous. Professionals competed, after all, in the labor market and typically offered their services in exchange for a fee. Yet they explicitly served public, even transcendent, ends. Public values are necessary in order to secure the goods of civilized life, but they can be secured for each citizen only when all, or nearly all, citizens contribute to their support. This is plain in the simple case of a public good such as security. If there is too little general contribution in the form of law-abiding mutual trust, then individuals find themselves put on a defensive posture, forced to restrict contact

with strangers and dependent upon private defenses, in an escalat-
ing spiral of defense and withdrawal until the once-sought public
good is lost altogether.

For the nineteenth-century free professions, the problem was
to convince not only the public at large but also the mercenaries
and eccentrics calling themselves doctors, lawyers, and preachers
to act toward their clients with fiduciary responsibility. The laissez-
faire environment of American life made it difficult to establish the
idea that to be a professional means acting in the interest of one's
client. The client often depends on the wisdom and integrity of the
professional's judgment. The professional, by contrast, cannot be
simply the client's tool or instrument. The professional is accountable *to* the client as to whether the former is serving the latter's best
interests, but the professional is also accountable *for* the public purpose for which the profession exists. Thus the lawyer is rightly
called a counselor and attorney, since the lawyer's task is to apply
trained judgment in acting for the client in seeking his or her best
interest in regard to justice. The same is true in the case of the
physician with regard to health, and similar responsibilities apply
to the other professions.

The common problem for the free professions was—and is—to
establish and safeguard standards of practice that ensure public
authority and confidence. But how could this be done in so mili-
tantly egalitarian and utilitarian a society, and when so many
would-be professionals were either incompetent or venal, or both?
The problem paralleled the one de Tocqueville traced for the arts.
In practice, the choice was between seeking to establish individual
professional authority through personal charisma or seeking to
persuade public opinion of the value of granting and enforcing fiduciary responsibility to a professional body. The former strategy was
the dominant one through the middle of the nineteenth century.
Much in the manner of celebrity painters or musicians, leading
lawyer-orators, star preachers, and celebrated doctors became influential, and sometimes wealthy and powerful, figures.

But the unmet challenge, one more in keeping with the civic mission of professionalism, was to educate public opinion toward institutionalizing professional standards through such devices as licensure and accountability. This strategy depended upon many professionals' and their nascent societies' assuming the role of civic actors so as to spread and win acceptance for a vision of reciprocal responsibility between professionals and the public. When this effort succeeded, it did so mostly where professionals were able to make of themselves valued members of the local civic culture. However, later in the century professionals would finally begin to gain public stature on a national scale not so much by identifying themselves with public ends and fiduciary responsibility (though these values played a role) but through their embrace of the increasingly spectacular achievements of science and technological progress.

Authority Through Expertise: The Organizational Professions

The Civil War that Lincoln waged to save the Union did more than destroy the slave society of the Old South. It set in motion forces that would rapidly change American life almost beyond recognition. Under Lincoln's leadership, the United States began to come to a sense of itself as a single nation. In the ensuing decades, the nation would expand geographically and yet also grow closer toward forming a unified society. What was at the time of the war a dispersed agrarian and rural nation, boasting a few commercial cities and industrial centers, would become the world's leading industrial power by century's end.

In the process, vast migrations to the West, immigration from Europe, construction of national systems of technologically advanced communication and transport, and the burgeoning of unprecedented industrial cities would call into being new forms of human organization hardly imagined in antebellum America. Work moved out of the household into the shop, factory, and office. It was less the self-reliant independent citizen and more the self-made entrepreneur looking for the main chance who set the pace. The expanding national market made possible the sudden rise of fierce captains of industry. Their quest for dominance opened the testing ground for new organizations exemplified by the railroad and the industrial corporation.

By 1900, the chaos of economic laissez-faire was being recast by the leaders of business and finance, and fitfully encouraged by government, into a new mold historians describe as the age of corporation capitalism. Economic life came to be regarded as less a field of random forces and more an interconnected system on whose management national prosperity depended. The key institution through which these changes were taking place was the business corporation itself, "a form of organization designed to accumulate large amounts of capital, resources, and labor and apply them to the rational, planned conduct of economic activity through a division of labor and bureaucratic routine."[17] The principles embodied in the corporation would spread widely (though not without resistance) throughout American society and give rise to new forms of professional life. Everywhere groups sought economic stability and protection from the punishing unpredictabilities of the unregulated market. They formed associations and organizations to give themselves market shelters, areas of activity protected by law or contractual agreement from encroachment by competitors from other sectors of the economy. The result was an upsurge of agricultural cooperatives, trade unions, and new or revived professional organizations.[18]

This was a social environment considerably more receptive to aspects of the professional enterprise than antebellum America had been. If Jacksonian Americans thought about opportunity largely in the horizontal terms of an expanding frontier for self-reliant household enterprise, increasing numbers of Americans would come to understand opportunity in vertical terms. The image fit with the reality of a career in a large and impersonal organization, operating as part of a national system and taking over area after area of economic life.

The new era was to be the age of the career. The stability of a career in a prestigious occupation lifted those who could attain educational credentials toward the possibility of dignified and well-paid work within the expanding national network of commerce. The new universities, themselves sometimes founded or funded by the wealthy creators of the corporation economy, were critical to this development.[19] Professionalism, often defined less as a civic art and more as the capacity to solve technical problems, would over time enable the middle class to make peace with the plutocrats. The unsettled social conditions of the time also created the opportunity for enterprising profession builders to persuade influential publics of their value to the nation.

For this was also the age of the expert. The organizational professions of the late nineteenth and early twentieth centuries, such as engineering and management, introduced into the professional enterprise a new emphasis upon science, efficiency, and technical expertise. The expert (in the sense in which Americans of the nineteenth century might have recognized the term) was typically the learned judge, the theologian, the scientific scholar, the ingenious inventor who benefited the community. Such expertise derived from learning, and often from demonstrated practical wisdom as well. It carried overtones of the fiduciary qualities characteristic of the professions of office and the free professions. In its new sense, however, expertise connoted someone who knew how to get things done, the person able to wield sophisticated techniques as means to produce desired ends. At its most expansive, the new notion of expertise meant the capacity to solve problems, the kind of skill that expanding industrial America greatly needed and very much admired.

"Little noticed in the heat of the nineties," wrote Robert Wiebe, "a new middle class was rapidly gathering strength." That "class . . . covering too wide a range to form a tightly knit group" included significant groups of those "with strong professional aspirations in such fields as medicine, law, economics, administration, social work, and architecture." Notice that this list includes not only two of the three traditional professions but such newcomers as academic social science and professionalized administration. Wiebe also noted that "consciousness of unique skills and functions, an awareness that came to mold much of their lives, characterized all members of the class."[20] This was to be professionalism's heroic age, when it came forward as a new American moral ideal. It was also a time of major conflict over the meaning of professionalism. That conflict would result, by the early decades of the twentieth century, in identification of professionalism in many fields with technical expertise, to the detriment of the civic orientation characteristic of earlier professional ideals. This development continues to produce negative effects today for the larger society as well as within the professions.

What made possible the appearance of the organizational professions, far more tied to large formal organizations than the free professions were, was a revolution in both social organization and attitudes toward specialization. The change, though, was not accomplished easily or without painful conflict. It is hardly an exaggeration to say that the organizational professions were born out of profound social crisis. By the late nineteenth century, many Americans could no longer make sense of their social world in the inherited terms of their local civic creed or through the idiom of open opportunity. As farmers and townsfolk were drawn into the geographic and cultural orbit of the industrial metropolis, the familiar idea that some benign natural harmony underlay the apparent randomness of market society was in retreat. Those who could make sense of things were suddenly in demand. Social analysts and prophets abounded.

It seemed clear to all that the optimistic republican dream of a harmonious and classless civic community was being torn to pieces in conflict between opposed economic interests. Members of the middle class felt themselves caught in a squeeze. On all sides, they saw powerful forces that were essentially outside their familiar cultural and political world.[21] The middle class was horrified by class struggle, sensing that it marked the end of the old American ideal of civic community. The United States was changing dramatically in a way that created new differences and antagonisms among groups. The age of specialization and differentiation was at hand. The question was whether and on what terms a new social integration was possible.

"The fate of classes," wrote the economic historian Karl Polanyi, "is much more often determined by the needs of society than the fate of society is determined by the needs of classes." In terms illuminating the rise of the professions, Polanyi argued that at moments of major social change the success of classes and groups "will depend upon their ability to win support from outside their own membership, which will depend upon their fulfillment of tasks set by interests wider than their own."[22] All the segments emerging out of the industrial maelstrom faced the problem of securing public legitimacy. Populist farmers appealed to the Jeffersonian heritage, while Samuel Gompers's trade union movement sought approval on grounds of the fairness of labor's demands. Socialists such as Eugene Debs invoked the republican heritage to condemn the new system of industrial oligarchy. The leading financiers and industrialists invoked the social Darwinist vision of progress through competitive struggle to justify their rise to dominance.

In similar vein, the new professional middle class strove to cast its new occupational specialties as the bearer of a better future. The new professionals sought to establish themselves by bringing new techniques for coping with the challenges presented by urban, industrial disorder. They also linked themselves to the wonders of technology, appearing as ministers of the better life promised by scientific enlightenment. In early-twentieth-century America, the professions thus waged a two-front battle for legitimacy. The developing professional fields strove to attract members by providing obvious benefits such as rising salaries and improved conditions of practice. Their other challenge was to convince the public of their value to society and their worthiness for legal protection and philanthropic largesse.

Professionals were often at the forefront of efforts to find solutions to the new problems of the industrial era. In time-honored American fashion, these efforts typically went forward through a maze of voluntary associations led by local notables, often one organization for each issue, such as public health and sanitation, immigrant resettlement, charitable work, and the rest. Now, however, the emerging middle-class professionals received unexpected assistance from some of the very plutocrats they feared and distrusted. Great captains of industry, among them Andrew Carnegie and John D. Rockefeller, were by the turn of the century also attempting to win the hearts and minds of the public they had so often outraged just years before. The industrialists sought to soften their public image, and genuinely to adopt positive civic roles by establishing vast new philanthropic foundations. Scientific medicine, for example, received a major boost by attracting the attention of the Rockefeller philanthropic interests.[23]

The philanthropic foundations established by the corporate empire builders invested in a host of new or expanded institutions designed to ameliorate the conditions of economic and social turmoil their founders had done so much to cause in the first place. So what was typically done in other societies by institutions of general competence (chiefly church and state) was done in the United States by the most powerful private persons to emerge from the competition of the civil society. Whether the new philanthropy did a great deal to change public attitudes toward the donors remains debatable, though it certainly moved some of the plutocracy toward a larger sense of social responsibility, linking their aspirations—and sometimes their lineage—to those of the nineteenth-century gentry.[24]

These same developments aided the organizational professions' search for legitimacy and importance. The philanthropies of the plutocrats, the universities, specialized institutes for research and training, and settlement houses and other organizations aimed at easing the horrors of mass urban poverty each became in turn a crucial site of training and employment for the developing professions. Through their association with these causes and these new institutions, professionals gained greater public acceptability as a key resource for expertise in meeting the threatening challenges of an urban, technological society.

Expertise Makes Itself Indispensable:
Frederick W. Taylor

Of the many heralds of the new scientific and technological virtues of the professions, none was more successful, nor ultimately more important, than the engineer Frederick W. Taylor. He was to the organizational professions roughly what Morgan, Rockefeller, and the others were to corporate capitalism itself. The corporate economy promised a vast increase in productivity, national wealth, and individual opportunity. Taylor, who began his career as a mechanical engineer and went on to fame with his time-and-motion studies of worker efficiency, intended to be far more than a mere servant of corporate wealth. His purpose was to spread the benefits of efficiency and productivity into all sectors of American life.[25] Taylor set out to show that by applying rational principles of "scientific management," not only industrial productivity but the whole of modern life could be made far more dependable and efficient, opening a vista of unlimited satisfaction for all. Not coincidentally, Taylor's vision also included the prospects of new and exciting careers for the effectively educated.

Though he thought in terms of the public interest, Taylor's chief means toward that end was emulation of the organizational patterns of business, a conception that, also not surprisingly, found widespread approval among influential businessmen. The impulse toward bureaucratic organization was for Taylor a historically significant innovation that would stabilize the dangerously antagonistic social relationships threatening the cohesion of the United States. Nonpolitical, neutral experts could work to reshape these conflicts by acting as mediators between big capital and labor, and by staffing new institutions of government that would put social "efficiency" ahead of partisan advantage. As Taylor saw it, the key to scientific management was replacement of personal authority and judgment with rules developed scientifically, by experiment.

"Questions which are under other systems subject to arbitrary judgment," Taylor wrote, "are therefore open to disagreement." By contrast, under scientific management these same questions "become the subject of the most minute and careful study in which both the workman and the management have taken part."[26] These rules could then be codified and applied impartially, to govern both worker and manager. On an expanded scale, the same approach might be applied to the operations of whole industries, cities, even the national government. The vagaries of discretion were to be traded for the predictability of formula and algorithm.

One of the direct effects of the growth of professional management along Taylor's lines was to sanctify with professional certification the complete subordination of employees to their employers. Taylor's principles insisted on the need to strictly divide and define tasks for maximum efficiency. The minutely specialized operations could then be coordinated from above by the manager. This was to be done in the interests of economic, and ultimately social, efficiency. Rising productivity in mass production would ultimately lower the costs of goods and so benefit everyone: workers, managers, and the owners of capital alike. But scientific management also removed from workers all discretion in organizing and controlling their work.

The spread of scientific management through industry and into government and all large organizations created a demand for new kinds and levels of knowledge skills, but it also worked to "deskill" many of the artisans whose capacities previously were essential to industrial life. The rise of scientific management thereby marked the irreparable decline of traditional skilled labor of the artisan type, and with it the loss of one version of American republicanism.[27] Organizational professionalism on the technical managerial model thus complemented the dominant organizational form of the new order. The notion of administration or management as an ethically neutral, technical body of knowledge has long outlived Taylor's direct influence. It has been the dominant approach to administration in American organizational life, in the public sector as well as the private, ever since. Likewise the organizational career usurped the older aspiration toward private practice as the typical pattern for many a professional career, at least until the onset of large-scale restructuring in American organizations at the end of the twentieth century.

Success in a professional field is often now a story quite similar to success in a business organization. It means a climb toward a higher degree of competence in a narrower area of responsibility combined with expanded supervision of more similarly specialized subordinates. This structure is predicated, in a way Taylor would have applauded, on the supposition that the skilled specialist, properly organized and deployed, is the key to solving the problems of living as well as those of producing. Along with establishing the research university as the model for the educational enterprise, developing the notion of expert problem solving through organization set the context within which the organizational professions of the twentieth century would come of age.

The Professions Enter the University—and Vice Versa

By making their own the prestige of expert knowledge, the new organizational professions solved the previously daunting problem of professional authority. The institutional basis that made this possible was the new research university. Possession of higher educational credentials gave the aspiring professional a kind of movable capital upon which to trade in the increasingly specialized marketplace. Through the new model of education it advanced, the university became the one institution shared by all professional fields, aspiring and established.

Harold Perkin has called the university the "axial institution of the modern world." Even though its roots and some of its forms date from the premodern era, Perkin notes that the university was essentially reinvented in Europe during the nineteenth century. The key innovation was to link the traditional function of preparing students for a career that required special training, usually a profession of office, with a new one: the advance of knowledge itself. Worldwide, the foundation of universities has been one of the crucial marks of modernization. It is typically in universities that members of national elites are identified and trained, and since the revolutions of nineteenth-century Europe university students have often been the vanguard of political change. Yet increasingly it is the growth of knowledge through specialized research that has come to seem the core purpose of the university.[28]

Until the time of the consolidation of the corporation economy, the United States had a diverse array of academies and colleges for preparing future leaders and free professionals, but no universities of the modern type. The American university appeared on the scene quite suddenly after the Civil War. Sometimes new as with Johns Hopkins, Cornell, or Chicago, and sometimes a renovation of an old college as with Yale and Harvard, these institutions set out to both advance knowledge and produce skilled graduates. Just as at this time the founders and key personnel of the leading economic enterprises began to coalesce into a national (as opposed to merely local or regional) elite, research universities were spurred by their own interest as well as by patronage from the same sources to become the site where ambitious Americans could obtain the credentials and connections to make their way in this new national society. The period of the foundation and early growth of these new national educational institutions, like that of the modern professions and indeed the whole industrial system, coincides with the two decades on either side of 1900.[29]

The new American universities were eclectic in drawing upon British, French, and especially German university patterns. In Germany, the universities were developed principally to train expert personnel and advance scientific research. They were directly tied to the state, which provided support and access to a host of careers, from teaching and the ministry to much of engineering and medicine. In the United States, by contrast, private trustees and businesses came to share the role of patron with state governments. It would not be until after World War II that the American university would assume a role of comparable social centrality, but the basic pattern for that development was set in those formative years around the turn of the century. This was the time when the pattern of the university teacher and researcher crystallized, displacing the clergyman and sometime scholar as the archetypal figure in higher education.

Though more diverse and competitive than British or European systems, the American universities also came to standardize the requirements for a degree, particularly in the growing professional schools. This was a gradual and difficult process. In the late nineteenth century, professional education appeared as a potential rival for the new system of higher education. Nevertheless, the growing prestige of the new research institutions, which was based upon the ideal of scientific knowledge, made collaboration a better strategy than competition. Early in the century, most professional degrees demanded little collegiate preparation. By the middle of the twentieth century, however, medicine, law, and divinity all solidly required a graduate degree of their practitioners. Engineering developed graduate education for a higher degree, as did teaching and finally nursing, but these fields never succeeded in making a collegiate degree the prerequisite for their professional schools. By early in the twentieth century, the once common conflation of professional status with anyone who could claim higher educational experience was already being differentiated into a clearer system of credentials: the bachelor's, master's, and doctoral degrees connoting a pyramid of increasingly prestigious learning, in which scientific research held pride of place, with "clinical" practice always second.

The new basis of professional authority in specialized expertise, like the research university itself, represented a departure from the earlier pattern of the free professions. For the free professions, the question of authority and standards was tied to social acceptance of the professional's claims to public value, what Brint calls "social trustee" professionalism. In the earlier pattern, technical competence was visibly linked to civic involvement, since the professional's livelihood depended upon his reputation with the public for good practice, judgment, and benevolence. Parallel to de Tocqueville's observations concerning the arts, American professionals struggled throughout the nineteenth century to establish their claim to status independent of their link to elites of property. In these efforts, they were largely unsuccessful, indicating the limited authority of expertise or even scientific knowledge per se at the time.[30] When all this changed around the turn of the century, it is not surprising that not just the new, aspiring fields such as management or engineering turned eagerly to appropriate the prestige of expertise for legitimacy; the old learned professions successfully did the same.[31]

Through these developments, the new universities came to resemble in organization and ambition the great corporations, as their critics liked to observe. The ties between the professions and the universities would involve the professions in much of the criticism the universities began to receive. "The men who stand for education and scholarship have the ideals of business men," complained John Jay Chapman of early-twentieth-century Harvard, going on to say that the university's administrators "are very little else than business men, running a large department store which dispenses education to the millions."[32] Of course, Chapman was exaggerating. Only a small percentage of the nation's youth were actually attending college or university, and those who did were overwhelmingly white, male, and from comfortable backgrounds.

There were exceptions to this generalization. Beginning with the founding of Vassar in 1865, women's colleges afforded a way of successfully challenging the assumption of separate male and female spheres of competence and concern. African Americans too often made their way more effectively in their own liberal arts colleges and theological seminaries than in the national universities. Black intellectuals such as W.E.B. Du Bois invoked the ideal of the civic professional in a new context when he argued that educated and professional blacks had a responsibility to take on the task of community leadership, with an ultimate aim of leavening the materialism of American culture.[33] Still, Chapman could have added in his critique of Harvard that the ultimate purpose of higher education was indeed the kind of social standing conferred by a career in a professional field.

Within the universities, a battle was going on among faculty, trustees, and presidents over how this education for the millions was to be organized and at what it should aim. Led by Harvard's charismatic and innovative president, Charles W. Eliot, many advocated specialization to foster social usefulness. Elsewhere, especially among representatives of the old colleges, the notion of a generalist education in which a "man of learning" would have "an uplifting and unifying influence on society" continued to have force. However, the premise of that older vision was that "higher learning constituted a single unified culture."[34] More and more, however, curricular integration seemed more an act of political will than a natural complement to the contours of modern learning.

At Johns Hopkins, for example, the emphasis from the start was on graduate training for specialized scientific research. Unlike the traditional American college, Johns Hopkins (at first an all-graduate institution) operated on the assumption that the old unity of culture had been surpassed by the progress of the sciences. Standards for a degree and the basic organizational structure became general fairly quickly. In this sense, the structure of the American university became fixed by the first decades of the century, but no single model of curriculum and organization appeared that fully and successfully resolved the differences in educational philosophy.[35] In one important sense, however, critics such as Chapman and Thorstein Veblen were on to something. Like major philanthropy, the universities seemed to receive the largesse of the barons of business in large part because they appeared to exemplify the idea that social progress was primarily an affair of an ever-more-effective application of expertise.

From such a perspective, the civic ideals of the old liberal arts college appeared as outmoded as the classical curriculum. The literary and rhetorical culture of the gentry elites was shouldered aside in the curricular battles of the time, in favor of more useful knowledge. The model for this notion of useful knowledge was the scientific-technical culture exemplified in fields such as engineering. The contest was, as the contemporary German thinker Max Weber described it, between the traditional ideal of the "cultivated man" that had provided the basis of social esteem nearly everywhere (including among the British and American gentry) and the new "specialist type of man." The trained specialist, argued Weber, was increasingly in demand—and in charge—thanks to "the irresistibly expanding bureaucratization of all public and private functions of authority." This fight, wrote Weber, "introduces [itself] into all intimate cultural questions."[36]

The Professions and the National Society

The professions thus began to win their battle to gain social support for expertise. The tentative new middle class of educated knowledge workers of the 1890s was on the road to becoming a growing, confident, and successful sector of the society. A career in a profession became a mainstay of educational ambition as state after state moved to license professionals in a variety of fields, and money poured from corporations and philanthropies to universities and hospitals. Meanwhile professional organizations such as the American Bar Association and the American Medical Association emerged as the voices of socially significant groups, and aspiring fields such as nursing, social work, accounting, and architecture struggled to find their niche. The professions were taking up positions within the new national economic order, according to that order's own organizing principles. Within this national system, the professional's role was typically specialized and technical, so that collaboration among differentiated fields increasingly depended upon the skills of still other specialists, the managers and financial technicians, all as Taylor had theorized it should. The old, personalized ways of doctoring or pastoring or the life of the bar seemed simplistic by contrast and decidedly out of date.

By contrast, the nineteenth-century free professions lived and took their direction not from a small and distant federal government but within the civic order of the American town. Compared to the smoothly managed processes of the new national order, the civic context was a contentious one, far more interactive and demanding of the individual's loyalty and active engagement. As we have seen, that cultural world, though regionally diverse, shared the ideal of a unified, morally responsible character: the independent citizen, who embraced the disciplines and limitations of local civic life for the sake of the dignity and purpose it yielded. American civic culture also supported a genuine public space (open at least to all male citizens), a forum of often raucous contest over the terms of the civic compact. Free professionals frequently sought to enhance their prestige and public leadership through painstaking demonstrations of impartiality and benevolence in community affairs.

Civic culture played a key supporting role as a civilizing and stabilizing influence upon the main protagonist in the American drama, the heroic push beyond all boundaries in the quest for expanded individual opportunity. By the turn of the twentieth century, though, the national drama's principal theme was being orchestrated by an industrial economy that transcended and despised the constricting boundaries of those local civic cultures. Wherever possible and convenient, the huge national corporations simply colonized local communities. Yet those eclipsed civic cultures "multiplied local winners" while protecting "the self-respect of many citizens with small incomes but good reputations." Instead, the expanding national system "funneled a few winners to the top, dramatically extended the distance from there to the bottom, and stripped an anonymous poor of their residual sources of respect."[37]

This new order was truly national in reach and advanced by the great, hierarchically integrated corporations. Here the comparative weakness of the country's national core again proved decisive in setting the United States on a course of social development different from that typical of Europe and Japan. Private considerations of profit and competitive victory would determine the pattern and pace of economic development, with little admixture between public concerns and national welfare or social justice. Centered upon the raw industrial cities, these corporate giants married technological advance to financial and administrative technique, thereby setting a new model for efficient and businesslike organization of social functions. As we have seen, the new organizational professions excelled at the very functions the new order needed: specialized expertise, scientific research, planning, and managerial coordination.

Professionals thus came to the forefront among the growing segment of the population that was oriented more to this national system than to local society. Compared to the citizens of the towns and rural communities, these metropolitan Americans were more narrowly specialized in work but less bound by convention in the rest of life, opening up the possibility of a uniquely private realm in which the individual could aspire to sovereignty. A sharp division developed between these two groups, the one looking outward to nationwide and even international networks, the other focused inward on the local civic community. The ensuing clash of perspectives, values, and ways of life would become an increasingly significant and conflictual cleavage in American life. Professionals would be central actors in this twentieth-century story, functioning both as a bridge between the two groups and as the chief agent by which metropolitan values and practices would penetrate popular life.

While this new industrial order was growing over the heads of most Americans, its captains defeated the efforts of populist farmers and urban workers to bring political controls to bear upon it. By the turn of the century, though, the vast hopes and angry energies generated by these changes gave rise to new efforts to reassert the values of American civic culture within the emerging metropolitan society. These currents took form in a series of reform movements collectively known as Progressivism. The old American civic order relied heavily upon voluntary association and involvement. The effort to develop a contemporary and national version of that civic creed would likewise rely heavily on voluntary participation in social movements to win the minds and hearts of Americans. Just as the lack of a powerful, centralized state enabled powerful groups to push their interests until they overreached themselves or encountered strong opposition, so the lack of a center also meant that reformers had to struggle in the public forum to win over the minds and hearts of Americans to a new vision of a more civic national society.

Professionals and their aspirations would be central to Progressivism. In the ensuing debates and struggles, some influential members of the new professional class would develop a conception of professionalism opposed to the narrowing implicit in its technical form, a professionalism designed to complement and strengthen a new civic politics. We will call this development civic professionalism.

Chapter Three

A Metropolitan Maturity

The Progressives' Struggle for a Civic Professionalism

The professional enterprise of the twentieth century has been at its core a metropolitan phenomenon. All the critical sites of professional development, from the university to the teaching hospital, the corporation, and government, expanded and proliferated in industrial cities. It was also against the stormy backdrop of America's twentieth-century urban expansion that professionalism found convincing formulation—or, rather, formulations, for the meaning of professionalism was a disputed matter throughout the crucial formative period of the organizational professions, those two decades on either side of 1900 that also witnessed the nation's epochal transformation into an industrial, metropolitan society. It was a time of extraordinary social and political volatility as the nation struggled toward a new institutional order appropriate to the changed circumstances. The resultant institutional order set the basic pattern for American life throughout the twentieth century, and professionals were very much a part of this ferment, especially in the social movement known as Progressivism.

Progressivism and the Professions

The major aims and themes of the Progressive movement fit well with the need of the growing professional middle class to find a place within the emerging industrial order. In broad outline, Progressivism represented an effort, particularly congenial to the middle classes, to bring the giant financial powers of the corporation economy within the American civic order. Like the populism

of farmers and the socialism and labor activism of industrial workers, the Progressivism of the professional middle class sought both
social justice and a place for themselves in the emerging metropolitan society. It was a crusade to reenfranchise citizens dispossessed
or overawed by brutal new powers.

Progressives generally sought neither a return to the unregulated
market economy of the nineteenth century, which had given rise to
the financial giants, nor the extirpation of private property by the
state. Rather, as a middle class whose capital lay in occupational skill
as opposed to the dividends or rents of the upper classes, adherents
of Progressivism espoused adoption of common civic values and
standards, enforced by new governmental initiatives, to bring equity
and balance into the economic order. Progressives championed
gradual social reform to extend democracy to the social and economic spheres through governmental planning, subvention, and
regulation of the economy for the sake of social justice. Intellectually, American Progressives shared with certain contemporary
European currents of reform a new confidence that knowledge and
judgment could be founded in experience rather than abstract reason or ideology.[1] This confidence took its most influential form in
the philosophy of pragmatism, as exemplified in the influence of
William James and John Dewey.

As a social movement, Progressivism contained diverse currents. It could be both cosmopolitan and hostile to immigrants, confident of the eventual triumph of universal moral principles over
parochial attachments and shrill about the corruption of political
bosses. Progressives embraced expansion of the division of labor;
they thought of scientific knowledge and the new technologies of
transport and communication as potentially civilizing forces. They
opposed social Darwinist ideas of progress through competition to
the death, as they sought ways to institutionalize social purposes
to counterbalance the relentlessly utilitarian tendencies of the market economy. They exalted education and, what was new to the
United States, many Progressives saw urbanization as a potentially
positive transformation away from the rapacious mores of the frontier rather than as a corruption of rural virtue.

The mutual influence between the Progressive movement and professionalism was ongoing, and long after its eclipse following World War I Progressivism's impact on professionalism remained considerable. Professionalism became one of the pillars of the Progressive movement by positing, in the professional career, a design for living that promised to give individual occupational achievement moral meaning through responsible participation in a civic life. In practice, however, the Progressives' efforts to articulate a new social whole revealed fissures in their projected edifice, which ensured that their dreams would never be fully realized.

Like the modern metropolis, to whose genesis it was so tied, Progressivism contained within itself contradictory tendencies. On the one hand, many Progressives promoted scientific expertise and technical efficiency as the keys to a more advanced form of society. On the other hand, Progressives also looked to civic ideals that seemed to require a moral and political integration of life that could only be achieved if modern citizens were educated to a high level of public participation. Were social action and political reform to be conceived as tools wielded by superior experts, or as a process of mutual involvement between civic educators and organizers seeking to enlist a broad public? This opposition within the movement was simultaneously played out in the evolution of the professions as the tension between technical and civic models of professionalism.

Progressive Professionalism: The Case of Louis Brandeis

An uneasy tension between reliance upon technical expertise and the traditional civic loyalties of the professions was one of the enduring legacies of the Progressive era to professional life. More clearly than any other figure, Louis D. Brandeis, the "people's lawyer" appointed to the Supreme Court by Progressive and former university president Woodrow Wilson, embodied the clashing features of Progressivism. His career and teachings left a considerable imprint on both the bar and the bench. But they also dramatized an interaction and clash between the technical and civic emphases of professionalism on a nearly heroic scale. What seemed to him but two complementary aspects of responsible practice appeared to later generations of lawyers as more often mutually exclusive directions of the professional enterprise.

One side of Brandeis enthusiastically endorsed the utilitarian quest for efficiency in business and government, nearly as a social panacea. This was the Brandeis who used the latest results of social science in his briefs to argue for the desirability of a decision, the Brandeis who thought of law as an instrument for social reform, who sought for "social inventions" designed to make the mechanisms of society less prone to friction. Yet Brandeis also brought to the bar and bench traits of mind characteristic of the practical social intelligence espoused by the pragmatist philosophy of John Dewey. This Brandeis could argue for a "right to privacy" in order to protect the free unfolding of individuality. This Brandeis celebrated the enlarging effects of legal practice on the character as well as the mind of both client and attorney. He could also enunciate and hold fast to legal principle, to the despair of more consistent (or simple-minded) practitioners of "sociological jurisprudence," or legal realism, for whom law was an instrument reflective of its times and no more.[2]

The more technocratic side of Brandeis took classic form in the celebrated Eastern Rate Case of 1910–11. This legal battle over whether the economically pivotal northeastern railroads should be granted a freight rate increase against the united opposition of shippers and consumer interests established the term *scientific management* in the public mind. It was Brandeis's famous brief that proposed a solution was to be found in the enhanced economic efficiency resulting from the railroads' adoption of Taylorite principles of management. Applying the social invention of scientific management, Brandeis argued, would preserve the railroads' profits while keeping shippers' rates down, allowing a reasonable wage increase for rail workers *and* benefiting the public, all at the same time. Thus enlightened expertise, personified in this case by Taylor, could resolve what appeared to be intractable political conflict among opposing parties.[3] In Brandeis's view a legal process informed by the "facts" was itself the chief means for social progress through reform, as it had been for Bentham and the British utilitarians of the nineteenth century and was for his contemporaries, the intellectuals of the British Fabian Society.

Social engineering from above the conflict, such as he advocated in the Eastern Rate Case, fit with a prominent aspect of Brandeis's view of modern society. He saw society as a complex interplay of frequently blind forces that required the intervention of individuals gifted with wide and disinterested intellect to remain in balance. Seen under the corresponding metaphor of a social invention, law could appear as simply a means for effecting results rather than as a charged medium of connection shaping both the participants in the conflict and the nature of the ends pursued. Brandeis's view was not as icily technical as the mechanical metaphor might make it seem, though. It also included a large element of noblesse oblige, which Brandeis shared with the patrician reformers of his adopted region, the province of greater Boston.

Born to immigrant German Jewish parents in Cincinnati, Brandeis early acquired an enthusiasm for the transcendentalist culture of New England, which he happily embraced as a Harvard student. He made the New England tradition of patrician reform his own, exhorting a Boston audience to recall "the great heritage of an honorable, glorious past, handed down to us by our fathers."[4] Part of Brandeis looked to the past. He favored a world of middling-sized enterprise, protected by government, in which the traditional Calvinist virtues of hard work, probity, and concern for the public weal could continue to flourish under twentieth-century conditions. In other equally central attitudes, he anticipated and helped shape much that would characterize liberalism from the New Deal onward: reform from above, but in the people's interests, especially through legal regulation and control.

Brandeis set out his conception of the lawyer's vocation most clearly in a lecture he delivered to prospective law students at Harvard in 1905. In that lecture, titled "The Opportunity in the Law,"

Brandeis argued that legal practice offers a great opportunity for those so motivated to improve social life. Brandeis was arguing in deliberate opposition to another understanding of the opportunity in the law, put forward by a very different publicly engaged attorney, Elihu Root. It was Root who epitomized the conception of the lawyer as technician of business effectiveness by insisting that it was the lawyer's job to tell the client how to do what the client wanted to do.[5] For Brandeis, on the other hand, the practice of the law works to develop capacities in the practitioner that are of special value in a democratic society.

Brandeis asserted that the lawyer's training and experience "fits him especially to grapple with the questions which are presented in a democracy"—questions, Brandeis added, that required a cast of mind different from that of "the scientist or the scholar."[6] Rather, Brandeis argued, the lawyer's practice, if general and not confined to a single specialized area, finally "extends into almost every sphere of business and of life." This range "ripens his judgment" while "his mind becomes practised in discrimination as well as in generalization. . . . He is apt to become a good judge of men." These qualities, taken together, fit the lawyer for a "position materially different from that of other men. It is the position of the adviser of men."[7] The upshot of all this, for Brandeis, was that the lawyer was both fitted for and obligated to a role quite different from a simple effort to advance the client's interest. As counselor, the lawyer was to inject the larger perspective of the public interest as it bore on the matter at hand. Ideally this made the attorney a "lawyer for the situation," as Brandeis put it.[8]

This highly civic conception of the lawyer's calling corresponds to ideas advanced by the idealist philosophers of the previous century, whose thought carried much influence in the Cambridge circles Brandeis admired and frequented. In his celebration of the kind of practical judgment he saw as the lawyer's best skill, Brandeis was echoing a venerable tradition that ultimately reached back to Cicero and Aristotle. In this view, a good life for individual and society depended less on applied intelligence of the abstract scientific sort than on a trained capacity for judgment that Aristotle called *phronesis*, or as Cicero Latinized it, prudence. Practical judgment results from a kind of reasoning Aristotle called deliberation. Its aim is decision, not simply reflection. "In an unqualified sense," wrote Aristotle, "that man is good at deliberating who, by reasoning, can aim at and hit the best thing attainable to man by action."[9] In Brandeis's rendering, the aim of legal education and practice was to develop professionals expert in this capacity for practical judgment. Such professionals could be trusted to educate their clients and the public at large to see the ethical and civic dimensions of even routine legal matters. They would give living texture to Progressive institutional reforms.

Embracing the Whole: Toward a Civic Professionalism

In the struggle of the new middle class for an identity, the organizational professions constituted the model. Part of the world of corporation capitalism and at home in the bureaucratic settings of administration, professionals also seemed not entirely of that world. Brandeis, for one, placed considerable store on the prospects of professionalizing business not only because he thought it would improve efficiency but also because he was convinced that professionalization would have a moralizing effect, upholding purposes and motives beyond the utilitarian goals of the marketplace. This sense of higher purpose helped steady the nerves of middle-class professionals.

Professionals were, in the main, aware that their lives had to respond to two pulls. On the one hand there were the claims of conscience, identification with the values of vocational integrity and a justly ordered polity. On the other, there was essential concern for technical competence and practical efficiency, the components of successful modern enterprise. The challenge—and the need—was to bring these two kinds of concern into complementary relation. Then, conscience, by producing a sense of connectedness, could guide enterprise, while prudent enterprise posed the material basis

for ethical life. In this context, the contribution of pragmatic philosophy was vital, especially the highly influential pragmatism
developed by Dewey.

While Progressives such as Brandeis embraced Taylor's "scientific management," and Taylor's collaborator Morris Cooke hoped
to realize the new metropolis by applying scientific management to
city government, others, including Dewey, were drawing from the
idealist philosophy of figures such as T. H. Green a broader social
vision of progress that could serve as an alternative to the utilitarian notion that progress meant increasing the sum of individual satisfactions. In Britain, by the early nineteenth century, the idealist
current had found expression in Samuel Taylor Coleridge's proposal
for a new elite of "clerisy," a public-spirited, educational leadership
concerned with social and cultural life, supported by institutions
independent of government. Similar themes reached a wide public
through such writers as Matthew Arnold; by late in the century the
early crudity of the utilitarian philosophy of Jeremy Bentham had
incorporated important features of the idealist politics of conscience into a new middle-class ideal of professionalism that was
based on service, responsibility, and efficient use of resources for the
public good.[10]

The British idealists' approach had a formative influence upon
the orientation of Dewey's pragmatism. It also had affinities to de
Tocqueville's argument that a strong social consensus about public
aims and the ethical norms to guide their pursuit would be the best
way to realize the positive potential of a democratic society. Besides
Dewey, in differing contexts Jane Addams and Herbert Croly also
worked, from the 1890s through the coming of World War I, to formulate a Progressive public philosophy that was the rationale for a
professionalism with a strong civic focus.

Croly, for example, sought to persuade his readers that a modern
society needed public commitments broader than simply impersonal
rules to guarantee fairness. The old small-town morality, which as
de Tocqueville had seen was grounded in a fuller moral ecology than
mere rules of procedure, was in decay. In its place, Croly warned,

came the growth of an amoral pursuit of self-interest blind to the larger whole. The earlier homogeneity of society was daily receding, "and no authoritative and edifying, but conscious, social ideal has as yet taken its place."[11] Croly proposed that a new spirit of professionalism could become the moral salvation of the individual through membership in a reformed national American society, mediated through occupational and local institutions. An ethos of shared loyalty, well institutionalized, would create the milieu within which individual achievement could be developed and rewarded. For Croly, it was the task of intellectuals, in the spirit of Coleridge's clerisy, to provoke, inspire, and criticize these developments.[12]

Significantly, Croly, Dewey, and Addams all sought to marry idealist values to pragmatic philosophy, and they did so in trying to come to grips with metropolitan life. It was at the new University of Chicago, located in the most dynamic of the new industrial centers, that Dewey began to develop a persuasive philosophy of education and practical life. In the same city, and also during the 1890s, Jane Addams was developing at Hull House a new kind of urban service institution, the social settlement. During the following decade, Herbert Croly, also influenced by idealist philosophy through Josiah Royce at Harvard, took up editorship of the *Architectural Record* in New York. Through that journal's particular attention to the problems of building and city planning, Croly began to formulate a new view of American democracy. In 1914, he established a national pulpit for these views as editor of the *New Republic*.

All three thinkers accepted the growing specialization and interdependence of modern society that the industrial metropolis dramatized, but they sought to render its complex functional interrelationships intelligible and mutually responsive. Providing this intelligibility was for them the professional calling par excellence. By bringing the interdependence to vivid public awareness, they hoped to provoke political action. Aroused publics would then struggle for conscious regulation and planning of what would otherwise have remained but dimly perceived, disconcerting developments, benefiting the powerful few and harming the many. Once the public began to discover itself in this effort to control its environment, these Progressives reasoned, the possibility would open of turning awareness of interdependence into a cultivated disposition toward mutual trust and solidarity among citizens. Their common political and cultural vision was in this way both optimistic about the potential of democracy under modern conditions and educational in a basic and radical sense.

In the imagination of these thinkers, a vision of the reformed metropolis began to materialize. This new city was not conceived as simply a healthier and more efficiently administered marketplace of skills and goods. City life was to be transformed. Not merely an unfortunate economic means, life in the metropolis was to become an end, good in itself as well as in its consequences. The final justification of reform was to make the metropolis a school—and laboratory—of democracy. Inclusive of all, open by communications and commerce to the world, sustained by an efficient and professionalized government, and unified by popular participation and celebration, the metropolis would become a whole greater than the sum of its parts.

An ecology of civic institutions, extending from neighborhood, school, and church through clubs, sports, and occupational associations to libraries, theaters, and museums, would be nurtured as sites at which a diverse body of citizens could develop and celebrate both themselves and their city. As Dewey put it in 1916, "A democracy is more than a form of government; it is primarily a mode of associated living, of conjoint communicated activity." In practical terms, this meant "the breaking down of those barriers of class, race, and national territory which kept men from perceiving the full import of their activity. These more numerous and more varied points of contact . . . secure a liberation of powers" which it was the office of the reformed Progressive school to elicit and harmonize.[13] This description could have served as a vision of the new city as well.

Lawrence Cremin writes that the master purpose at work in this brand of Progressivism was rooted in a long tradition of Western culture that reached back to Plato. It was to "transform all politics into education." This was true of Jane Addams, for example, but it was preeminently true of Dewey: "The Progressive foresaw the responsible and enlightened citizen informed by the detached and selfless expert, the two in a manifold and lifelong relationship that would involve every institution in every realm of human affairs."[14] Dewey's philosophy focused on his expansive understanding of science as a method of social formation that he aimed to actualize on the local level in the school. More than merely one specialized institution among others, Dewey wished the school to take on something of the role the church had once played in Western society: it would be the site where the individual could discover and be grasped by the spiritual current of the age and make it his or her own. For Dewey, science and education, properly understood, contained the creative nucleus of a whole social order, a society that could learn, reflect, and take action in common.

During the 1890s, Dewey articulated this philosophy of what he would later call "creative democracy" at the new University of Chicago, founded through the philanthropic largesse of John D. Rockefeller and its first president, William Rainey Harper. Harper sought to make the new institution a contributor to the city's life through such experiments as an extension program and the Laboratory School. There, with his wife, Alice Chipman Dewey, as director of the Lab School, Dewey presided over an expansive department combining philosophy, psychology, and education.

If democracy's promise of human dignity and community was to be redeemed in the new conditions, Dewey was convinced that the spirit of reflective inquiry he identified with science had to play a major role in everyday life. As a leading pragmatist, Dewey contended that thinking was itself a kind of doing, a mode of action. It followed that, like any skill, thinking could be learned and practiced only in appropriate social contexts. He concluded that developing a democratic public would require creating institutions within which learning could become a continuous practice in all areas of life. This meant reforming existing institutions to offset the narrowness of outlook bred by the pursuit of specialized interests.

The institutions to which he looked were those he judged able to foster an informed public: the mass media, voluntary associations, and above all education. As professionals were becoming crucial to all these institutions, Dewey sought to develop a cultural understanding that would orient professional life there toward public concerns. Through the agency of teachers, social scientists, journalists, and administrators, the experimental outlook would spread throughout the society.

Dewey argued that inherited American individualism, because it denied the dependence of the individual on social nurture and support, had become irresponsible. But individualism seemed worse than useless as a guide to action in the twentieth century because it was an unrealistic description of contemporary conditions. Society was growing constantly more interconnected, and individuals increasingly interdependent. Citizens could fulfill their potential only if they could grasp the whole of which they were part and collectively work toward improving its life for all concerned. As Dewey put it, "the attempt to cultivate it [wholeness] first in individuals and then extend it to form an organically unified society is fantasy." The only way to bring individual purpose to harmonious fulfillment would be "membership in a society which had attained a degree of unity," and this could be achieved only "through personal participation in the development of a shared culture."[15]

The researcher and the journalist were to act in the larger social context much like the teacher in the setting of the Progressive school. He or she was to define for the other members of the group the context in which they find themselves—and assist them in learning how to take part in that process of defining and problem solving through experiment and interpretation. Dewey was surely too sanguine when he imagined a future of public-spirited experts seeking to assist the lay public in discovering itself, just as the American university would not turn out to embody the public purposes embraced by Chicago in its early days. Had Dewey paid more attention to the power of the tendencies running counter to his vision, he might have better understood the difficulty of the project he was urging.

In the same city, and for a period in collaboration with Dewey, Jane Addams was pioneering at Hull House a more radical response to lives disrupted by immigration and rapid social change. In contrast to the more bureaucratic approaches that came to dominate much of social work, Addams did not emphasize rules and sanctions designed to separate "deserving" from "undeserving" recipients of aid. By integrating her clients into a professionally sustained community of work, education, and discussion, Addams sought to make possible their development as active and responsible family members, workers, and citizens.

Jane Addams had to struggle to forge for herself a public career and identity at the end of the century, a time when genteel, middle-class women were expected to remain comfortably, if passively, at home. Addams studied at a ministerial college and then tried medical school. In the end, her personal quest for a vocation helped define a new profession. Unlike most of her contemporaries, she saw the settlement house movement as more than a form of charity or moral uplift carried out by the middle classes for the poor. Instead, she conceived Hull House, her experimental settlement of 1889, as a center for community education and organization. Its aim was to enable the impoverished immigrants of the raw boomtown that was industrializing Chicago to become full participants in the life of the society they were joining. Her Chicago was three-quarters foreign-born, and she was aware that the old pieties of small-town America were of little value to these workers and their families. What was needed, in her words, was "an institution attempting to learn from life itself"—an institution capable of developing a truly metropolitan, democratic sensibility.

In this endeavor, Addams early on enlisted the assistance of interested faculty from the new university, including John Dewey. But better than Dewey, Addams realized that it was difficult to mesh this organic and activist understanding of the work of settlements with even the best of the research university model. "It seems," Addams complained, "as if the men of substantial scholarship were content to leave to the charlatan the teaching of those things which deeply concern the welfare of mankind." Confronted with the fragmenting—and, she thought, often trivializing—effects of specialist knowledge, she invoked the medieval clergy as a model for the kind of general understanding she thought most valuable. "The beginner in knowledge," she noted, "is always eager for the general statement, as those wise old teachers of the people well knew, when they put the history of creation on the stage and the monks themselves became the actors."[16] Addams sought a new kind of clerisy, public-spirited and attuned to the problems of new times.

Hull House organized a variety of social services for its clientele. It became deeply involved in research and political agitation in support of labor and sanitary legislation. But its heart was in its educational endeavors. Addams aimed to give young men and women who were often only a short remove from their peasant origins an understanding of the industrial metropolis. By imparting a sense of the history and nature of the emerging industrial society, Hull House tried to give the immigrant a sense of the whole and his or her particular part in it. By intellectually grasping the context of their new lives, Addams hoped, the immigrants would also become better able to shape and fulfill themselves in practice. Through experimenting, Addams developed an understanding of the possibilities of social work that was, and continues to be, remarkable, rooted in her vision of a "Christian humanitarianism" whose central tenet was "a deep enthusiasm for humanity, which regarded man as at once the organ and the object of revelation."[17]

Addams was seeking to involve the entire community in an educational effort whose aim was to form active and responsible citizens. She was impressed by the intellectual eagerness of her clients. "A settlement soon discovers that simple people are interested in large and vital subjects," she wrote. "Simple people did not want to hear about simple things; they wanted to hear about great things, simply told."[18] This approach to education led Addams, in an era when American fear of the foreignness of immigrants often took wild and punitive forms, to encourage her clients' knowledge of and pride in their ethnic heritage.

Addams encouraged students in the Hull House English classes to write, in the new language they were struggling to acquire, "some of those hopes and longings which had so much to do with their immigration." She described a young Russian immigrant girl trying to describe the vivid inner life of her relative, an old Talmud scholar. This man had previously appeared to many of the other hard-pressed immigrants, especially the youth, as lazily self-absorbed. "Certainly," Addams concluded, "no one who had read her paper could again see such an old man in his praying shawl bent over his crabbed book without a sense of understanding."[19]

For Addams, the settlement was a new model institution, part school, part church, and part community-organizing project, which social work was to staff and develop. But the purpose of the settlement, as of social work, lay beyond itself. Philanthropy had a civic, political, end: the formation of citizens through the repair and promotion of public life. Addams saw her calling as an open-ended responsibility. She was a founding member of the National Association for the Advancement of Colored People; the Progressive Party led by Theodore Roosevelt; and, later, a national leader of opposition to America's involvement in World War I.

Characteristically, Addams was often at work developing collaborations of professionals. She involved the architect Allen B. Pond in designing new settlement housing, supported Margaret Haley's drive to gain professional status for school teachers, and joined John Fitzpatrick of the Chicago Federation of Labor in promoting workers' rights. Addams, then, understood professional expertise in anything but a narrow sense. She saw professionalism as linked to the broad social vision of participation and trust among citizens that she called democracy. In this she was extending into the world of complex organizations the best ethical aspirations of the free professions. She aimed to help her fellow citizens see their world and themselves not as problems to be solved but as participants in developing settings for a life worth living.

If every writer's dream is that life should pay his or her art the supreme compliment of imitation, then Herbert Croly, after turning forty, must have been a happy man. In those heady years of change prior to World War I, Croly witnessed a meteoric ascent of his fortunes. He went from life as an obscure architectural journalist and sometime Harvard student to becoming a sage; overnight he became the inspirer of an influential public and an advisor to the charismatic Theodore Roosevelt. The vision Herbert Croly presented to the world of 1909 in *The Promise of American Life* was stirring people to action.

Just a few years after his book's publication, Croly was sought out by the well-to-do reformers Dorothy and Willard Straight and given a free hand to organize a journal to spread his ideas. The result was the *New Republic*, and Croly brought together on its first masthead a powerful set of journalistic talents, prominent among them Walter Lippmann. The new magazine was soon attracting America's foremost intellectual and literary lights as contributors, while it quickly drew a readership that included Woodrow Wilson, Louis Brandeis, Jane Addams, and John Dewey. Its subscription list was a virtual roll call of Progressivism.

The Promise of American Life was at once a sharp criticism of existing American institutions and a plan of social "reconstruction." At the center of the book was the vision of a new type of American hero. America's folklore exalted all-round individualists: frontiersmen, self-taught yeomen, and adventurers. Often enough, they were represented as holding a rather tenuous connection to settled society. But, argued Croly, the social context in which such figures made sense no longer existed in the United States. In sharp contrast, Croly's new hero was to be part of the society, committed to a specific sphere of activity within a complex division of labor. This new kind of citizen was also to be a person of special training and awareness. Croly's hero would be loyal to a deeper destiny than individual success. The new type of American Croly thought he could discern struggling for self-definition was the civic professional.

These new heroes would still be committed to advancing the national promise of individuality and emancipation. But each would now be "doing his own special work with ability, energy, disinterestedness, and excellence." Croly exhorted his readers to grapple with an apparent paradox: to become truly free, the individual had now to learn that self-fulfillment came through public service in loyalty to a larger purpose. "What the individual can do," wrote Croly, "is to make himself a better instrument for the practice of some serviceable art; and by so doing he can scarcely avoid becoming also a better instrument for the fulfillment of the American national promise."[20]

Significantly, when Croly was asked where he derived the idea for this new vision, he responded that its source lay in a novel of a decade earlier, *Unleavened Bread*, by the popular Boston writer Robert Grant. In the part of the story that struck Croly, an idealistic young architect intent upon using his skill to address the problems of poverty and distress in New York is undone by his effort to placate his wife's social and financial ambitions while remaining faithful to his own sense of responsibility. By trying to serve two antithetical purposes, the architect loses everything: he pays the price of divided loyalty and dies from the stresses of overwork and a bad conscience.

However melodramatic, *Unleavened Bread* hit home to the young Croly, then deeply immersed in the architectural world of New York. Commenting on the fictional architect's situation, Croly later commented, "It struck me as deplorable . . . I began to consider [its] . . . origin and meaning . . . and the best means of overcoming it."[21] What struck Croly was the architect's lack of a "well-domesticated tradition that would . . . make him build better than he knew."[22] What destroyed the fictional architect was a problem Herbert Croly found endemic in many of the most important areas of American life: the lack of well-institutionalized professional traditions that could support individuals in their quest to serve the public need. Croly rediscovered the paradox of democracy that Tocqueville had commented on regarding the arts of his day. The problems of architecture in the industrial city were the organizing insight for Croly's analysis of the deficiencies of American institutions more generally, and they set him on a quest for a public philosophy able to recover the promise of American life through a civic professionalism.

Facing the Challenge of the Metropolis:
Architecture and Planning

Not by accident, it was as an architectural critic that Croly came upon his insight that a civic professionalism, as part of a broad public philosophy, could resolve the problem of civic purpose in American democracy. Because they so visibly affect the lives of all, architecture and city planning have posed in an especially vivid way the question of professional responsibility in a democracy. In this century, the metropolis served as the supreme symbol and symptom of the emerging global civilization. It was architecture and urban planning that for a time gave most visible embodiment to the hopes that professional expertise could clarify and uplift the conditions of metropolitan life. The several paths of response to those conditions that we have noted running through American political and professional life attained concretely visible form in the directions taken by the old profession of architecture and the new field of urban planning.

In its origins and the social forces directing its development, the modern metropolis is a great marketplace. It has remained fundamentally the City Economic. Still, in Europe, urban reformers appalled at the conditions generated by the uncontrolled commercial and industrial expansion of the nineteenth century could draw upon a long heritage of architectural thought concerned with moral and social improvement of cities, and their efforts would have important consequences on the development of the American design professions.

In the old urbanism of Europe, the aim of its architecture was to imprint a clear sense of center and hierarchical order on the built environment by means of focal religious and civic structures. Thus European cities were memorable chiefly because of the churches, palaces, guild halls, markets, and government buildings defining their layout and focusing the circulation of people and goods. In earlier periods, their town walls had literally bounded and shaped the visual order of city life. Baroque city planning was described as trying, generally successfully, to unify "the opposites of order and freedom," by focusing "all movement around fixed points," the monumental structures that came to identify Rome, Paris, and London.

This was a planning tradition reaching back to the cities of the classical world. For Baroque city planning and architecture, it is "the space that governs the design, and the solids are entirely in the service of its dramatization."[23] Such architecture was a visual rhetoric; it represented the primary purposes and values of its society. It aimed to persuade those who encountered it to understand the city from the viewpoint of its sacred and noble centers by placing them in a commanding relationship to the secular, peripheral, and private aspects of life. For this tradition, it was indeed true that architecture was the supremely public art, "the total environment made visible."[24] This humanist architecture had, since Vitruvius and Alberti, spoken a confident language of form. Just as in the classical cosmology there could be only one perfect form for each function, so the classical architectural orders and forms were thought to represent a unique, universal rationality. At their best, buildings and urban designs were thought of as microcosms, revealing and celebrating in human scale the timeless rational harmonies of the larger cosmos.[25]

The shock effect of the revolutionary social transformations worked by industrial capitalism ended the plausibility of traditional humanist architecture as a conception of urban design. Fear of incipient chaos, spiritual as well as social, stalked the established cities of Europe as much as the less formed environments of the New World. By the end of the nineteenth century, two major programmatic responses appeared to the baffling situation in which it was "already the end of the old, humanist, man-centered world with its fixed values—and the beginning of the mass age of modern history, with its huge environments and rushing continuities."[26]

One response had by that time achieved worldwide recognition. It was embodied in the dramatic transformation that the Emperor Napoleon III and his planner, Baron Haussmann, worked on Paris. Haussmann turned the old city, centered on the life of its antique and varied *quartiers*, into one vast workshop, market, and showplace interconnected by the most spectacular street design constructed: the famous boulevards that have become the trademark of the City of Light. The other, less exampled response sketched out an opposing direction in which reconstruction of community life and a sense of the public welfare became guiding principles. In his much-noted work of 1889, *City Planning According to Artistic Principles*, the Austrian architect Camillo Sitte opposed the open city of traffic circulation with one focused instead on a series of public squares around which the life of the reformed city was to pulsate.[27] Both were to have important echoes in the American metropolis of the twentieth century.

The United States had few traditions of urbanism outside the eastern seaboard. As they spread across the continent, Anglo Americans established few cities in the European sense of centers of government, religion, trade, and culture. Once beyond the port cities and the ordered towns surviving from colonial New England, the nineteenth-century American landscape drew amazed (and usually appalled) comment from Europeans because it seemed to lack meaningful shape or center. Instead, the United States appeared as a series of campsites, in which individuals and families struggled to wrest from nature, machines, or each other the elements of personal well-being. America indeed embodied in its contours its promise as the land of liberal capitalism, with little government, few cities, and apparently limitless individual mobility.[28] But all that changed quickly, painfully, and without plan as industrialization drew millions from all over the nation and the world into ramshackle, swarming concentrations of industry and housing somewhat euphemistically called cities.

With the sudden shift of economic gravity to the cities, the principle of allowing the unguided market to decide how land was to be used was visibly producing intolerable conditions. The well-to-do fled to new railroad suburbs beyond the smoke belt, but the more farsighted among even those fashionable refugees realized that something had to be done, if only to make their place of business less revolting to prospective customers and clients. Thus was born in the metropolitan middle-class public—particularly among physicians involved with public health, social workers, architects, and social scientists—a movement for reform. Women were often conspicuous as leaders in these efforts, which offered them new possibilities for service outside the middle-class home. The reformers sought public sanitation and order, but they also desired appropriate physical forms to civilize the new forces of market and machine. In this process, the aesthetic visions of European critics of industrial life such as Sitte, John Ruskin, and William Morris found resonance in the work of such Americans as Frederick Law Olmsted, the creator of New York's Central Park and a pioneer in designing a new urban environment.[29]

Shaping the Things to Come: A Profession Finds a Mission

Architecture in America was then just at the point of establishing itself as a profession. The generation of architects who came into prominence at the turn of the century—Stanford White, James McKim, Louis Sullivan, Daniel Burnham, John Root, Frank Lloyd Wright, and others—differed profoundly among themselves about the direction architecture should take. But they were all acutely aware they were breaking new ground and creating the visual forms for a new America. Their style of professional practice too expressed this sense of excitement and mission.

Following the lead of the European-trained master H. H. Richardson, with whom a number of them apprenticed, these architects at first modeled their offices on the cooperative *atelier* system developed by the French architectural academy, the École des Beaux-Arts, the leading exponent of the classic style. The *ateliers* of the École were in effect design studios in which students apprenticed with masters in a heady atmosphere of mentorship and camaraderie.

As American architectural schools developed and the scale of building finance and construction grew, this early heroic moment was superseded. In the growing centers of commerce, the nature of the architects' clients was shifting as the scale of the demanded work began to grow vastly larger and more complicated. Banks and large corporations demanded new kinds of expertise than did private clients wishing a new residence. In place of the *atelier*-style office, large new architectural offices appeared, organized not as a collaboration among artists but, like a business firm, a task group of specialized experts, often mixing engineers with architecturally trained personnel.[30]

The leader in this transition from small office to large and businesslike architectural firm was the Chicago architect Daniel Burnham. Perhaps not so coincidentally, Burnham was also the originator of the first city planning movement in the United States. Through the last decades of the nineteenth century, the architectural firm of Burnham and Root prospered in the new Chicago that rose after the fire to become the nation's second metropolis. The firm's prosperity derived in at least equal part from the engineering background of Root and Burnham's extraordinary capacity to provide eloquent architectural metaphors to express the needs and desires of their clients. Burnham was like many of his generation in having had no formal architectural training. He developed his considerable gifts through a series of apprenticeships.

Burnham and Root helped pioneer the great architectural and engineering innovation of the age: the skyscraper office building. From their service to the business needs of the rising prairie metropolis, the partners prospered. To handle the surge in commissions efficiently, Burnham innovated organizationally, dividing the firm into effectively specialized units handling the complex tasks of design, construction, and supervision. In this work, Burnham and Root were not alone. Among their chief rivals was the equally innovative firm of Dankmar Adler and Louis Sullivan. Sullivan remained famous as a precursor of the later modern style and the mentor of Frank Lloyd Wright. Louis Sullivan could see in the new skyscraper, in whose design he was a master and which was in one sense simply the epitome of the commercial urge to economize on space, "in some large elemental sense an idea of the great, stable, conserving forces of modern civilization."[31] Sullivan had only contempt for what he saw as Burnham's Philistine preoccupation with adapting historical forms as decoration for the new technologies that were transforming both building and cities. Yet, like Burnham and other Chicagoans of his time such as Dewey and Addams, Sullivan wished passionately to construct a content within which modern people could orient themselves toward a vigorous democratic community life. But what should be the guiding norms for this enterprise, now that traditional norms could no longer serve naïvely as a source of aesthetic and moral order and unity?

The City Beautiful

Burnham was less original an architect than Sullivan. Yet he was considerably more than simply a business or professional innovator. He thought of himself as an artist, and in his midforties Burnham found the great opportunity of his life. He was retained, together with his partner Root and the already-famous landscape architect Frederick Law Olmsted, by the commission planning the Chicago World's Fair of 1893—the enormously successful World's Columbian Exposition. The result was the famous White City, which was destined to have such enormous impact on the future of American cities—and which Sullivan, though a contributor, would later describe as a backward-looking disaster for American architecture. It was the first large-scale project of unified social and aesthetic planning to be undertaken in the United States. In the White City's grand plan of neoclassical civic architecture, boulevards, parks, fountains, and vistas, Burnham first developed the conception of urban planning that he would apply to Washington, D.C.; Manila; San Francisco; and the city of Chicago itself. It would be known as the City Beautiful ideal, and it became a feature of Progressive Era hopes. In its style it pleased both many Progressives and a segment of the business elite for whom its classical allusions embraced a welcome international symbolism that proclaimed their sophistication and status as urban benefactors.

Although Burnham certainly saw no ultimate conflict between the market economy that supported his work and his civic goals, he moved in a direction coinciding at many points with Progressive reform. Like the Progressives, he sought "to restore to the city a lost visual and aesthetic harmony, thereby creating the physical prerequisite for the emergence of a harmonious social order."[32] A little over a decade later, the young architectural journalist Herbert Croly enthusiastically endorsed Burnham's comprehensive plan for a new San Francisco, again linking social advance and "national aesthetic aspiration."[33]

The sensibility Burnham sought to embody in his vision of the City Beautiful was perhaps best portrayed in his own interpretation of his purposes. "While the keynote of the nineteenth century was expansion," he wrote, "we of the twentieth century find that our dominant idea is conservation." This observation, which paralleled Sullivan's search for forms appropriate to the "great conserving forces" of the age, led Burnham to the classic questions linking economics to the ends of politics. "The people of Chicago," he observed, are now asking: "How are we living? Are we in reality prosperous?" Burnham saw that these concerns about the quality of life were grounded in economic considerations of whether the city was a convenient business site and whether it was a "good labor market" in which "labor is sufficiently comfortable to be efficient and content."[34] But the economic considerations did not wholly determine the ends of the City Beautiful.

Later critics would point out that City Beautiful proceeded from the point of view of the great new fortunes of a booming Chicago and the mobility of modern capital, considering the needs of other classes only paternalistically from above. Burnham was vividly aware that good planning could be sold to business leaders because it raised land values. He certainly grasped the rhetorical appeal of planning, as in the famous quote attributed to Burnham to "make no little plans. They have no magic to stir men's blood."[35] He also understood the mass appeal of the visual "production values" of his neoclassical visions, an idea that would be elaborated into a hugely successful "Magic Kingdom" by the son of one of the laborers on his White City project, Elias Disney. But Burnham's interest pointed beyond the concerns of a good business climate to questions of the kind of character and social fabric the city's arrangement would form and attract: the classic issues of political philosophy.

The kind of happy symbiosis between art, commerce, and civic morality Daniel Burnham sought to embody in his great city plans was to prove elusive. Yet, Burnham had intuitively hit upon a professional role very like the sort of civic professionalism Croly advocated in theory. Unlike Frank Lloyd Wright, who solved the problem of the lack of secure cultural standards by overwhelming his clients with sheer charismatic power, Burnham's appeals to civic leaders and organizations were significant gestures toward building social consensus for a public vision of the city. In this process, the architect's role was that of advocate as well as the artist who could give vague aspirations evocative form. Burnham went beyond providing a desired service to clients; by redefining the city's needs in a strikingly attractive way, he actively brought into being a new public as his client.

The City Beautiful ideal, however, like many of the disparate features of the Progressive movement, failed to sustain the mediation it promised or to gather sufficient public support. Business was often wary of its costs, and reformers, concerned with urban poverty and health, worried that the monumental improvements would deflect resources and attention from urgent social needs. During the 1920s, the planning impetus would continue, though in the form of "metropolitan planning," a mode of thinking that took expansion and economic development of cities as an unquestioned goal, seeking to enhance the business climate while furnishing the growing middle classes with housing. In the tradition of metropolitan planning, architecture continued to adapt to the corporate world, while the evident need to coordinate overall efforts gave rise to a new profession: the scientific urban planner. In this vision, the architect was closely yoked to the engineer in the search for economic and social efficiency. On the other hand, after World War I a new approach to urban planning appeared, calling itself the regional vision. For the regionalists, the architect was one of a group of craftsmen-professionals who would serve as guides and pedagogues in the transition to a new ecological vision of civilization.[36]

A Metropolitan Ecology: The Regionalist Vision

In the 1920s, a group of intellectuals representing several professions, including architects Clarence Stein and Benton MacKaye along with the young generalist writer Lewis Mumford, formed a small organization they somewhat grandiosely styled the Regional Planning Association of America. Their common belief was that the industrial era that had concentrated population and machinery in the great urban clusters, with all the resultant pathologies by then long familiar, was past its prime. The new technologies of electricity and electronic communication were opening the possibility of a new form of life both healthier and more humanly fulfilling. Those possibilities could only be grasped by a more holistic approach to the problems of economics and politics, one rooted in a new awareness of the connections of city and countryside. They would call these connections, by analogy to the newly developing subfield of biology, ecological.

The import of this vision was conveyed by Lewis Mumford, who came to maturity just after World War I, when he described the "essence of the art of building cities" as guided by the realization that "life has, despite its broken moments, the poise and unity of a collective work of art." The office of the city was "to create that background, to achieve that insight, to enliven each individual capacity through articulation in an intelligible and aesthetically stimulating whole."[37] Substitute *professional* or *architect* for *city* and one has a new statement of the ideal of civic professionalism.

In his treatment of the status of the architect in the developing corporate society, Mumford epitomized the new regional planning movement's critique of the direction in which the profession had developed. "Cut off from his true function to serve and beautify the community," Mumford complained that the architect had come to be "made an accessory of business itself, like the merest salesman or advertising agent." Given this reality, it was no wonder, according to Mumford, "that the architect speedily lost his leadership; and that the initiative went once again into the hands of the engineer."[38] For Mumford, architecture was first and foremost a social and cultural achievement. It "sums up the civilization it enshrines, and the mass of our buildings can never be better or worse than the institutions that have shaped them."[39]

The regionalists were scathing critics of the modern city's total subjugation to real estate values and business enhancement. They criticized the class order and inequalities of capitalism while also strongly attacking the forms of state coercion then appearing in communism and fascism. But the regionalists' primary concern was constructive rather than critical. They sought to reshape the human habitat so that cities, towns, and their regions would become schools of a responsible democracy, able to live in harmony with the natural and larger human world. Drawing on precedents such as Ebenezer Howard's regional "garden cities" proposals, their goal was environments in which modern individuals could recognize their unique possibilities and appreciate their common destiny. They believed that in this project the imaginative artist, especially the architect, had a special creative role to play.

For the regionalists, the architect did not act alone. The architect's calling was a collaborative one, to share the formative and educational function in society. Architecture was the art of designing environmental forms to enhance the full development of all society's members. Though socially radical, the aims of the regionalists were also deeply continuous with the classical Greek and Roman roots of architecture—and the democratic tradition. Thus Mumford could write that one must ask what functions the city performs in order to know what the architect and planner must do.

Like Aristotle, Mumford insisted that the city is formed "not merely by the agglomeration of people, but by their relation to definite social and economic institutions." The purpose of "community planning," then, was "to express these relations clearly, to embody them in buildings and roads and gardens in which each individual structure will be subordinated to the whole." The regionalists' scope was even wider. They insisted that the city had developed as the integrating node of an interconnected region that included a variety of habitats, natural and social. The aim of regional planning was to recapture for its citizens this life-sustaining web of interconnection, to render legible their present position in the environment and in history. Why, then, should all this be the special concern of architects? Because, Mumford argued, the modern architect, "cut off though he is from the actual processes of building," still remains the "sole surviving craftsman who maintains the relation toward the whole structure" that had once been typical of all craft workers.[40] Like Burnham, Mumford too saw the architect by training and tradition as a potential mediator, a figure able to grasp interconnection and render it physically as well as intellectually visible.

Modern individuals could act freely and responsibly, argued Mumford, only if they could grasp the whole context of their lives, including the linkages among home, work, and public life. Architecture and city planning were to make these linkages less abstract and render them obvious. Like Dewey, Addams, and Croly, Mumford and the regionalists were searching for forms of democracy appropriate for the urban and technological era. Much in the regionalist conception of human society recalled the idealist philosophy of the nineteenth century and, through it, the classical tradition. For the regionalists, as for Aristotle, the city was above all a public place. The chief goal of city building in this tradition is well described by Hannah Arendt when she speaks of the function of great works of art. To provide a "home for men during their life on earth," a "world," Arendt wrote, "the human artifice must be a place fit for action and speech . . . the measure can be neither the driving necessity of biological life and labor, nor the utilitarian instrumentalism of fabrication and usage."[41]

Mumford's sense of the overriding value of the city as an intelligible social whole, and of the purpose of practices such as architecture and the other crafts, echoed the Greeks. Arendt argued that the public realm needs artisans in their "highest capacity," the "help of the artist, of poets and historiographers, of monument-builders, or writers because they alone can provide, through works of art, enduring expressions of the ends that give focus and meaning to the story of a society's life."[42] Mumford and the other regionalists certainly wanted the architect to take on this office, and for similar reasons. They knew, however, that they were struggling against the utilitarian drift of American society in the twenties. Where was the institutional structure needed to support these aims to come from? Where was the public to sustain and vitalize this conception of collaborative professional activity? No more than the Progressive advocates of the City Beautiful were the regionalists to find a lasting institutional home for their civic conception of artistic and professional identity.

The Limitations of the First Effort at Civic Professionalism

The figures we have surveyed lived through a key moment of national restructuring. The pragmatist Progressives made it a visionary moment. They proposed a vision of how an industrial, metropolitan United States could develop its democratic potential beyond the local communities of the nineteenth century to become a more inclusive and unified national society. With their differing emphases, Brandeis, Croly, Dewey, and Addams sought to unite scientific progress with humanistic institutional reform. They looked toward a society of skilled, specialized groups working collaboratively to render conditions more like those depicted in the new city and regional plans. The pragmatist Progressives were confident that it would be possible to educate experts in scientific inquiry who were also attuned to matters of equity and inclusion in an increasingly interdependent yet ethnically pluralistic society. Their models of such collaboration came from the great causes of their era, such as public health, in which physicians and nurses worked with social workers, engineers, educators, and journalists to create new standards for city life and administrative agencies to protect them.

Their moment did not last. American entry into the Great War brought big business and the national government together, a collaboration that marked the triumph of a different version of the national society. This was a system in which the organizational professions, working in vertically structured enterprises, would set the dominant model. The mechanism of the market, guided by corporate and governmental management, would order priorities and the terms of collaboration. Consequently, though many of their ideas found incorporation piecemeal in the maturing national society, especially after the New Deal and World War II, the pragmatist Progressives' synthesizing vision of civic cooperation was not sustained. Fellow-traveling critics of the "pecuniary values" of the new industrial order such as Veblen despaired of reform.[43] Their cultural heirs among the younger generation who came to maturity in the twenties, including Mumford, found few political embodiments for their own hopes and adopted instead the stance of cultural critic, while refusing to place trust in either the market system or the growing federal government.[44]

What was the weakness of the pragmatist Progressives' vision? Part of the answer lies in their diagnosis of the American situation; the other part concerns the kind of response they made to that diagnosis. Succinctly, thinkers such as Brandeis, Croly, Dewey, and Addams saw nineteenth-century democracy decomposing into a series of fragments under the impact of the uncontrolled market and industrial system. The old moral code of American democracy, centered on the town, the church, and the household, seemed to be giving way. On the social level, this meant the breakdown of the controlling moral order that had guided America's provincial communities, especially the household order, releasing women as well as men into a wildly uncertain marketplace.

Instead of the generalist Independent Citizen, who was expected to play a variety of roles in society and was judged by similarly general notions such as reputation and character, the new economy demanded specialists. Specialists came to exalt competence as judged by their professional peers above the old moral norms. At the level of the individual, this decomposition liberated new possibilities but also threatened moral and psychic chaos. Thus, Lippmann, one of the younger Progressives, could comment during the twenties that "the modern man is unable to think of himself as a single personality, so that . . . morality thus becomes a traffic code designed to keep as many desires as possible moving together without too many violent collisions."[45] It was inconceivable to the pragmatist Progressives that so vast a transition could be negotiated without recourse to a new synthesizing public philosophy. Here they showed themselves the spiritual, if more secular, heirs of liberal Christianity and idealist philosophy.

As we have seen, the pragmatist Progressives attempted to popularize just such a mediating, synthesizing public philosophy. Although embracing science and modern metropolitan conditions, it nevertheless taught the need to achieve a measure of wholeness, a rational harmony among life's ends, in the organization of society as well as in individual aspirations. Thus, even though they criticized the narrow cultural homogeneity of nineteenth-century society—particularly those who wished to confine women to permanently domestic roles—these thinkers also disliked the tendency of the industrial order to split life into separate worlds of work and leisure consumption without permitting moral mediation between the two. Accordingly, the pragmatist Progressives focused on development of a revitalized sense of the public and civic life. Their more cosmopolitan civic culture aimed to enable specialized groups and freelance individuals to grasp their interdependence. Such a civic culture would give rise, they thought, to new social institutions, such as professional communities of function, through which an awakened public could find itself amid the complexities of modern life.

By the 1920s, however, metropolitan opinion was changing. With immigration cut to a trickle and the economy surging upward for nearly everyone but the farmers, intellectuals worried less about social and moral fragmentation and more about a stifling provincial conformism they felt to be endemic in the broad American populace. This change of focus was symptomatic. It marked a growing chasm between the metropolitan culture of expert competence and those provincial worlds that still adhered to the inherited moral ideals of character. The opposition set off a series of cultural-political conflicts during the 1920s, in the struggle over repeal of Prohibition, the Scopes trial, the rise and fall of the Ku Klux Klan. These cultural cleavages signaled the failure of Progressive hopes for successful democratic mediation between elite and popular understandings, a development that would return to haunt enlightened American opinion at century's end. With the eclipse of the Progressives' mediating vision went hopes for reorganizing professional life on civic principles.

Instead, the institutional order stabilized in the form that corporate reorganization of the economy had given it at the turn of the twentieth century. In this order, work was part of the "public" realm, carried out in specialized enterprises aiming at efficiency and guided by market and government. The logic of the organizational professions fit this pattern. Professionals, at least in the leading metropolitan centers, became specialized experts who advanced knowledge by subdividing tasks and applying the results according to formal procedures. As much as possible, government, management of public services, and even politics were reshaped to accord with these norms. This rationalized world of work and enterprise contrasted sharply with the "private" sphere of personal life, supported by a widening variety of consumer goods. There, enlightened individual choice in the pursuit of happiness was to prevail over restrictive small-town morality.

In the decades after 1920, the cleavage between metropolitan and provincial lives and attitudes was not so much mediated as stabilized. Metropolitan professionals, in contrast to their locally bound peers in the provinces, embodied a secular consciousness and led the way in experimenting with new permutations among the available options for happiness in personal life and relationships. The national news media, staffed by metropolitans and sponsored by the corporation economy, brought these attitudes into provincial life. Despite friction, however, the result was less overt conflict than gradual accommodation, with local life slowly coming to reflect metropolitan models. Economic growth, which brought more Americans into the national system of corporation employment and consumption, proved a remarkable lubrication system. Education, especially the research universities, also constituted a continuous route for mobility upward from the local to the national networks of business and professional life.

This process was first slowed by the Depression and then greatly accelerated by World War II and the explosive postwar boom. These developments muted questions about the relation between professional expertise and civic life through the middle of the century. Even so, just as the contemporary culture wars between traditionalists and modernists (and postmodernists) have suddenly reactivated the fault lines separating metropolitan and provincial moral orders, so the collapse of steady economic improvement has reopened the pragmatist Progressives' concern for mediating philosophies and civic renewal. As we shall see in succeeding chapters, the return of those repressed elements of the early-twentieth-century national debate is also reawakening interest in the nature of professionalism and its desirable location in the national life.

Chapter Four

No Center to Hold

The Era of Expertise

"Thus in the beginning," wrote John Locke, "all the world was America."[1] Locke was referring to the Americas before the European conquest, when he imagined an abundant nature appropriated by native peoples unencumbered by civil government. However, Locke also believed that labor, the willingness and ability to turn nature to productive use, established a right in property for the industrious and the able. Locke thereby installed the conquest of the world through tools and work, together with the individual's secure appropriation of the resulting abundance, as the basis of human happiness. This idea has been an essential aspect of the spirit of the United States throughout its life, but at no time more centrally than during and after World War II.

At that time it would have been only a slight exaggeration to say that all the world wanted to *be* America. Even her enemies envied the undeniable prosperity and strength of the United States. At that zenith of power and prosperity, which lasted a quarter of a century, from 1945 into the early 1970s, the nation seemed Locke's vision updated, a uniquely modern and successful society, built on the basis of heroic labor in the form of advancing technology. America's ingenuity, our ability to "roll up our sleeves" and "solve problems," had triumphed over the ideological fanaticism of the Axis powers. Victory had gone not only to the more virtuous cause, but to the more resourceful and flexible kind of society.

In postwar America, expertise took on a charismatic power. To possess it, to be linked to it, simply to bask in its wonderful effects, made life sparkle with promise. The radiance was signaled by the triumph of American scientific and organizational know-how in the war. Aircraft engineering, radar, computers, the world's greatest industrial output, construction projects that dwarfed the pyramids, the atomic bomb—these were the visible tokens of a people's power and pride. Beyond the military gains of the war, science and engineering daily demonstrated their capacity to control nature for human benefit. Advances in military medicine drastically improved the odds of survival outside the battle zone for combatants and civilians alike, as wonder drugs such as penicillin loosened the grip of pestilence. Medicine, now firmly anchored in the research institute and teaching hospital, went on to achieve such stunning breakthroughs as the eradication of polio, promising successful future wars on the old enemies of infirmity, mental illness, perhaps mortality itself.

Not only technology but systems of social control and management appeared to have taken a quantum leap as a result of the prodigies engendered by the wartime marriage of science and administration. At the climax of the postwar era, the space program of the 1960s would bring to the world its most attractive symbol of Promethean technology: the astronaut out for a walk on the surface of the moon. Accidentally, that same mission would also bring a reminder of the fragility and connectedness of the human world, our "spaceship earth," through the stunning scenes of an "earth rise" broadcast live from space. That image, itself the direct result of rocketry and electronics integrated through modern management techniques, helped touch off a powerful reverberation of concern about the effects of those systems of technology and organization on the human habitat.

But those sentiments grew strong only toward the end of that postwar era. Its predominant tone was captured in the advertising copy of Madison Avenue and television. There American industry, more and more guided by expert management, was translating scientific knowledge into the marvels of synthetic materials, while automobiles and jet aircraft delivered new opportunities of mobility. By the 1960s, in a kind of parallel to the technological glory of the space age, the destructive business cycle seemed to have been tamed by expertise, banishing depressions and opening hope that longstanding social problems such as poverty and racial discrimination were on the verge of solution. Under the banner of expert problem solving, the professional knowledge class seemed to have at least come into its own.

War is among the most revolutionary agencies in human experience. By focusing the energies of a population upon the single goal of victory over the enemy, war can generate a profound sense of common destiny and purpose. World War II instilled in the American population at large the belief that its national purposes embodied moral righteousness in an invincible collective power. At the same time, war also brings to the fore instrumental rationality in all its sublime, ruthless power. Instrumental thinking concerns itself with means rather than ends or final values. It asks, relentlessly: How well is this approach working? Could it be improved? What kinds of improvement will be most effective for the least cost?

The achievement of a balanced and sustainable form of cooperative life, if not collective purpose itself, can only coexist tensely with the indiscriminate pursuit of instrumental rationality. The latter, as modern experience has shown, often works to undercut the former. The use of war and preparation for war as a unifying strategy is thus for any nation a dubious and dangerous strategy over the long run. Without the overwhelming pressure of mortal threat, most societies have striven to contain the inherently disruptive effects of unrestrained instrumental thinking within constraining customs, the social equivalent of the lead shields in which American technicians learned to shroud atomic reactors. War may or may not be the "health of the state," as social critic Randolph Bourne put it. But for the United States it certainly proved an ideal forcing house for instrumental thinking and its near kin, technical problem-solving rationality.

In World War II, the practice of "total war" demanded mobilization of the resources of whole continents, human and natural. This process accelerated the economic and technological trends that had long been pushing the world's leading nations toward a new kind of human society, one conferring historically unprecedented importance on figures who could combine a high level of technical expertise with organizational skill.

These global developments also set the stage for the postwar American achievement of historically unprecedented prosperity. This context, in which enormous economic growth and technological progress took place against the backdrop of actual or "cold" war, was both the cause and the consequence of an enormous expansion of the professions. It brought professionalism, with its capacity to deploy technical and organizational ingenuity in defining and solving social problems, to the top of the agenda.

Already during the war, governmental and business leaders were busy discussing and planning the basic direction American society should take after victory. Their immediate motive was to prevent another massive economic downturn on the scale of the Great Depression following the sudden demobilization of the economy and population that victory would bring. Not surprisingly, then, the focus of the discussion was almost entirely on economic issues in the narrow sense. What emerged was remarkably clear-sighted about the economic and technological features of the postwar world. But the experiences and challenges of American city planning had little impact on that historic discussion.

The dominant postwar conception of the good society would prove very different from the vision of twentieth-century democracy proposed by the pragmatist Progressives Jane Addams and Herbert Croly, drawing on the pragmatism of John Dewey. Their vision of a metropolitan nation rested upon developing the social capacities by which interdependent but dispersed and anonymous citizens could recognize each other and themselves as members of a public and so organize for action to achieve a rich, shared form of life. In that vision, professionals were to assist and support the nascent publics in developing the understandings and institutions that could make the modern public viable.

By contrast, postwar reality defined professionalism in predominantly technical rather than civic terms, as rightly concerned only with improving the means by which individuals and groups could pursue their opportunities in an expanding economy. Rather than the civically active metropolis of the pragmatist Progressive vision, there emerged a dispersed, suburban America in which the good life was remarkably uniform yet narrowly individual and private in orientation. The increasingly influential patterns of professional life were organizational in form and focused on applying technical knowledge to the material environment (as in engineering) or the human (as with medicine and management).

Consider, for example, the Sunbelt of the southwestern United States, including California, Arizona, New Mexico, and Nevada. Beginning with the Hoover Dam on the Colorado River during the New Deal and increasingly during the war, the region became the beneficiary of vast federal outlays for military installations, weapons plants, water projects, highways, and other features now called infrastructure. (These infusions of governmental subsidy continued throughout the postwar era, especially through the close government-industry cooperation practiced in the defense-oriented aerospace industry.) During the war years, a report by the Pacific Southwest Office of the National Resources Planning Board, a New Deal institution later scrubbed by a hostile Congress, noted that "technological progress," by promoting an "ever widening flow of employment opportunities," had enabled California and nearby states to absorb "huge population increases decade after decade." After the war, the Council predicted, "a new frontier will be awaiting exploitation—an economic frontier opened by technology."[2]

The report stressed the role that private enterprise would have in exploiting this new frontier, though it also highlighted the needed partnership between industry and government that the wartime experience had fostered. The report concluded with the prescient observation that the region needed to prepare for a long-term decline in the proportion of the workforce employed in agriculture and industry, with growth in the service and distribution areas. These admonitions were taken to heart, with the key role to be played by private industry in generating new jobs, and government working to provide the needed assistance. The institutional patterns that emphasized private enterprise and individual mobility were mostly taken for granted, even as they generated the dispersed suburban workplaces and automobile suburbs (with decaying older cities), segregated by race and social class, that have become the American norm. The long-term effects of these patterns on the land and on quality of life were hardly imagined or considered.

The society envisioned amid the stress of war and later etched in the physical and institutional structure of the nation contained three major components. First, as the emphasis on jobs in the Pacific Southwest Region's planning report indicates, it was a society focused, beyond all other values, on provision of economic opportunity for individuals. For most Americans this meant two interrelated but increasingly distinct spheres of life: work and leisure. Jobs were instruments, affording the means. The goals for economic activity were set by the expectation of a rising level of comfort and consumption. On the macro scale, this relationship was echoed in the economists' preoccupation with keeping demand high so as to create a continuing incentive for expansion in provision of goods and services, and therefore expanding opportunities for profitable investment. As the planners' reports indicated, the progress of technology was the key to this system; in practice this came to mean large private and public outlays for education, research, and management of the whole process.

Second, this was the economy of corporation capitalism in its mature form. It was an institutional order in which the great corporations and their investors played the starring role, with a vital but ancillary role for government, a legacy of the bitter experience of the Depression. The social philosophy of the New Deal was by no means universally embraced, but government was confirmed in its role of regulator and honest broker, whose task it was to ensure that as the economy expanded its opportunities and benefits continued to spread as well. The postwar period saw the highest proportion of the workforce ever organized by unions. Not coincidentally, those decades were marked by high wages and a steadily rising standard of living. Buoyed by great increases in productivity, the era was also characterized by expansion of administrative regulation and governmental intervention throughout society, which worked to finance housing for returning veterans and college education for the children of wage earners and aided tendencies toward greater equality, helping finally to enfranchise African Americans as full citizens. Often working in government or institutions associated with it, professionals came to be valued instrumentally, as key enablers of this vision of progress, which in fact they often were.

The third feature of postwar society involved maintenance of the larger context within which the intermeshing corporate and governmental arrangements flourished. The postwar era saw a great burst of institutional creativity, as the United States took the lead in establishing the United Nations, the World Court, the World Bank, and an international currency regime guaranteed by the American dollar. Here both private and governmental agencies played important roles, but the major hand was that of the state. For the first time in its history, the United States found itself not only inextricably tied into the international order but the single dominant power. A sense of historical mission to accompany this new role had already been enunciated before the nation entered World War II in publisher Henry Luce's famous declaration of the "American Century."[3]

These beliefs could launch great constructive enterprises such as the Marshall Plan of 1947. They were also easily pressed into service to sustain the long period of mobilization against the Soviet Union that came to be known as the cold war. This permanent, partial war economy ensured that the instrumental bent of war planning would continue to exercise a powerful—and in the long run distorting—influence on all sectors of American life. Everything from educational expenditure to the gigantic interstate highway program were justified on the basis of "national defense." These developments created a need for broad policies for managing so vast an enterprise, and for the expert personnel who could conceive and implement them. It was precisely the moment for the forceful touch of an expert elite.[4]

This core institutional order linked the corporation economy closely, though not necessarily smoothly, with government at every level. Though the United States was the giant of the postwar world, and in many ways the successor to the power of the British Empire, it did not stand in isolation. The smooth functioning of the postwar order depended on maintaining a favorable balance in its interactions both with wider global economic and social forces and with the cultural and political life of American society itself. The system also depended upon the natural resources and physical conditions of the nation and its partners in trade. At the beginning of the postwar era, the balance of power and benefit in each area was highly favorable to that corporate order.

By the late 1960s, the very success that the American order had engendered in Europe and Japan nurtured mature economic rivals in some ways more efficient than the United States itself. The cost of sustaining the united front against the Soviet menace continued to rise, especially thanks to the Vietnam War, putting the squeeze on the nation. That is, the patterns of interchange turned seriously against the good functioning of the postwar order. In domestic affairs the civil rights, students', and women's movements; in natural resources, rising prices and the beginnings of environmental protest; in international affairs, the Vietnam War, consequent inflation, and the weakening of the dollar all produced serious dysfunctions that ate into both the economic growth and the social confidence that had been the mainstay of the affluent society of the postwar decades. With these sea changes there would also begin a corresponding erosion of confidence in the professional enterprise.

The Anatomy of a Professional Society

At the height of American postwar success, social investigators began calling attention to the consequences of these developments for the basic structure of the society. Many believed they were witnessing the rise of a new social formation. It was characterized as the organizational, information, or service society, but most lastingly as the postindustrial society. By the early 1970s, social analyst Daniel Bell succeeded in making the term popular when he announced that the nation had reached takeoff into a new kind of society, one based less upon the extraction of natural resources and the "fabrication" of goods typical of the industrial era than upon "processing," a society in which the key to wealth is knowledge, the command of the techniques by which things and people can be shaped and reshaped.[5]

Bell's abstract generalization described what was different about the new industries and services of the postwar society, as compared to the smokestack industries of the past. The new economy relied upon expert knowledge and skills of social communication to a vastly greater degree than any previous social system. Compared to the establishment of the corporate capitalist order at the turn of the century, the knowledge class of professionally trained workers had doubled as a percentage of the American workforce. By the 1970s, the proportion of professionals in the labor force had risen to 13 percent and Bell was forecasting a further increase, approaching a full 25 percent in the year 2000. The numbers understated, if anything, the influence of these workers because of the range of their involvement in all sectors of society.[6]

In Bell's account, the success of the postwar society marked nothing less than a new phase of social evolution. This change of phase was being heralded by the momentous change from goods production to "services" and the new practical value of theoretical knowledge. The kind of knowledge produced in universities and scientific institutes became the key source of innovation, as in the electronics industries, and was, in the social sciences and management, the key resource for governing an increasingly complex society. Bell went on to locate four distinct "estates" within the "professional and managerial class." First came the pioneers of innovation, scientific researchers. Then came the technological estate, peopled by those who applied scientific knowledge: engineers and health care professionals. They were followed by the administrative and managerial professionals. Fourth and last came the "cultural, artistic, and religious professionals" whose major concerns were with the elusive but critical goods of value and meaning.[7]

For Bell, the crux of the issue posed by the coming of post-industrial society was that this growth in the number and technical quality of professionals was not in itself enough to make so complex a social order viable. (He was, after all, writing in the wake of the troubles of the late 1960s.) The very scale and complexity of the new society would make it imperative to "define some coherent goals for the society as a whole and, in the process, to articulate a public philosophy which is more than the sum of what particular . . . social groups may want."[8] In saying this, Bell defined the need without suggesting how it was to be filled.

Recently, British historian Harold Perkin described the long-term evolution of Great Britain toward what he calls Professional Society, one sharing many features with Bell's conception of the postindustrial society. In Perkin's account, as in Bell's, this new social form is gradually succeeding the early capitalist order that was based around the undisputed power of the property-owning class. This order is market-oriented and class remains an important shaping power, but it is no longer all-pervasive. Instead of a horizontal organization by class, Perkin argues that modern nations have come to resemble the Giant's Causeway in Northern Ireland. Rather than a field of class polarization, the social landscape is dominated by many competing hierarchies of power, each jealous of the others and each based upon a distinctive and unequal combination of ownership (class power) and expertise (professional power).

A cultural formation that Perkin calls the professional social ideal has come to counterbalance the dominance of specialized, technical processes in modern societies. Perkin argues that this social ideal, almost a kind of public philosophy, has during the twentieth century been spreading throughout modern societies, though at different rates and to differing degrees. Class society is permeated by the "entrepreneurial ideal based upon active capital and competition"; professional society is characterized by a rival emphasis upon human capital "based upon trained expertise and selection by merit" and exercised through cooperation.[9] In the conflict among social ideals, Perkin notes, the professional ideal tends to displace the old working-class ideal of common labor and cooperative endeavor, though certain features of professionalism— especially its concern for serving the community—also resonate with working-class solidarity in a way entrepreneurialism does not. The professional social ideal prizes mutual service, efficient use of resources, and responsible use of knowledge for the larger good. It also has some considerable fit with postindustrial trends and suggests a way to humanize the austere qualities of most depictions of the postindustrial world.

The larger implications of the professional social ideal received powerful restatement in the postwar period in Britain in the work of T. H. Marshall. In a famous essay of 1950, "Citizenship and Social Class," Marshall argued that although the dominance of entrepreneurialism weakened the old notion of social solidarity implicit in the idea of the body politic, public provision of important goods, such as health care, education, and culture, could be used to offset the power of money in order to nurture a more integrated society, one that guaranteed a civilized life for all its members.[10]

The British debate over the welfare state, which took place at roughly the same time as the postwar planning discussion was proceeding in the United States, forms an interesting contrast that emphasizes the strongly technical and utilitarian quality of the American professional era. The British debate, focused by the report of the Beveridge Commission, was explicitly about the moral requirements of citizenship and the social goals of a victorious, postwar Britain. In the United States, not only was the discussion in almost exclusively technical economic terms, with little or no moral criticism; the whole process was far less unified and focused. There was simply less real discussion and debate. The American plans for a postwar order were far less examined and debated than Britain's, and ours rather than theirs were more decidedly couched in nationalistic, even imperial terms, as in Henry Luce's declaration of the coming American Century.

In the 1960s, many of the worldwide developments Perkin describes were affecting thinking in the United States. In one of the most influential books of the decade, *The New Industrial State*, economist John Kenneth Galbraith hailed the consolidation of the "new industrial state," with the judgment that "power has, in fact, passed to the association of men of diverse technical knowledge, expertise, or other talent which modern industrial technology and planning require." Galbraith explicitly noted that the expert-guided economy was weakening the traditional appeal of labor unions to solidarity in favor of individual upgrading, leading workers to urge upon their children education rather than joining the union.[11] The professional social ideal was perhaps about to be extended and realized in the world's most advanced industrial nation.

The University at Center Stage

The American confidence in technical expertise echoed Louis Brandeis's Progressive Era enthusiasm for scientific management as the key to resolving social conflicts. Unlike Brandeis, however, the most vocal proponents of organizational professionalism rarely combined this technical emphasis with attention to the practical and moral dimensions of professional intelligence. But this was largely because they could still feel supreme confidence that the moral foundations of American society were secure and effective in guiding the events of their time. Those moral foundations, they tended to assume, once laid by the religious and civic authors of American culture, formed a kind of inexhaustible resource of hope, moderation, and fairness that could be counted upon tacitly to undergird social progress. The confidence many Americans felt in the nineteenth century that their system of laissez-faire economics would lead to automatic progress still clung to the national imagination.

This moral confidence, combined with an enthusiasm for scientific and technical progress, was extended by sociologist Talcott

Parsons to the professions. From an influential position at Harvard University, Parsons articulated the professional enterprise in a way that summed up the hope and confidence postwar America placed in professionalism. Parsons was emphatic in stressing the central importance of professional expertise. He called the "professional complex" the most important "component in the structure of modern societies," going on to declare that it was this and not "the special status of capitalistic or socialistic modes of organization" that was the "crucial structural development in twentieth-century society."[12]

What led Parsons to so strong and striking an evaluation of what he knew was a "set of occupations which has never figured prominently in . . . ideological thinking"?[13] It was his conviction that the modern professions represented an evolutionary social advance in the direction of a greater rationality in human affairs.

The professions, according to Parsons, gave special prominence to the intellectual component of cultural life, a quality he termed "cognitive rationality." By emphasizing formal training in technical thinking, professional education produced experts who could bring greater efficacy in suiting techniques to advance goals. These capacities were certified by educational testing and state licensing. But professional life, particularly for the modern organizational professions, also developed the "institutional means of ensuring that such competence will be put to socially responsible uses." This is to say that through the professional complex the United States solved the moral problem posed by the differentiation and inequality induced by division of labor; professionalism was advancing the technical efficiency of particular social functions while it simultaneously directed that efficiency into socially beneficial channels. The spearhead of these developments, in which Parsons suggested the United States was leading the world, was the modern research university.

There, in the universities that were expanding enormously thanks to government expenditure of unprecedented scope, Parsons described the cultural generator of these advances. It was the graduate school of arts and sciences, increasingly well funded and dedicated to pure research, on the analogy of technological progress through scientific investigation. In these faculties, Parsons noted, "the typical professor now resembles the scientist more than the gentleman-scholar" of the older American college, and the researcher is motivated by the need to achieve a "reputation in a national and international cultural forum" rather than relying upon "locally defined status."[14]

Thus, specialization and differentiation of function permitted technical rationality fuller application, freeing it from the constraints of the more "diffuse social responsibility within a collective system" that traditional academics, like their clerical progenitors, carried. To balance the situation, Parsons noted that this older, more diffuse culture of responsibility was actually being extended as more preprofessional students had to enroll in undergraduate college programs.

The concrete meaning of all this became clear when Parsons described how the new system worked. He took medicine as the pioneer in "marrying the university to professional practice and education," citing the Flexner Report of 1911 and Johns Hopkins as the key points at which medicine developed, through the teaching hospital, a flexible vehicle for "working out the application of research to practice."[15] The same model was being extended, Parsons noted, to field after field. Thus law, the venerable agency for implementing the moral consensus of society, had since Oliver Wendell Holmes and Louis Brandeis come to center its own thinking around the university-based social sciences. Similarly, education, social work, and psychotherapy were becoming branches of applied psychology, while engineering found its equivalent of the teaching hospital in industry and the military. Management, from guidance of the national economy to control of local organizations, was similarly the application of the social sciences and the new information processing field of cybernetics.

The common theme was that the university and credentialing system allowed American society to specialize more functions, improving each of them through application of technical rationality, while making them work in concert toward both a better material life and a society of greater inclusiveness and fairness. There runs throughout the discussion the presupposition that somehow the basic moral values of individual opportunity, fairness, and social harmony will prevail throughout the increasingly differentiated professional system. For Parsons, as for most American liberals of the era, there was little need to worry about nurturing that basic moral matrix. Shrill calls for "moral rearmament" could be left to benighted conservatives.

This peculiar moral optimism showed up in Parsons's claim that the clergy, though they were recognized as the distant progenitors of professionalism, could not be considered professionals in the full modern sense. The problem, for Parsons, was that they lack a specific technical competence and held "diffuse social responsibility within a collective system." Artists and intellectuals (those concerned with general social understandings as opposed to specialized sciences), were similarly disqualified because of their rootedness in social interests outside the research university.[16]

By contrast, no question was raised about how the progress of technical rationality, the assimilation of the university to the paradigm of scientific research and the practitioner to the role of technician, might affect the value orientation of the professional complex itself, not to mention its implicit moral base. The organizational society was institutionalizing the professions as ever more efficient extensions of the purified, specialized technical rationality of the research institute into the messy world of daily life. What neither Parsons nor other proponents of the new order questioned was whether this development was compatible with the long-run social purposes the professions were expected to serve. Was, in fact, the professional enterprise, seen as the cutting edge of the whole society's line of development, humanly sustainable? Or did it rest upon seriously flawed intellectual, moral, and institutional premises? The events of the late 1960s made such questions hard to avoid, as they made the benign confidence of the previous period hard to sustain.

Crisis of the Professional Era

If any one figure summed up in character and career the shocks and tragic turns taken by American society during the climax of the post-war era, the decade of the 1960s, it was perhaps Robert McNamara. During that fateful period, McNamara rocketed to fame as standard bearer of the capacity of expert management to solve problems. He served as secretary of defense in the Kennedy and Johnson administrations and was a chief architect of the American strategy in Vietnam, a strategy that was in many ways designed and executed according to the most technically advanced theory of expert control then available. The disastrous outcome of the strategy for the nation, both abroad and at home, stands to this day as the most poignant symbol of a turning point in contemporary history.

McNamara's career was, like those of so many other American leaders of that time, given effective direction by the events of World War II. Early in the war, Robert Lovett, a Wall Street insider who generously responded to the call to government service, recruited McNamara from his teaching post at Harvard Business School into his operations planning group in the Army Air Corps. This operation was an experiment, designed to test the potential of the emerging field of statistical control techniques for improving the combat readiness of American air power. McNamara arrived confident in the power of advanced statistical techniques to give managers a new level of command over the factors of production, human as well as material. It was simply a matter of adapting and fine-tuning the powerful new techniques of systems theory.

With the aid of early data processing machines just becoming available, McNamara helped Lovett's team to calculate precisely the life expectancy of its air crews and even how many planes could be counted upon each day in each theater of the war. *Fortune* magazine played up the new operation, describing this achievement of modern systems thinking as the application of "proven business methods to war."[17] After the war, McNamara and his associates were recruited in turn by Henry Ford II to turn around the floundering automotive giant. As the "Whiz Kids," they were to reapply those same methods to reproduce at Ford Motor Company a dramatic, much-imitated reorganization and turnaround into profitability.

In 1960, McNamara responded to John F. Kennedy's call to Washington to join his new administration. It had pledged itself to "get America moving again" by revitalizing the nation's sense of purpose. Here all the themes of America's postwar development reached a kind of crescendo. McNamara was to be a leading player in this development. He quickly became the star on the New Frontier's team of university-recruited experts, the then-celebrated "best and brightest." As secretary of defense, McNamara's application of proven business methods to war fit well with the administration's confidence that expert thinking could lead to improved control over events. McNamara proved a great innovator. He extensively reorganized the Department of Defense and the procedures of the military services around the sort of Whiz Kid principles that had so catalyzed Ford Motor. Where possible, the theme was to substitute procedure for individual judgment and quantitative measure for personal assessment.

This policy was to have dramatic, and fateful, consequences on the conduct of the war in Vietnam. One effort sought to bypass the usual methods of subjective assessment by military and intelligence officers in the field. Instead, during the war McNamara's staff developed a complicated and sophisticated set of quantitative indicators such as "body counts" and "kill ratios" in an ill-fated effort to quantify and so objectify judgments about the progress of the fighting.

The organizers of the new procedures, however, overlooked the propensity of the human parts of the system to modify their behavior to accord with their own interpretations of the directives handed down in apparently objective form from above. In time, commanders of combat troops began to organize their field activity around the indicators themselves, as distinct from traditional military objectives. From there, the forces in the field slid into manipulating or even falsifying their data. Promotions and whole careers came to depend upon the quantitative measures demanded by the new systems of control. The outcome was that military operations were often directed toward fulfilling strategically meaningless but objectively important kill and body count goals. The results, of course, were both monstrous and tragic.

McNamara's program was designed to modernize the organization of the military services themselves, to bring them into line with the latest management theory and practice. The goal, that is, was to recast the military profession as something more like, and more amenable to, civilian management on the business model. But by establishing a new system of quantified incentives and assessment, the program worked to play down or extirpate just those structures of tradition, loyalty, and *esprit de corps* that had given the armed forces their distinctive ethos and much of their effectiveness. With bitter irony, those efforts to "rationalize" war making contributed substantially to the breakdown in military effectiveness suffered by American forces in Indochina through their unintended but quite devastating effects upon morale. In short, the systems approach ran afoul of just those aspects of human society that its proponents ignored or believed could be reduced to formula and procedure.

In the end, despite the disaster of Vietnam, as a citizen and as a professional Robert McNamara showed himself to be better than his theories. Once he concluded that his judgment about the Vietnam War was tragically wrong, he resigned in early 1968 from the Johnson administration. To his credit, McNamara later reentered debate over defense policy by arguing that nuclear deterrence was a counterproductive policy at a time when it was not popular in Washington to say so. Still, the moral of this tale is the one a professional military officer become secretary of state preached at the beginning of the era of American predominance. George C. Marshall, in urging support for his plan to aid war-ravaged Europe (and in the process our own economy), argued eloquently that there is finally no way to ensure success through pure technique, and that the chief threat to any successful people is always its own hubris.[18] In the American case, this proved to be above all else the hubris of technique.

For thoughtful Americans, the self-inflicted wounds suffered by American government and society during the Vietnam conflict posed disturbing questions about the premises of the whole postwar structure of expertise. Could that order of affluence have raised expectations it could not fulfill, and that it in fact seriously undercut? For many troubled citizens it seemed for a moment that American society in general, and the university-centered professional complex in particular, was chiefly producing, in a way ironically different from Marx's famous adage, its own grave diggers.

The sixties were indeed a time of major questioning of the direction in which the nation was moving. During that decade a powerful polarization began to divide the previously broad "consensus" about the generally benign course of American development. On the one hand, many were determined to press ahead with the postwar agenda, eager to continue the patterns of economic and technological expansion, culturally powered by utilitarian individualism and nationalism, that had proved so successful for nearly two generations. Questioning and protest, however, stripped the veil of moral innocence from these hopes. By the end of the sixties, the leadership of this tendency passed from the consensus-seeking establishment figures represented in the postwar administrations of both political parties to more contentious representatives of the ambitious economic powers of the Sunbelt states who, though themselves major beneficiaries of governmental intervention and subsidy, strove to recall the nation to a banner of renewed anticommunism and laissez-faire.

This ideology by no means prevented the enactment of reforms in the areas of civil rights, occupational safety, and environmental quality—all areas of administration in which professional expertise played a central role. The inclination of these predominantly Republican leaders and their supporters, however, took a rather hostile stand toward the earlier equation of social progress with the prominent role of university-educated experts. By the 1970s, influential intellectual pundits styling themselves "neoconservatives" would single out the professional experts as a New Class, responsible for sowing seeds of amoral skepticism about national purpose.[19]

The other great tendency of the times proved no friendlier, though for quite different reasons, to the professional complex Robert McNamara embodied and Talcott Parsons praised. This tendency sprang directly out of the moral idealism of the New Frontier and the burgeoning movement for black civil rights that was taken up by the Great Society of the Johnson years. Particularly attractive to the young, the religiously liberal, and the university-educated, this movement sought to lay claim to core values of the American moral center that had been overwhelmed by the rush to affluence, especially justice and social responsibility. The upsurge of sixties idealism, like that of the Progressive Era half a century earlier, criticized virtually all institutions; like its Progressive predecessor it was generally critical of big business, but its sharpest attacks were leveled at the very institutional sphere in which it came to self-consciousness: the university.

Talcott Parsons was right to emphasize the new centrality of educational institutions to modern societies. He seriously misjudged, however, the pedagogical effects of the postwar system of education on the nation's youth. As student movements erupted across America's campuses, starting at the University of California in Berkeley in 1964, the themes of civil rights, equality, and opposition to the war in Vietnam mingled with a generalized outrage at the kind of specialized, achievement-oriented education that had settled into place in school and campus. As the postwar university was being expanded and rationalized to become a more integral component of the economic growth system, the nation was undergoing great social change. The student population, though much expanded compared to anything in previous history, was still overwhelmingly upper-middle-class, male, and white, with a preponderance of native-born Protestants. They were typically the children of the expanding professional middle class. The social movement set in motion by these "privileged" students, however, greatly accelerated efforts to open higher education to women, minorities, and the less privileged. The generation of sixties students themselves proved to be suffering not only from bad conscience about their privileges but also from a severe case of one of the most characteristic disorders of modernity: alienation.

The era of the multiversity and affluent class- and income-segregated suburbia, from which the students mostly came, was beginning to make a series of discomfiting discoveries about itself. It was the time when "the organization man" was criticized as a cultural ideal by claiming that organizations were the enemy of genuine individuality.[20] It was also the time in which "juvenile delinquency," "identity crisis," and widespread poverty were "discovered," while the "feminine mystique" came to define the life of postwar suburban housewives, alone all day with the kids. Above all, it was the time in which the injustice of racial discrimination and the drama of the civil rights struggle were brought into living rooms through television. In this climate of generalized self-questioning, the university seemed to many students to represent a suddenly obsolete culture of smug obtuseness. The culture of the specialized graduate and professional schools was spreading throughout the undergraduate curriculum, ousting older humanistic culture at nearly every turn. This institutional ethos of the university gave students a permissive context in which to experiment, yet it seemed (and in many ways was) closed to their deeper doubts and ideals.

The American research university embodied a faith in specialized, scientific, secular reason and was as ill-suited as the liberal political order to addressing issues involving fundamental matters of identity and purpose. At Berkeley, Clark Kerr, the chancellor of the University of California system, was hailing the knowledge industry as society's most valuable instrument for "the production, distribution, and consumption of knowledge in all its forms."[21] Against utilitarian emphases upon competitive success and individual achievement, which were the typical working values of the system, the students raised their banner of self-discovery and general understanding, of individual empowerment and social solidarity. It would prove a heady though unstable mixture. New prophets such as social critic Ivan Illich attacked the whole professional system as a threat to the nurturing of "autonomous individuals" which was subjecting them "to the domination of constantly expanding industrial tools." The result, Illich wrote, was that "people tended to relinquish the future to a professional elite."[22] The very tendencies that the proponents of the professions had been celebrating, the "antiprofessional" critics demonized and damned. An older populist suspicion of experts and elites lived again, now on the political left, as it would rise shortly on the political right in the neoconservative attacks on the New Class.

The tragedy of the times was that neither the romantic world of student rebellion nor the professional ethos of the technically oriented universities proved to have the needed imagination or commitment to invent a better form of life. The desire of the idealistic young for a life marked by wholeness, authenticity, and community collided with the widely perceived social fragmentation and personal conformism of American affluence, whose sources lay in the narrowness of division of labor generally and the technical focus of so much of professional life more specifically. Yet the modernity the students protested as alienation and dehumanization also opened new possibilities. Still, it proved beyond anyone's capacity at the time to grasp those possibilities coherently.

The reforms of that era began to correct some of the worst inequities of the postwar order, especially in regard to race and sex, but the criticisms of fragmentation and alienation went largely unaddressed, while the postwar marriage of private consumption and a militarized economy continued. Increased emphasis upon social justice and individual fulfillment helped promote growing concern about the quality of life, as opposed to a merely economic standard of living, paving the way for the rise of "postmaterialist values" such as concern about the natural environment.[23] However, the postwar economy had grown beyond the moral patterns of the family firm and local community. The informal controls of the old gentry ethic in the professions was being superseded by the bureaucratic structures of organizational settings. The suburbanized, postindustrial social patterns offered few integrating practices to replace the old ones. The substitution of rule and procedure failed to impart the desired sense of orientation and participation.

For a time in the early 1970s, the country saw efforts to translate some of the concerns of the movements for reform both into national legislation and into the professions themselves, as some theorists of the student movement were urging. Finally, however, even though the basic structure of the postwar order held, there was too little institutional experimentation and reform to revitalize the nation's self-confidence about the future. The abiding result was that most established ways of life lost legitimacy. Regrettably, though predictably, the consequence was a rising tide of cynicism, within as well as about the professions, plus ever more bitter culture wars fought over the unresolved divisions that surfaced during the turbulent sixties.[24] The cynicism about institutions and those cultural conflicts soon acquired massive power thanks to economic and social changes that began to engulf the United States during the 1970s.

Professionalism Under Stress

Beginning in the early 1970s, the dynamic stability that had characterized the postwar economic picture was replaced by a series of rapid and often violent shocks. Whole occupations, industries, and regions suddenly found themselves overtaken by foreign competitors and made obsolete overnight. Economic security became a subject of everyday worry and anger, creating the perception of rising stress throughout the population, including the momentarily secure. The root cause of these distressing events was the increasing disorder of the international economic system, a disorder that reverberated domestically with the breakdown of the informal social contract that had underpinned the interest-group bargaining typical of postwar politics. In this climate, the fragile social contract that had led labor and business to moderate their demands on each other reverted to a sharply oppositional stance. A similar tone of suspicion and hostility spread through much of American society.

During the years of these changes, the 1970s and 1980s, professionalization continued to grow in the United States, but the distribution of the growth shifted markedly. Resources and applicants shifted away from the public-sector fields that flourished before 1970, such as education and social services, toward fields directly related to business, military, and technological institutions. These shifts were partly due to conscious governmental policy and spending and partly resulted from changes in society itself, such as the educational effects of the decline in the number of school-age children. Professional growth occurred mostly in areas where technical understanding of professionalism was least likely to be broadened by the intrusion of moral and political concerns. Again, the causes and the results were mixed. Thanks to governmental policies of affirmative action to correct past patterns of discrimination, professional education was far more open to women and minorities than before. At the same time, professional life within such economic and social circumstances itself became more competitive and constrained to focus on economic success, or at least survival. The expansive professional era of previous decades did not return.

Within the tightening squeeze of economic pressure, work life—even for the professional middle class—became increasingly constrained by the imperatives of economic efficiency and organizational growth. This forced to the margins the traditional professional concern with the intrinsic purposes of work. The focused life seemed more than ever a luxury to be indulged in during leisure time. This period saw increasing assimilation of medicine and law, the core free professions, to the model of organizational professions. Law firms found themselves under growing pressure to emulate the standards of business. The ever more complicated and expensive world of high-technology medicine slowly catalyzed government and third-party insurers to take steps to bring physicians increasingly under the control of large health care corporate entities.

There was more at work in these trends than ideology. As the economy found itself exposed to unexpected shocks from abroad, the social bonds that the conflicts of the 1960s had strained began to give way. During this time the American economy found itself in an intensifying competition with Europe and Japan. The apparent prosperity of the nation during the 1980s was largely funded by massive military spending, the last gasp of the cold war era, which abruptly ended with the collapse of the Soviet empire at the end of the decade. During those years, American business was finding itself pressed to compete effectively in the now global economy. In the press, major organizational citizens, from banks to corporations to public agencies, defaulted on longstanding bonds of trust with their workers, their clients, communities, and the public at large. The result was an interdependence without mutual trust—the precondition for generalized hostility and fear. All sectors of the population possessing the means sought to defend their newly perceived vulnerability by organizing in their own interest.

This strategy of secession from the social contract was pursued most aggressively and successfully by affluent groups, including the professional middle class. In an economy that no longer enjoyed rapid productivity growth, the advance of some now had to occur at the expense of others. The prediction that the nation was becoming a "zero-sum" society was, by the 1990s, confirmed.[25] The "culture of contentment" enjoyed by the rich and the professional middle class improved gratifyingly, but the economic misery of the many worsened.[26] The postwar institutional order was in tatters, and with it the good conscience and social esteem of professionalism.

The appearance of the yuppie phenomenon during the 1980s gave these large-scale social trends an immediate and none-too-lovely human face. The young, urban professionals of the acronym were "discovered" in 1984, their reality certified by a *Newsweek* cover story and a great deal of additional media attention. Like so many social discoveries, this one called attention to a certain style, a way of putting life together, more than it described a clear statistical category. The term referred to a lifestyle concentrated upon occupational success, often in the recognized professions and particularly in fields tied to business, which sought proper reward for hard work in private acquisition and display of status goods.

In outline, the yuppie phenomenon simply advertised the basic goals of the postwar economic order in heightened and streamlined form. What made the yuppiedom of gentrified urban neighborhoods stand out against typical American middle-class life was the apparent willingness of yuppies of both sexes to subordinate all other life goals, including family and child rearing, to career success and consumption. The yuppies were, as Barbara Ehrenreich put it, "exemplars not of their generation but of their class, the same professional middle class that had produced the student rebels."[27] Alienation had not gone away. Instead, a new generation found another, less publicly oriented promise of a cure.

Beneath the envy and moral indignation stirred by the preening of yuppyism lay the continuing, unsettling presence of economic disorder. The most powerful and affluent professions became very much a part of the sclerotic condition of American society. This situation emphasized the often contradictory results of earlier efforts to amend the postwar order. For example, legislative reforms of the early 1970s opened political campaigns and the regulatory process to more direct public involvement. They also allowed, if unwittingly, well-organized and highly funded publics to assemble smaller versions of the powerful lobbying arrangements President Dwight D. Eisenhower had dubbed "the military-industrial complex." A medical-industrial complex soon grew up, along with specialized law firms whose entire clientele consisted of one agency or another of the federal government. In these highly politicized organizational contexts, the old client-centered, paternalistic ethics of the free professions proved to be a less-than-adequate guide to maintaining professional integrity amid severe economic strain.

By the beginning of the twenty-first century, the wracking changes in the economy were undermining old conceptions of professional identity and responsibility. In an era of radical economic instability, when investment capital shifted rapidly around the globe seeking the highest return, organizations themselves began to implode. In a mad effort to attract or retain investors—or to prevent hostile takeover from outside—business firms intensified their efforts to squeeze more out of their employees, professionals as well as others. The technical focus that had dominated postwar professionalism now tended to blur into a self-interested economic strategy for taking advantage of shifting market winds. In this swirl of uncertainty—the "casino capitalism" of the United States in the 1980s—whole new professional enterprises were born, with the rise of consultant firms.

The established professions were becoming domesticated for organizational life, but the consultant firms adopted, as often as not, the swashbuckling outlook of old-time entrepreneurial capitalism. The organizational push for predictability and efficiency has long worked to isolate technical proficiency from concerns with institutional responsibility. The intensified economic focus of the professional consultant reduced the civic dimensions of professionalism still further. The combined effects of these developments, however, has been sadly similar. They weakened integrity of function and public service, which are the special attributes of professional occupations. This at a time when the entire economic order was suffering from a breakdown of mutual confidence, the systemic consequences of pushing self-regarding instrumental rationality to the limit.

Under these circumstances, de Tocqueville's democratic paradox has returned with a vengeance. Observing the more dispersed and far less integrated civil society of the nineteenth century, de Tocqueville stressed that the long-term viability of free institutions, and thus of individual freedom, required some means whereby the intrinsic values of activities essential to the common welfare could be protected from meltdown into the cash nexus.[28] At a moment when the unregulated cash nexus of the market threatens to implode upon the social order it should serve, the reinvigoration and institutionalization of the ideals of integrity of function and public responsibility that professionalism represents would fill an essential need.

We need a new professionalism adequate to the changed circumstances of American life. The first step toward this reinvention of professionalism, however, requires that professionalism be understood as a public good, a social value, and not the ideology of some special interest. To make good on this claim, the positive features of professionalism must be extended to all work in the modern economy. By combining the dignity and security of occupational identity with the integrity and competence of social function, professionalism can be a major resource for rebuilding not just a dynamic economy but a viable public order as well. The chapters that follow are concerned with reinventing professionalism as a civic art, to reform the professional enterprise and extend its goods more broadly while helping to spark the renewal of the larger society. The succeeding chapters argue that, although it may seem idealistic, this cause will in the long run prove the most realistic strategy by which to address not only the crisis of professionalism but also the problems of work and meaning.

Chapter Five

Reinventing Professionalism

Few moments in history are more disconcerting yet so exhilarating as a time of interregnum, when an old order of affairs has ceased to operate but no new pattern is yet clearly in place. In the history of the sciences we are used to calling such moments revolutionary.[1] In social and political affairs it is perhaps more accurate to call them a period of historical discontinuity. At such times, specialized knowledge and routine functioning, which contribute both progress and stability in more settled periods, can become a menace rather than a blessing. Then the need is for criticism, but even more for reflective rethinking that can imaginatively conceive emerging novelties as a whole situation.

A Moment of Historical Discontinuity

When an era ends, as for example when the age of European world dominance ended after 1945, the effect is sudden, often unpredictable change. Europe, which had been at the center of world power, was suddenly reduced to one of several areas contested between the United States and the USSR, powers viewed by many Europeans as alien and dangerous to the values of a now-dwarfed Old World culture. Today, the conflict of superpowers, the cold war that was the central organizing fact of the past half century, has itself come to an abrupt end. Since the dissolution of the Soviet world before an astounded global television audience, it has become clear that we are today entering another such moment of historical discontinuity.

If taken as suggestive rather than precise examples, well-chosen historical analogies can ease the anxiety of such moments of change and bring the perspective and orientation necessary for effective response. For the United States today, the signs of major discontinuity are manifold: the evident breakdown of the once-successful postwar economic order at home and the uncertainty that hangs over the international economic scene; the resulting conflicts between suddenly unrestrained local interests following the cessation of the cold war; the destructive effects of an anarchic instrumental rationality at work in technologies and organizations with uncertain social mooring; the rising tide of cultural division in American life, accompanied by a frightening dissolution of the social fabric. The nation has not merely entered a period of readjustment in which the basic institutional order can be taken as sound; this is a time of massive decomposition. The only adequate response has to be an equally massive movement of criticism and reconstruction.

The last comparable moment in American history was neither the 1960s (despite the apocalyptic rhetoric of the time) nor 1945, nor the trauma of the Great Depression. These were times of major readjustment, but they could and did assume the basic adequacy of the economic, social, and political structure then prevailing. Rather, the scope of today's challenges suggests the period stretching from ca. 1880 to World War I. During that time the United States restructured itself from an insular and dispersed, racially divided, dominantly Protestant, agrarian-commercial society into an industrial giant and world power whose strength lay in a national economy centered in great cities with multiethnic populations.

Through that tumultuous period, immigrants, Catholics, Jews, women, and African Americans began aggressively to seek equality and full participation in American life. The nation's life was itself reshaped through a whole set of new institutions ranging from corporations to regulatory government to the university-led education system, all staffed by the new type of organizational professionals. This was the period of massive national restructuring, described in

Chapter Three, which set the context for the rise of the organizational professions.

During that time of discontinuity a century ago, Americans discovered they were living in a new world that presented important challenges to the nation's inherited, if still limited, dedication to democracy. Today's challenges are no less sweeping and unprecedented: how to invent a new global order while seeking to enhance the national well-being; how to adapt humanely to technological change while striving for ecologically sustainable economic growth with equity and inclusion. The effort of the pragmatist Progressives such as Herbert Croly, John Dewey, and Jane Addams to bring civic concerns to bear on the rationalizing tendencies of technological society may be our most valuable analogy for making our way in this moment of historical discontinuity.

Croly's thought and career seem especially suggestive for this effort at reconstruction. Like Addams and Dewey, he had frequent recourse to the idea of reconstituting an active public.[2] Responding to a moment of historical discontinuity that seemed to discredit the older American values of democratic civic life, Croly put forward the idea of the public as a new kind of civic community. He sought to promote a new process of social learning and moral deliberation. Croly understood, before most of his countrymen, the problems of interdependence that the new corporation capitalism posed for civic community in the United States. He insisted that the *sine qua non* of a complex, interdependent modern society was to make the growing differentiation of skills and social position an asset to democratic life rather than an obstacle. To guarantee that specialized expertise be employed within a wide horizon of common needs and aims, Croly sought a new equivalent for declining local civic communities.

Professionalizing work was to be a key part of this project. Finding individual scope and recognition, even within large organizations through craftlike dedication to public standards, professionalization would enable citizens to depend upon each other for the common goods of modern civilization. Educated middle-class professionals were to provide leadership in the opening technological, organizational era.[3] Croly looked to them to mediate between the often-closed domains of the emerging national economy and the provincial world in which most Americans felt most at home. In this way, professionals could stand as models of how to use knowledge for the general betterment, as exemplars of a democratic community appropriate to the twentieth century.

At that past moment of epochal social change, Croly also insisted that functional expertise and interdependent cooperation could be sustained only if all the participating groups recognized each other as sharing a common destiny and raised cooperation to the status of a conscious social value. This was the core meaning of his proposed "new nationalism." Croly's national purpose was to make concrete what his teacher, Josiah Royce, called the spirit of loyalty to a cause, the moral sense that Royce argued was the necessary foundation for justice and social trust. In this conception, the trendsetting middle-class professions were to become standard bearers leading the process of institutionalizing civic professionalism as a common social value. As we have seen, however, even though Croly was proved right about the nation's need for a sustaining public purpose, it would be imposed from above for purposes of meeting emergencies and preserving military strength instead of growing through interaction between leaders and participants in common civic projects.

Ours is a new moment, testing whether American democracy can develop new ways to advance its historical commitments. But social projects, like individual purposes, must be worked out in the context of historical contingency manifest in the actual state of economic development, the institutional order, and the sphere of culture. These conditions, as we have noted, are in many ways today characterized by decomposition, as the once-successful patterns developed during the period of postwar American supremacy prove less and less functional. Reconstructing professionalism, no less than other key projects of reform, must begin from sober assessment of the actual state of the professional enterprise and how professionals understand their own lives.

The Disintegration of Professional Integrity:
A Close-up

Contemporary professional life continues to be lived along parallel but unequal lines, the provincial practitioners and the metropolitan professional elites. Provincial practitioners, although usually trained at metropolitan institutions, find their most significant connection and purpose within localized settings. There, longstanding features of American civic life, especially the importance of public cooperation, moral character, and local community service, temper the allure of pure technique, the rewards of wealth, and the expanded personal options available within the metropolitan context. Here the community-trustee aspects of professionalism are still concrete reality rather than an abstraction of theory. However, the vastly increased integration of national markets and aspirations has steadily overshadowed those provincial loyalties, creating an undertow running against the viability of loyalty to place and local culture.

The same dynamism of the national economy and trendsetting metropolitan organizations and opinions pulls professional ambition toward high-status national institutions. Metropolitan professionals typically work at the center of their field and live within a geographically dispersed network of peers. They are often closely identified with the workings of national business, government, or professional organizations. They are far less tied to a local civic milieu and naturally identify most closely with their career and the settings of metropolitan life. It is not surprising, then, that it has been among metropolitan professionals that the most condensed symptoms of the stresses of historical discontinuity appear. The yuppie syndrome, as it was dubbed in the 1980s, called attention to tendencies that, in a more buffered form, have affected professionals, and indeed virtually all parts of the American population, to an increasing degree ever since.

The lifestyle adopted by the young urban professionals during the 1980s had a huge influence upon subsequent notions of the "successful" and the "hip" among the highly educated and professionals. It also exposed in a new and dramatic way the tensions that underlie professional life and that the intensified capitalism of the present renders more acute. The yuppie, it should be noted, confounded much accepted cultural wisdom. Contrary to the supposed contradiction between a sturdy work ethic and hedonistic consumerism, once argued by Daniel Bell in *The Cultural Contradictions of Capitalism*, these urban professionals work ambitiously while also consuming commodities and stimulating experiences with equal energy.[4] More recently, in *Bobos in Paradise*, David Brooks labeled this kind of cultural style "bourgeois-bohemian," a blend of previous opposites, united by the opportunities of the knowledge economy that Bell had correctly diagnosed.[5] The problem of this mode of life (it has become indeed the mode) does not seem to be conflict between work and hedonism but the discovery that both success and pleasure are often capricious and without moral significance.

The ethos of what can still be called the yuppie style is characterized by a high level of material security and a vast number of opportunities for personal exploration and fulfillment. It is also a life of intense competitive pressure and little free time. Yuppie life is thus riven by harsh dichotomies. Competence and adaptability are the presiding values in work. This cult of competence is at the same time curiously detached, engendering few lasting ties to employers, coworkers, or organizations. More recently, this aspect of the current style was also ambivalently celebrated by Richard Florida in *The Rise of the Creative Class*.[6] The yuppie, the Bobo, or the Creative Class wannabe must travel light, emotionally as well as physically. The demands and stresses of highly competitive work are expected to be balanced or at least relieved in the intimate realm of personal life. Yet even there, relationships, including marriage and family, are a source of enormous anxiety and often severe disappointment. The conflicting demands of such a highly segmented life require a strategy for managing it all and ultimately soothing the hurts of an inevitably wounded self. Metropolitan professional life is therefore marked by massive consumption of professional services, from personal financial management to child care to psychotherapy. They further the fragmentation of existence, threatening to transmute the effort to live well into an exhausting battle for psychic survival.

This dichotomy between the harsh demands of the market-place and the private sphere of personality is familiar to many of the metropolitan professionals' fellow citizens. It is rooted in the characteristically sharp differentiation Americans now experience between the public and private spheres. Our economic as well as public institutions are increasingly governed by instrumental and utilitarian standards, pushing workers to narrow their concerns to technical competence and self-protection. In other capacities, however—as consumers, members of associations, and private persons—Americans expect a different logic to apply, one giving expression to individual yearning and the desire for a satisfying life.[7]

While many Americans become "gradgrinds" at work, bent on improving efficiency and payoff, in the recesses of private life (where they believe they can be themselves) they often seek compensation as "Bloomsburies." They find themselves emulating the Bloomsbury set of Edwardian Britain, who, finding little meaning in the public culture of their time, sought fulfillment by cultivating a romantic sensibility tinged with terminal irony. The consumer economy provides essential support for this private quest, especially in its marketing of the nostalgic delights of an upscale, autumnal hedonism. Not only metropolitan professionals but most citizens of modern societies (even self-described postmodernists) must negotiate a compromise between these two ways of living, sometimes adopting the no-nonsense seriousness of a gradgrind while now and again affecting a Bloomsbury style of aesthetic detachment. This division of life into contrasting spheres of value was what Max Weber identified as the modern fate. Earlier, it seemed to G.W.F. Hegel a description of alienation, a state of unhappy consciousness.

Louis Auchincloss's *Diary of a Yuppie* takes its readers into that ethos via the world of corporate law as practiced in the go-go financial scene of New York in the late 1980s. The novel tells the story of attorney Robert Service and his wife, Alice. Both are in their early thirties. The book takes them through the near-ending of their marriage while Bob bounds from conquest to conquest, playing the casino world of corporate takeovers in which manipulation of financial assets displaces the nurture of enterprise. The story is a chance to observe close up a character type, a moral philosophy, and also the deformation of old-time blue-chip law firms into unprincipled competitors for clients in the world of business services. The old gentry ethic of the free professions is here ousted by the purely strategic orientation of finance under conditions of reduced governmental regulation. A blatantly mercenary professionalism evolves as a response to an increasingly dangerous and bellicose economic scene. The vehicle for the tale is Bob's private journal, over whose shoulder, as it were, we are allowed to peek as events unfold. As for Alice, a former literature major at Columbia, Service's literary heroes were aesthetes, especially Walter Pater and his ancient Epicurean alter ego, Marius. Like Pater's Marius, Service is incapable of profound loyalties, but unlike Marius he insists that he is fundamentally like everyone else, except that Bob Service can accept this fact in sangfroid, without illusions.

Service harbors no illusions about the law, either. He sees his superior realism setting him apart from both Alice and his professional mentor, Branders Blakelock. "The trouble with you," Service instructs Alice—and through her, Blakelock—is that she doesn't grasp the "moral climate in which we live today. It's all a game, but a game with very strict rules . . . but there is no particular moral opprobrium in incurring a penalty."[8] Service's great talent is his ability to manipulate, as it is his peculiar character flaw that he cannot distinguish manipulation from genuine persuasion. Service insists, however, that his view is not exceptional, only exceptionally honest. Thus he is not surprised later in the story when his own protégé turns on him. Neither is he surprised when Alice, who has all along deplored his cynicism, at the story's end apparently accepts not only him on his own terms but also the possibility that he may be right about humankind. Service (who bears an ironic cognomen, to be sure) fits well into a time when the educated middle class sees discontinuity all around: in the breakdown of professional and personal mores, in the loss of any sense of calling beyond a financially successful career.

Service can move easily between the harsh world of business and the softer climate of the personal sphere because for him these transitions involve no difference in principle, only change in modulation. Service's ability to modulate his presentation of self to charm or force the other to his will serves him well in the venue of corporate law. This, of course, is precisely Auchincloss's point. Service literally refuses to credit any other way of relating to the world. Yet the novel gains its savor from the reader's belief—or at least hope—that there is a richer moral world, though an alternative to the protagonist's invincible cynicism casts little shadow in the book.

The yuppie strategy, as pursued in this tale, is a relentless organization of life in instrumental terms. Its social consequences are suggested by the wrecked relationships and broken trust Service leaves in his choppy wake. But this approach to living is revealed as failing even on its own terms. The private satisfactions of winning, having, and achieving fail to stem an anxious agitation that, like an addiction or an obsession, presses on toward yet more struggle. Service cannot achieve a stable and satisfactory form of life. The instrumental life is seen to implode upon itself.

Robert Service is a literary creation. However, achieving a meaningful, satisfying life while gripped by a devouring orientation toward career success is a real and widespread problem in contemporary life. In the absence of an ethic of calling, the quest to "become one's own person" through instrumental achievement cannot, for most, support satisfaction in practicing a profession over time. In the absence of social confidence in the value of the work done, ambition must become paranoid and even self-destructive. Without shared confidence in the value of the task, there can be no secure recognition for individual achievement, leaving individuals endlessly anxious, having to validate their self-worth through comparative ranking along an infinite scale of wealth and power.

When winning isn't possible, or its personal cost is too high, or when one's career has plateaued, the instrumental orientation toward success reveals its poverty. It fails to yield an enduring sense that life is worth living and even, ironically, that this would-be imperial self has value.[9] Then begins the search for authenticity in expressive identity or secretion of a hardened shell of cynicism that are such prominent features of today's society.

By contrast, a professionalism unfolding as part of a cooperative civic culture permits an escape from this unhappy consciousness by focusing the person's energies outward, engaging the challenges presented by social reality. But such a professionalism depends upon a certain kind of institutional development that sustains the intrinsic values of professional work while connecting professionals with other citizens. Without such institutions, professional morale must wither, and with it the objective dependability of those professional functions so vital to the life of a modern society.

The Underlying Problem: Negative Interdependence

The entropic forces tearing away at metropolitan professionals point up the paradox of global interdependence. As the units of the global system become more tightly linked, the prosperity of each depends upon close cooperation with the others. Yet this very interdependence seems to generate intensely distrustful, competitive, and hostile response. We might describe this condition as one of negative interdependence. That is, interdependence turns negative in outcomes when it is inescapable yet neither acknowledged nor taken as a shared responsibility by those involved.

In an interdependent situation marked by uncertainty and limited trust, participants with dominant market positions or political power are tempted to resist those cooperative activities that imply immediate cost to themselves, despite their recognition that it would be generally beneficial if all complied. Similarly, individual social actors are tempted to seek unilateral advantages, even when they realize that all would suffer if everyone did the same.[10] But whatever their short-term benefits, these strategies inevitably increase social entropy, with negative consequences for the individual participants as the social environment on which they depend erodes and finally collapses. In even the moderately long run, no purely individual strategy can overcome the underlying logic of interdependence. Either the actors learn to cooperate, regulating and sharing responsibility for the collective effects of their individual actions, or they continue to suffer the downward spiral of negative interdependence.

Consider the contemporary consequences of the decomposition of the postwar order of national economic regulation. As we have seen, it sets off a suspicion-driven strategy of increasingly desperate, unregulated competition among nations as well as among interest groups within them. By intensifying the pressure toward instrumentalizing relationships, unmediated competition makes loyalty hard to sustain, undermining the moral infrastructure of civilized freedom. Among the secure, the result is the cultural fragmentation characteristic of the yuppie syndrome. But among the urban poor, as Cornel West has shown, the consequence is a far more immediately destructive nihilism.[11]

Neither is unregulated competition likely to prove economically sustainable. The era of the Great Depression witnessed a particularly vicious cycle of negative interdependence. Then, firms that sought to shore up their market position by the familiar tactic of shedding workers so as to lower costs discovered that what appeared individually rational turned out to be collectively ruinous. What lightened the costs to individual firms also depressed the collective purchasing power of their markets. Only the governmental management of the national economy that sustained postwar growth proved able to compensate for the disastrous logic of negative interdependence. It should not be forgotten that even then, this solution had to be imposed over the loud protests of some of the very firms thereby rescued from oblivion.

The contemporary metropolis, as we have seen, shows a similar tendency toward destructive negative interdependence. The flight from compact industrial cities into the suburbs was promoted by both government and business in the postwar decades as the opening of another American frontier, a technological return to a pastoral golden age. Nearly half a century later, however, this vast experiment is producing increasingly negative results. This is the case not only in the depressed and crime-ridden central cities but also in the stressed-out, overextended "edge cities" where mounting infrastructural costs, social problems, and consequent demands for services continue to exceed citizens' capacity to cope—or willingness to pay. Interdependence again seems to have overtaken the uncomprehending individuals whose lives depend upon it.

The scope of the contemporary challenge of interdependence is graphically laid out by Robert B. Reich in *The Work of Nations* and his updated sequel of 2000, *The Future of Success: Working and Living in the New Economy*.[12] Reich places his analysis within a longer narrative reminding the reader that America's postwar middle-class society, unlike the more state-directed and cooperatively organized European social democracies, was very much the consequence of an expanding consumer economy ruled by the great corporations. The key change of the past quarter century was the end of the nearly self-contained American national economy.[13] This new world-spanning web of enterprise no longer gives competitive advantage to the massive, hierarchically controlled corporation that once ruled the marketplace. The new unit of enterprise focuses on "high-value" products and services, pursuing fast-changing specialized market niches, the competitive targets of profitability. It has no need "to control vast resources, discipline armies of production workers, or impose predictable routines." Instead, the high-value enterprise, like a centrifuge, is rearranging the once-familiar contours of the workforce. The nerves and sinews of the new enterprise are "problem-solvers, problem-identifiers, and strategic-brokers."[14] Such enterprises must be unencumbered by bureaucracy. They depend upon speedy information flow and timely application of expertise to shifting problems.

These trends set the context for the increasing importance of expertise, but expertise that can be flexibly deployed through collaborative activities. Today's economy is increasingly divided into three occupational groups. Reich calls these the "routine-producers," the semiskilled and unskilled workers who were the backbone of the high-volume economy; "in-person servers," among whom are found a disproportionate number of the women in the workforce; and the new and dynamic factor, the "symbolic analysts." Among this last group Reich clusters researchers, engineers, bankers, lawyers, consultants of all types, systems analysts, journalists, "and even university professors." What they have in common is symbolic analysis: a set or sets of "tools for doing conceptual puzzles." Symbolic analysts now make up about 20 percent of the nation's workforce but reap half the total income. More than raw materials or simple labor, the symbolic analysts are the key resource for high-value production. Their particular skill is to "solve, identify, and broker problems by manipulating symbols."[15]

Much of *The Work of Nations* is given over to discussing the education, work styles, and social organization of symbolic analysts, these human counters in the economic game of the future. The surprising upshot of Reich's argument is that these developments are rendering obsolete much of professional life as it is now structured. Reich sees the traditional professional career, based upon certified training in a fixed body of knowledge and progressing through a fairly fixed occupational ladder, as passing away with the bureaucratic organization. Along with the corporation economy of the past century, Reich is forecasting the demise of the narrowly specialized, technically oriented, organizational professions.

In the new economy, Reich argues, the important thing is not mastery of a body of knowledge—that can increasingly be obtained through a few computer keystrokes—but "the capacity to effectively and creatively *use* the knowledge." Practical, multisided intelligence, that is, will become more valuable than narrow technical capacity. Or rather, the two are being combined in new ways so that the practical and general orientation often has the upper hand over the technical and the specialized. However, Reich also calls attention to disturbing features of the emerging culture of the symbolic analysts, which tend to reinforce the fictional picture of yuppie culture sketched by Auchincloss. "The symbolic-analytic mind," Reich summarizes, "is trained to be skeptical, curious, and creative."[16] Indeed, symbolic analysts increasingly carry over their strategic and instrumental thinking from their work to their social and personal lives. The result is what Reich calls "the politics of secession."

Reich descries the appearance among the ascendant symbolic analysts of "the darker side of cosmopolitanism." He writes: "Without strong attachments and loyalties extending beyond family and friends, symbolic analysts may never develop the habits and attitudes of social responsibility. They will be world citizens, but without accepting or even acknowledging any of the obligations that citizenship in a polity normally implies."[17] Reich fears that such people will resist any calls for common sacrifice and commitment on the basis of justice and fairness, ideals they may find to be "meaningless abstractions." Reich concludes his gloomy coda with a hope that somehow a "sense of national purpose" might arise to rescue us—especially the losers in the ruthless game of global high-value capitalism—from the devouring logic of unfettered problem solving, problem identifying, and strategic brokering.

There are clear echoes of Reich's analysis in the otherwise more enthusiastic portrayal of today's symbolic analysts in David Brook's "bourgeois-bohemian" high achievers and Richard Florida's "creative class."[18]

The Future of Success, which we encountered earlier when trying to place contemporary professions within the much-discussed new economy, shows the continuation of those trends during the decade between Reich's two books. In essence, the expansive, entrepreneurial economy of the American 1990s produced great growth in wealth, large gains in the application of information technology, and a brief decline in the rate of poverty and in inequality of wealth. The boom, however, proved temporary; more important—since all booms are by necessity intermittent—it intensified the pressure to avoid being left behind in a less equal world. Reich gives a vivid image of this socially entropic trend through the image of an ever more frenzied pursuit of the terrific deal.

Improvements in communications technology make possible a much more fine-grained marketing of products, precisely tailored to specific consumer niche markets. The Internet simultaneously enables consumers to trade around (and if possible trade up) for the highest-quality or most appealing goods and services for the best price. If the earlier kind of consumer society was based upon brand loyalty and mass markets, the new, electronically enabled version is about hopping nimbly from product to product, provider to provider, always in search of the terrific deal. As the system evolves and improves, argues Reich, consumers really are able to get closer to that elusive goal of whatever one wants when one wants it. But, he points out, the balance between making a living and leading a life does not thereby become easier or better. On the contrary, the logic of the new situation pushes in the direction of placing more attention on work and less on personal life and leisure.

The irony, of course, is that an enhanced quality of life was the ostensible purpose of the speeded-up consumer economy in the first place. So the world of the terrific deal has a darker side. As Reich points out, "What it means for the rest of our lives—the parts that depend on firm relationships, continuity, and stability—is acutely problematic."[19] Of course, the forms of professional work and the way in which professionals typically deliver their services are highly dependent upon just such things as "firm relationships, continuity, and stability." This culture of the terrific deal is in several ways antithetical to the premises that underlie professional ideals. It creates strong economic and social pressure to pursue the main chance whenever and however it appears.

This situation strengthens the appeal of the "secession of the successful" strategy that Reich highlighted in the earlier work. As the macro institutions of the less regulated economy favor big winners—and many large losers—the result on the micro level is that "the rewards of the new economy are coming at the price of lives that are more frenzied, less secure, more economically divergent, more socially stratified." Thus "as our earnings become less predictable, we leap at every chance to make hay while the sun shines. As the stakes rise . . . we'll do whatever we can to be in the winners circle and to get our children safely there as well."[20]

This picture of a winner-take-all society is not Reich's alone. Economist Robert Frank argues a case that it is this dynamic that is driving, and distorting, today's economy in *Luxury Fever: Money and Happiness in an Age of Excess*.[21] David Callahan has produced a stinging account of how the social climate Reich is describing gives rise to a "culture of cheating." The fear is that, since all is precarious and the powerful mostly succeed when they break or bend rules, not to do likewise is to consign oneself, and one's children, perpetually to that large "anxious class" that has so far failed to gain more than crumbs from the table of the past decade's great expansion of wealth.[22]

Making Interdependence Work: The Civic Alternative

The great promise and hope of the market economy has always lain in Adam Smith's confident prediction that, through exchange, the division of labor will produce such efficiencies in the deployment of talent and resources to raise the level of what he called "opulence" or material well-being. Historically, that promise in fact depended upon a great deal of statesmanship in designing and fostering institutions, both government and social forms of "civil society," which operate according to quite different principles and so serve to mitigate the otherwise socially disruptive and often humanly destructive forces Joseph Schumpeter aptly named creative destruction.

Today, the question of whether we are living through a period of resurgent religious fundamentalism is much discussed.[23] It is less commonly remarked that we have also been caught up for two decades in a revival of what could rightly be thought of as *market fundamentalism*. The negative connotation of religious fundamentalism is akin to the general mistrust of fanatics. Just who fits the category is a matter of perspective, but the notion of fanatic or true believer is a common one. It means a person whose zeal for an idea or ideal renders the individual blind to consequences for human welfare of acting on that belief. The worry about those accused of religious fundamentalism is that they may be fanatical. Certainly, this is how the perpetrators of the attack of September 11, 2001, are most often thought of. The fear is that, like fanatics, religious fundamentalists will disregard the cost in human suffering and other evils of their adherence to what they believe to be supreme goods and ideals.

Market fundamentalists are those who allow their enthusiasm for the ideals of market performance to develop into fanaticism. Arguably, elements of the Utilitarian movement in nineteenth-century Britain who imposed laissez-faire policies upon Irish famine victims were such, as were some enthusiasts for Social Darwinism at the turn of the last century. In each case, it is the extremity, the refusal or inability to see complexity in the form of negative consequences, that marks market fundamentalism. In the United States, notably, market fundamentalism has long been linked with an old fear and hatred of government. Since the 1980s, such opinions have become more and more determinative in U.S. economic and social policy. This is the sense in which we live in an age of market fundamentalism.

One prominent aspect of the resurgence in market fundamentalism as it began to gather impetus was an attack on the legitimacy of professions. In 1962, for example, Milton Friedman, the Nobel laureate economist from the University of Chicago, argued in his influential *Capitalism and Freedom* that professional licensing was unnecessary. In a well-functioning market, information circulates nearly perfectly. Therefore, in all fields quacks are soon separated from effective practitioners once death rates are published for physicians, trial outcomes for lawyers, and so forth.[24] Translated into public policy two decades later in the United Kingdom, the Thatcher government attacked professional prerogatives at every turn, including the once-sacrosanct self-regulation of the "ancient university" faculties of Oxford and Cambridge.

Missing from these market fundamentalist visions, of course, is any account of what might be supplied to the equity or amenity of social living through nonmarket institutions, such as universities, professions, churches, or even the state. The mark of fanaticism is unwillingness to acknowledge any need to balance one's deeply held beliefs and wishes with any concession to contrary—or simply different—principles. Therein lies the conflict between market fundamentalists and advocates of the "mixed economy," which represented efforts to moderate the outcomes of the market's creative destruction by means of supporting nonmarket institutions or by directly intervening through the state.

By 2000, political analysts such as John Judis could argue that the often dreaded elites of the much-maligned Eastern establishment of the postwar decades, including elements of leadership from the professions and the academy, were often critical players in balancing forces for social inclusion and equity.[25] A public-spirited elite, that is, embodies the ethic of community trusteeship amid the important negotiations between the conflicting but interdependent elements of the political economy. The choice for the leading professions is really between slow self-extinction through emulation of pure entrepreneurship and a rethinking of how their aspirations can meet and help inform a broad democratic consensus about how to make interdependence work for all.

The alternative to worsening social entropy, then, is a politics of positive interdependence. The outcome of interdependence becomes positive when the interacting parties develop the breadth of understanding, skills of cooperation, and willingness to share responsibility that enable them to turn the situation to their advantage. They learn to increase the complexity and stability of their environment rather than deplete it. In other words, positive interdependence is the result of successful application of capacities for civic cooperation. The viability of every society, as of the emerging global economic and political order as a whole, is now highly dependent upon the ability to manage the strains of interdependence toward positive outcomes. What is wanting, and wanted, in the current disorder is the stabilizing gravity exerted by shared social purposes and adequate institutions.

A reformed professionalism fits logically within this general perspective. To achieve the dependability and creativity in economic and social functions upon which everyone's prosperity increasingly depends, the individual players—organizations and individuals alike—must cooperate as well as compete. But they can do so only if they are able to sustain a stable consensus about where their common interests lie. They must also learn to recognize that upholding standards of excellence and reciprocity is a common necessity. For this, consensus-building leadership and active participation in sustaining a shared enterprise are needed at many levels of modern organizational life.

The restructuring process demands the civic virtues of political imagination and institutional citizenship. In these circumstances, professionalism with a civic orientation could go a long way toward fostering the core virtues needed to revitalize institutional citizenship. Even in its present state, the professional spirit boasts one of the most widely understood languages and conceptions of functional integrity, a language widely used by the professional middle class that heads and operates most of the society's central institutions. It is one of the most potent and widely spread understandings, capable of being reshaped to articulate the contemporary needs of building a new institutional order. The important question is how professionalism can be reconstructed to respond better to the imperative of positive interdependence.

Reconstructing Professionalism: A Pragmatist Approach

Reconstruction is a term of art in American pragmatist philosophy. It was popularized by John Dewey and invoked by other pragmatist Progressives such as Addams and Croly. As a critical approach, it is especially apt for social and cultural questions about which no one can pretend to a totally objective viewpoint but that demand serious and responsible effort at understanding and response. As a species of practical reasoning, reconstruction is a modern descendant of the practical philosophy developed by Aristotle for dealing with ethical and political questions. Reconstruction is thus implicit in every exercise of critical intelligence. This is the core insight of pragmatist philosophy.

Reconstructive practical reason aims to better attain goals inherent in a practice that has become problematic—that is, lost, confused, or self-defeating. Reconstruction proceeds by taking apart the components of the problematic situation to reassemble them in a new form so as to unblock the constricted or dissociated patterns of activity. Reconstruction, then, is intelligence at work to better fulfill the purposes implicit in a certain practice. It proceeds by seeking a more successful way of understanding or acting toward the goals of the practice, thereby realizing more fully its potentiality.[26]

Reconstruction always involves interpretation, in the sense of a construction of the situation in terms of an imputed purpose. But the truth value of the interpretation is always provisional. The proof of its validity is itself always subject to further challenge and amendment on the basis of future experience. The judgment that the defining purpose imputed to a situation has been sustained is a complex reflective process. Its most important indicator, though still a provisional one, is that the new understanding permits thinking or activity to go on in a way that restores or augments the complexity and coherence lost to the practice in its formerly problematic condition.

In its present problematic state, professional life is a ripe candidate for a reconstructive effort. Its aim will be both to better understand the intrinsic purposes of the professional enterprise and to suggest the lines along which the enterprise needs to move if it is to reclaim those purposes more vigorously and coherently. As a starting point, we can begin by summarizing what our survey of the historical evolution of the professions suggests about their purposes. Professional life is concerned with applying trained intelligence to the business of modern life. It is also about bringing the intricacies of technical processes within the sphere of moral meaning and social purpose. Professionalization is not, then, simply a reflex of the expanding division of labor; it is also an active social response to it. As new knowledge grows and new instrumental systems expand, every society needs to restructure itself not only for efficiency but to improve equity, to reweave the bonds of trust and responsibility so that they encompass the emerging areas of human activity. Professions thus stand on the boundary of interaction between systems of technical capacity and the moral and political processes that aim to integrate these powers into humanly valuable forms of life.

Professionals take part in the commercial life of civil society. Like other workers, they make their living by trading upon their capacities in the labor market. However, professionals enter the labor market with credentials, and sometimes state-certified licenses, which establish them as the owners of a marketable type of property, a kind of human capital. This capital is the result of their development of skills and acquisition of knowledge in institutions designed for that purpose, especially the university. Like physical capital, professional capital is appropriated by individuals and negotiated in the market. In this way, possession of professional credentials confers a measure of independence upon its possessor, giving scope for individual potential.

Professional credentials do this in two ways. In the external sense, the professional degree or shingle fosters social recognition. It confers upon its possessor a socially significant identity, a standing from which to advance a career "open to talent." In an internal sense too, the professional's acquired knowledge and skill open possibilities for finding challenge and satisfaction in applying these capacities to a situation in resourceful and even innovative ways. Indeed, one distinguishing mark of professional life is the expectation that the practitioner will dependably carry out routine functions and be able to contribute to improving the practice of the field. One expression of this norm is the requirement of original research for the Ph.D. degree. In other words, by possessing their peculiar form of human capital professionals gain both dignity and opportunity for creativity, thereby enhancing the opportunity for self-realization.

The security and negotiability of the professional's human capital exists, however, only as part of the public order of civil society. Even more than most other kinds of property, professional capital depends upon civil society's structure of legal procedures and reasonings. For example, the law benefits professionals by regulating the market for their services; it protects society by defining enforceable standards of practice. Professional status is in principle open to all, regardless of social origin. Yet individuals can garner the benefits of professional credentials only by joining a corporate group defined by moral expectations as well as standards of technical competence. As is vividly the case with physicians and clergy, by becoming professionals individuals integrate their personal identity in an important way with a collective project and find themselves held publicly accountable for reliable performance of services according to prescribed procedures.

Entering a profession, then, does more than open up opportunity. It also makes the individual dependent upon the disciplines and control of a quasi-corporate form of life. Without this, the individual is in a far more precarious market position. In a sense, professional property is shared property. To be able to make use of professional capital, the individual must be licensed by a professional community. This demands of the individual a demonstration of the character as well as the expertise that defines being a doctor, lawyer, accountant, scientist, or teacher. To extend the economic metaphor, we can say that the professional's human capital can produce effects only within the network of social capital, the expectations of competence, trustworthiness, and honesty generated by a community of practitioners through sustained cooperation.[27]

There is significant tension between these two features of professional life. The first feature, the freedom to employ one's human capital to maximum advantage and personal satisfaction, strains against this second feature of dependence upon a demanding, collective enterprise. By contrast, professional freedom of opportunity is realized only through the individual's acceptance of responsibility for the purposes and standards that define the profession. Individual initiative and collective loyalty depend mutually upon each other and yet pull in opposite directions. This tension is inherent in any interdependent situation, but it could be argued to be a particularly salient feature of modern societies based upon an extensive division of labor. That this is heightened in professional life only indicates how representative the professions are of the larger social world of modernity.

For professionals, this tension is heightened by the fact that the negotiability of professional capital is highly dependent upon a third, civic or public, factor: the public legitimacy of professional services. These services, after all, are often beyond a layperson's ability to understand fully or judge. There is thus an inescapable relationship of trust between practitioner and client involved in any successful professional enterprise. In the United States, this means both implicit civic compacts between particular professions and the public, such as exists in higher education, or development of an explicit charter of relations between public and profession in the structure of the bar, medical boards, and various kinds of certification.

The third civic dimension of professionalism thus emerges from the fact that professional capital is so visibly a social and political artifact. In a democratic society, professional legitimacy is always precarious because it can be secured only so long as a general balance is maintained between the kinds and degree of professional privilege and the public's perception that professional services contribute significantly to the public welfare. The importance of recognizing this third civic dimension to professional life becomes apparent from the consequences of its neglect, when professionalism is viewed in abstraction from its civic context of negotiated interdependence. Then, professionals find their enterprises appear either as fixed features of society whose legitimacy is taken for granted—or as strikingly successful monopolies that exploit public credulity to manipulate legislatures into granting them outrageous privileges and power. Neither view holds out either reason or hope for constructive engagement with the serious tensions outlined here.

By contrast, this effort at intellectual reconstruction has construed professionalism as a still-incomplete project whose eventual outcome remains unclear. It has, however, uncovered three constituent features of professionalism: (1) professional skill is human capital that (2) is always dependent for its negotiability upon some collective enterprise, which itself (3) is the outcome of civic politics in which the freedom of a group to organize for a specific purpose is balanced by the accountability of that group to other members of the civic community for furtherance of publicly established goals and standards.

Through this process of reflection, professionalism's implicit aim has begun to emerge into some clarity. It is to organize the conditions of work so that workers can develop and express their individual powers, by engaging them responsibly in ways that ensure individual dignity through being recognized as contributing to enterprises of public value. This purpose links expertise, technical innovation, and freedom of enterprise to individual fulfillment through responsible discharge of socially recognized tasks. Its chief enabling condition is the practice of social cooperation, both within the community of practitioners and between them and the other members of the public.

As disclosed by this intellectual reconstruction, professionalism's inherent logic addresses a central problem of modern life. This is the question of meaning, much discussed in some circles today. Meaning refers to the sense of value people experience when they understand their own lives to be linked in a significant way with the larger processes at work around them. It has both an inner and a public face. To discover meaning is to find a point to living by recognizing oneself as a participant in a worthwhile enterprise whose accomplishment calls out one's energies and whose purposes define and vindicate one's having lived.

To live with meaning is to discover the secret to fulfillment. In the modern world, the sources of meaning are plural—a significant advance over the narrow possibilities offered to most people in traditional societies. This is in part the result of the extension of freedom to ever greater sectors of the population, enabling women, the young, and ethnic and racial minorities to begin defining their own lives. Meaning, then, can lie not only in work but in family life, in religion, the nation, friendship, the arts, knowledge, national and global concerns. In modern societies with a highly differentiated yet relatively open division of labor, however, work plays a key role in furnishing the means by which individuals can develop their capacities and express their individuality. Work is also a key source of solidarity through pursuit of shared goals and values. In its broadest sense, the value of professional life resides in its having served as a continuing collective experiment, or series of experiments, in devising an answer to the question of how meaning can be institutionalized in work.

Making Interdependence Work: Civic Professionalism

The professional enterprise represents, in varying degrees across its many forms, so many institutions of civic cooperation planted within the workings of economic life. The vital mission of professional work is to infuse economic activity with opportunity for individuals to develop themselves through contributing to public values. At its best, professional life models this aim in practice. When successful, the professionalization of work is not only a means toward intense individual satisfaction but also a source of integrity helping to unify and justify personal effort. Civic professionalism means becoming more conscious of these defining values. Its achievement requires sustained, long-term effort at the project of reconstruction.

One key to that project lies in grasping the importance of institutions. As the enduring patterns of interaction through which human beings live, institutions are the most common and most powerful of educators. Thus American society's heavy reliance on market mechanisms to allocate opportunities and essential services in areas ranging from skills to health care teaches its youth effective lessons about the need to get ahead and the disgrace of failure. Professionals too have been educated to numerous understandings of their work in various historical moments and social contexts. The more closed moral cultures of regional society have inculcated the civic qualities associated with the traditional free professions. On the other hand, the organizational professions taught the superiority of meritocratic promotion and bureaucratic classification in formal organizations to untidy negotiation among professionals, employers, and clients. Institutions can have this deep effect upon attitude and character because they structure attention and impose sanctions to reinforce the dispositions appropriate to their ends.[28]

Institutions are the entering wedge through which moral meaning comes to affect technical and instrumental activities. Institutions "moralize" the performance of instrumental functions by embedding them in a network of social expectations.[29] Institutions are thus a key generator of social capital, resources of trust upon which individuals can draw as they pursue their own purposes and to which they contribute by practicing their occupation responsibly. Thanks to institutions, the task of making a living or solving a technological problem, or practicing the arts, or figuring out how to live together can become a focus for enriching character, friendship, and self-transcending loyalty. These processes in turn generate vital social energy upon which civic culture can draw.

Professionalism, we can now see, is itself a protean institutional form. It can give moral significance to the instrumental functions of work so as to allow its participants to control and take responsibility for their actions as free persons. But the reverse is also true. The professions do not fulfill their promise, nor do the positive qualities of professional work reach more people, unless professionals can reconceive their role within enhanced civic interaction. Especially in the case of the symbolic-analysis occupations proliferating among and outside established professional fields, the resulting fluidity and instability need to be turned into positive interdependence. This requires serious effort to reconstruct professional work and the relations among providers of skilled services. The task requires leadership, since it is unlikely that purely routine performance is enough to correct the dysfunctional state of many professional enterprises.

Leadership for reconstruction is inconceivable without a common language and frame of reference within which to make sense of the current situation and through which to articulate a strategy for achieving positive interdependence. A key means toward this end is articulation of a public philosophy. The aim of a public philosophy is to bring into view the human possibilities and goals tacitly presupposed in society's day-to-day life. A public philosophy aids the practical work of reconstruction. It interprets institutions by giving an articulation of their purposes and of the values they aim to sustain.[30]

By making purposes explicit, a public philosophy does not just idealize or celebrate these purposes and values. It also generates discussion and debate about the supposed purposes by focusing critical attention upon them. In this way, a public philosophy serves to frame social discourse, creating common ground for discussion where varying understandings can strive to make sense of an intricate and equivocal, yet shared, social life. Articulating a new public philosophy that can describe the possibilities of stronger civic cooperation is no detached, theoretical matter. It demands development of social partnerships that embody positive interdependence in practice. Forging those relationships is the work of professional leadership. Its work is integral to the larger effort toward professional, and social, reconstruction.

The Challenge of Civic Professional Leadership

The renewal of professionalism through reconstructive leadership is perhaps best illustrated in the work being done today by trailblazing civic professionals. At first glance, the grisly epidemic of violence among the nation's young minority poor would not seem a likely catalyst toward such revitalization. Yet at least one contemporary professional argues persuasively that, properly understood, it could be just that. Deborah Prothrow-Stith, M.D., is a dean at the Harvard School of Public Health and a former commissioner of health for Massachusetts. She is also the author of an unusual study of teenage violence, *Deadly Consequences: How Violence Is Destroying Our Teenage Population and a Plan to Begin Solving the Problem.*[31] The book describes the situation of poor, inner-city minority youth, one in which the effects of the loss of social capital are tragically apparent. It is a world in which the breakdown of trust and mutual account-ability have proceeded to a terrifying point whose consequences are all too well-known: unemployment, drug addiction, premature preg-nancy, and violent—often deadly—crime.

This is a situation that has proved, by tragic negation, that interdependence is an inescapable feature of modern societies and that nurture of the integrity of family and community matters des-perately. For the urban poor, particularly the African American poor, the familial and institutional networks they had once con-structed with great courage under considerable hostility and assault have shattered. In America's devastated urban areas, the mutual accountability upon which civic life depends has been unraveling for decades, and the major institutions of our cities have proved unable or unwilling to prevent the slide into despair and violence of young men born to those among the poorest of the poor. How-ever, the book also documents the widening eddies of destructive violence, now turned inward, manifested by the rising rate of teenage suicide among the white, the suburban, and the middle class.[32]

In the usual division of professional labor, violence is an affair for the criminal justice system and perhaps social work, but not medicine. Yet, as Dr. Prothrow-Stith points out, "more violent crimes show up in the emergency rooms of our hospitals than make it onto the police blotters."[33] Indeed, it was during her medical res-idency at a large northeastern medical center that Prothrow-Stith first encountered the enormity of the problem of youth violence. It was, she reflects, "a shocking contrast to my previous understand-ing of young male life" gathered during her African American upbringing in the South. This contact propelled her to search for an adequate professional response to the problem. The search led her toward a more comprehensive understanding of the missions of public health and medicine, and toward action to reshape professional education and practice.

Deadly Consequences begins with the story of that search. For Dr. Prothrow-Stith, it turned into a gradual discovery that the technical orientation and organizational structure of today's professions are inadequate to their common purpose, which is to mount a first defense against the unraveling of the social fabric. From the typical expertise expected of physicians, that of being technically good at specific medical interventions, Prothrow-Stith moved to ask what might be done to lessen the need for treating the bloody results of street violence. Her first thought was that prevention might be sought through the criminal justice system, with its several component professional groups of law enforcement personnel, lawyers and judges, and social service providers. But here too she encountered a tendency similar to what she found typical of medicine: to define the problem in terms of the field's favored methods. Here was positivism in action.

"There is," Prothrow-Stith reflects, "a self-perpetuating industry built around putting people away, just as there is around various forms of acute care provision in medicine." What makes this purely technical approach troubling is that soon increased use and effectiveness of the intervention itself comes to be seen as progress toward solving the problem. Thus more people in jails is touted as controlling crime, just as a better survival rate from heart surgery is identified as progress against heart disease. But in fact, comments Prothrow-Stith, "we are gradually coming to see that our major diseases today, such as heart disease, a typical 'modern' affliction, are caused by environmental and, often, behavioral factors such as diet, stress, lack of exercise, and so forth." Thus, she argues, public health is a more effective long-term response to the problem of disease than any amount of medical intervention after disease is already advanced.

From criminal justice, Prothrow-Stith moved to the mental health fields as a possible site for developing a more comprehensive approach to preventing youth violence. But here too she was disappointed, and for broadly parallel reasons. The technical orientation of psychotherapeutic intervention, whether by means of drugs or dynamic therapy, focuses principally on the individual. She found that mental health professionals were reluctant to shift their focus, in either clinical practice or research, from the interesting (and often lucrative) problems of acute individual malfunction toward a strengthening of social bonds that could make these malfunctions less likely and less destructive. She found psychiatry in particular to be busily extending the typical medical focus on biological research into the realm of behavioral disorders, usually with minimal reference to factors in the social and cultural environment. Once again, the problem was not that these approaches were valueless but that their exclusive dominance in the profession made a grasp of the complex sources of the problems they were trying to treat nearly impossible.

It was, then, virtually by process of elimination that Prothrow-Stith settled upon public health as the professional and institutional context in which to pursue her concerns. Public health, like the related and less well-established fields of community or preventive medicine, has remained an essentially interdisciplinary effort. Although a large portion of public health professionals are drawn from medicine as well as nursing, Prothrow-Stith argues that it is far more attentive to practical concerns with social well-being than medicine. Research and teaching in schools of public health is not only more interdisciplinary than in medical schools; it is also less driven by purely academic concerns and more interested in the interrelations between the biological sciences and human social life. It is to public health, then, that Prothrow-Stith urges us to turn in pursuing the problem of removing the scourge of youth violence through a major commitment to prevention.

A strengthened, encompassing field of public health could function as a useful catalyst toward wider professional reorganization.

Thus Prothrow-Stith notes that law enforcement agencies come gradually, and often not very willingly, to recognize that beyond a higher arrest rate and better electronic surveillance systems, partnership between enforcement agencies and communities emphasizing enhanced community responsibility—like Town Watch—are ultimately needed to handle crime. Similarly, she believes that "medicine is coming gradually to pay more attention to behavior and education."

These parallel developments, Prothrow-Stith argues, are widespread today. What is still inchoate is awareness of what is common in all these areas: the need to strengthen civic connectedness by developing partnerships between professional schools and organizations and other vital institutions of civil society. Like law enforcement, ". . . the problems of family viability, education, and much of medicine demand an approach that could be called preventive, one that focuses upon the whole context of the problem in order to find solutions."

What is bringing such approaches to public attention is economic necessity. The existing methods, which define a solution in terms of technical repairs, are simply so expensive that, with today's proliferating manifestations of breakdown, they cannot be paid for much longer. Here lies an opening for the civic orientation to prove its value in a variety of professional fields, including some parts of medicine. "We have almost no choice but to change," muses Prothrow-Stith, yet "we need what amounts to a change of ethos, away from a system geared to intensive, acute care toward a much greater concern with prevention and maintenance." A change of such magnitude is not necessarily to be expected. To succeed, it needs validation from the traditional core fields of the technically oriented professions, among them medicine. The change will go forward, according to Prothrow-Stith, if and when these fields "see themselves as part of the answer rather than the whole solution."

If such changes begin to succeed, and new intellectual linkages grow in the professions, all this will encourage more comprehensive organizational connections. If these institutional innovations take hold, professional education will change and new attitudes result. The meaning of such a change in ethos includes broadening the working definition of health care from acute care to encompass prevention; moving from a professional fixation upon individual achievement to concern for collective responsibility; advancing from a spirit of professional exclusivity and control to one of cooperation. Such developments also highlight the key role of professionals willing to take responsibility for the institutions they serve in light of their professed purposes, and so provide ideas and leadership in addressing problems.

There is some basis for hoping that such changes may find fertile soil within the professional ranks. "Some physicians," observes Dr. Prothrow-Stith, "find their practice quite frustrating. They are seeking a sense of calling beyond being technically good at doing a particular specialized task." They are also seeking an alternative to the moral absurdity of using vast resources to repair problems that are often preventable. These physicians, like many nurse-practitioners, are looking for a way to combine acute care practice with education and prevention. Restructured institutions could allow a professional to shift emphasis over time, making for a more flexible career path than is the norm. We might think of this as a kind of deindustrialization of health care, in line with similar increases in career flexibility emerging in other professional areas.

Even if these things do not soon develop, Prothrow-Stith seems quite confident that her efforts have significance. Her account of her own reasons for this hope reveals, perhaps, the power of the human connectedness that her policy proposals seek to extend to those who lack it. Besides her work as physician, teacher, administrator, and citizen, Prothrow-Stith is a mother of two school-age children and the wife of a minister. In fact, her familial and religious commitments are deeply interwoven with her professional and civic advocacy. Her private life and her public involvements seem to flow together and mutually strengthen each other. In this she is fortunate as well as resourceful. Her public hope is to make this sort of richness of life less unusual.

Dr. Prothrow-Stith seems to have come by many of her convictions naturally, as it were, having grown up in a strong family that, despite a long history of racial oppression, was supported by a vital religious and social community. With her generation, conditions of racial exclusion finally began to change, but it was from the context of family and church, she believes, she drew the strength that propelled her career in the mainstream of professional life. She credits religious faith as the source of the moral truth that "it was not OK just to be interested in me . . . that part of my purpose was to participate in making the world a better place." Perhaps because of this larger context of meaning, Dr. Prothrow-Stith has been able to struggle toward an understanding of the vocation of healing that has called her, like other leaders in forging a civic professionalism, to exploration and service beyond the comfortable boundaries of a conventional career.

The professions are today facing a serious choice. They can continue the default strategy of defending their narrow interests in the style of so many petty oligarchies oblivious to the long-run damage they are doing to their own legitimacy. The alternative is to reinvigorate the civic purposes of professional life. Leaders need to persuade their own constituency, as well as the public at large, to join in a common effort to place immediate self-interest within the perspective of the field's larger purposes and to focus on its health, integrity, and long-term survival. Such a reorientation would be the beginning of a major reconstruction of professional life, one true to professionalism's own deepest aims and potentials. With strong leadership, the professions could serve on the national level in many areas, including health care, as creative social nuclei for reshaping American institutions for the global era. In many local contexts, individual professionals, as well as their associations, could become key social partners, bringing expert knowledge and practical imagination to improving the life of the nation and world.

In this regard, Dr. Prothrow-Stith's turn to the synthetic field of public health is suggestive. Professions have historically developed in between the imperatives of the market economy, the impulse of technological advance, and the norms of civic life. Universities, and especially the entities such as schools of public health that connect academic fields, are the real and symbolic nodes of interchange among these jostling involvements and loyalties. In this time of resurgent market fundamentalism, the gravest threat to the integrity of the professional enterprise spring from decay within as the most favorably placed are enticed to abandon the common lot for some terrific deal. The resulting demoralization of many practitioners, to say nothing of the loss of public trust, is the often unintended consequence.

To counter these effects, all the professions have a stake in reaffirming—and rethinking—their distinctive character and defining purposes. Since these are most represented, and likely to have their greatest formative power, in training future members of the field, it is to professional education and the professional school that reformers need to look in developing a base and a rallying point for their efforts. The practical philosophy that Dewey and his collaborators once developed might again serve as Ariadne's thread, needed to escape the dead end of professional dissolution.

Chapter Six

Renewing Professional Education

A pivotal part of the story of the rise of the professions in America was their entry to the university. As in most other modern nations, the professions' self-understanding and character was formed importantly by their symbiosis with the modern academy. In broad terms, this meant a movement away from apprenticeship (with its intimate pedagogy of modeling and coaching) toward reliance upon the methods of academic instruction (with its emphasis upon classroom teaching and learning carried out far from the sites of professional practice). Just as the most successful groups of practitioners were consolidating a guildlike structure for organizing recruitment, standards, and admission to practice, they began simultaneously to outsource the crucial component of education. That they did so, rather than organize competing training institutions, is testimony to the great prestige that university-based teaching and research had achieved by early in the twentieth century. But it also bequeathed a legacy of crossed purposes and even distrust between practitioners and academics, as well as between the academy and the public.

The challenge for professional education is how to teach the complex ensemble of analytic thinking, skillful practice, and wise judgment upon which each profession rests. The university setting, and even more the prevalence of the academic model of thought and teaching, facilitates training analytic habits of mind. It does far less, however, to further students' progress in developing practical skills and capacity for professional judgment. It would be naïve to attempt to restore the old forms of apprenticeship, which often concealed exploitation and abuse of apprentices, but the predominance of academic theory tends to overshadow the importance of learning from and through practice. Moreover, the relative isolation of academic research and training from public concerns, though it fosters some intellectual development, has pushed the professions' social contract out of students' sight during the critical years of schooling. It is in this lack of integration among the parts and several aims that modern professional education confronts its greatest challenge. This chapter is an exploration of this challenge, to be followed by suggestions of how it might be better met, in the interest of reconstructing a vital contemporary professionalism that is both expert and civic.

From Apprenticeship to Schooling

What was entailed in the shift from apprenticeship to schooling? In the most obvious sense, the change meant transfer of authority over the formation of future professionals from practitioners to academic specialists. By agreeing to jointly administer examination procedures for admission to practice, the academics and the practitioners struck a kind of compromise. Students sought entry to professional school mostly in order to join the ranks of practitioners, of whom only a handful would stay on as full-time teachers. Yet on a day-to-day basis during the novice's most impressionable period, the faculty, the curriculum, and the teaching practices of the school represent the world of the profession. For practical purposes, the school with its demands and expectations defines the domain for the student. With little or no direct exposure to the experience of practice, students have slight basis on which to distinguish between the demands of actual practice and the peculiar requirements of academic life.

As professional schools accommodate to the organizational model of the research university, the most prominent result is the gradual remaking of the professional school faculty in the image of the faculty of arts and sciences. Professional school faculty continue to bring distinctive traits of their domains of engineering or law or medicine, but they have also come to espouse many of the central values of the professoriate, among them an analytical and detached, skeptical cast of mind; enthusiasm for abstract representation and theoretical argument; high valuing of original discovery or design; and often subtle denigration of the messiness of practice. The result is ever greater emphasis upon the intellectual training in which academics take pride, with the sometimes unintended result of this training being largely separated from, and generally eclipsing, the kind of practical and moral formation that was long the focus of professional apprenticeship organized by practitioners.

Because the academic model has been generally triumphant, it is difficult to recognize that its ascendancy does not represent unalloyed progress. In comparing across several modern nations the fates of practitioner-controlled training by apprenticeship, Michael Borrage described the usual, university-centered viewpoint on these developments as Whig's history. What is forgotten are the "opportunity costs" involved in the transfer of most training to the academy, which has been nothing less than the loss of "viable, traditional institutions—of practiced-based forms of professional education—directly under the control of practicing professionals."[1]

The strengths of the academic model are efficiency in systematic transmission of ideas and information, along with at least some guarantee that the knowledge communicated to students is reputable and up-to-date. Its weaknesses lie in relative abstraction from actual application of knowledge to practice, along with general avoidance of the embedded knowledge of practice itself. The crucial aspect of apprenticeship—initiation into the wisdom of practice—remains on the margin of academic training. Thus triumphant academics hold only part of the promise of professional advancement.

To compensate for this imbalance, many fields of professional education have introduced, or reintroduced, important elements of education by apprenticeship. Years of clinical training under practicing physicians has long been the norm in medical education. Generally, however, emphasis upon apprenticelike pedagogy is at the insistence of either the organized guild of practitioners or the licensing public authority. From within the academy, enthusiasm for internships, clerkships, clinical experiences, and the like is usually modest. The clearest indication of this is the typically lower status given to those who teach in such areas. Medicine, as we will see shortly, is the exception that proves the rule. Part of the problem is that studies have long piled up evidence that most actual learning of the practice of a profession takes place on the job, which is to say within a context of practice rather than a classroom. This inconvenient finding spurs periodic educational innovations, such as simulation of practice experience within a controlled environment, to bridge the gap between the cognitive command of ideas and practical mastery of technique and judgment. Such efforts are a partial exception to the generalization, as we will see in more detail later in this chapter.

The cognitive revolution within psychology during the last several decades has given new clarity to these issues. Schooling, as an organizational form, goes back millennia. Schools seem to have been contemporaneous with the development of literacy and numeracy while they emerged as the technologies by which to organize a complex society. In *Actual Minds, Possible Worlds*, one of the leaders of cognitive psychology, Jerome Bruner, argued that modern societies depend upon two broadly different modes of thinking that do not fit easily together.[2]

One mode of thinking is based upon narrative. Here, things and events derive significance through being placed within a story, an ongoing context of meaningful interaction. This is a mode of thinking that integrates experience through metaphor and analogy. It is employed in the arts and in all practical situations, including professional work. Critically, this mode of thought is the source of meaning and value, even in contemporary society. Bruner called the other cognitive style analytic or paradigmatic. Here, by contrast, things and events are detached from the situations of everyday life and represented more abstractly and systematically. Writing and numeration are the media through which the intellectual skills of classification, argument, and proof can be represented and learned. It has been essential to the development of science and technology, as well as the systems of law, administration, and communication that sustain modern civilization. It is this cognitive style that schools, at every level, exist to foster.

In this perspective, a school quickly appears as an ambiguous site for forming future professionals. In as much as professionals require facility in deploying abstract, analytic representations— symbolic analysis—schoollike settings are a good environment for learning. At the same time, professionals must also be able to integrate, or reintegrate, this kind of knowledge within ongoing practical contexts organized by narrative modes of thinking and judging. This key dimension of professional practice was captured by Eliot Freidson when he described the aim of medical education as forming a "clinical" habit of mind for "consultants who must intervene [with specialized, esoteric knowledge] in everyday, practical affairs."[3] Like analytic capacity, the clinical habit of mind necessary for skillful intervention in patients' lives can also be developed and trained. Successful apprenticeship instills these habits of the practical mind through the pedagogy of modeling expert judgment and then coaching the learner through similar activities. To be effective, professional education must build a foundation in both kinds of learning.

The blending of analytic and practical habits of mind that professional practice demands represents a complex pedagogical challenge. Take medicine as an example. It relies heavily upon the kind of scientific knowledge that is the result of analytic thinking. Yet the profession is rooted in practical concerns and considerations. As a profession, it exists in order to address pressing human needs relating to life, health, and relief of suffering. At the same time, medical practice relies upon, is informed by, and participates in analytic inquiry carried out by a variety of scientific specialties.

In approaching a case, the physician's first objective is to reach a diagnosis of the patient's condition, and then to develop a plan or regimen of treatment. To do so, the doctor needs to draw upon a vast and complex body of biological knowledge. Like the research biologist, the physician must be a curious scientific investigator as well as a competent scientific analyst. However, in contrast to the researcher, for the physician the patient's condition is not only an object for study and experiment but also a means toward general knowledge about nature. For the physician, it means first of all engagement with a human being in need. It is this therapeutic purpose that creates the imperative of clinical judgment. The physician must decide what course of intervention, if any, is good for this particular patient, at this time, and in this situation.

What kind of thinking does the physician call upon to do this? Medicine, it is often said, is more art than science. The larger meaning of this cliché is that medicine is a practical endeavor. It is part of a world of human meaning concerned with bodily functioning and well-being, not simply with scientific fact or technological possibility. To admit this is to acknowledge that medicine is dependent upon narrative understanding and practical judgment, that it is an art deeply informed by scientific knowledge but finally guided by concern for human well-being. The overarching, commanding perspective is a form of Bruner's narrative or practical rationality. This is the kind of rational reflection that relates means to ends and evaluates the appropriateness of possible means for particular goals under certain conditions at specific times. It is practical reason of the kind we encountered in the previous chapter and will explore further in the next. It is important to realize that in this, medicine is not unique but representative of the situation of all professions.

The actual history of professional education in the university, however, has institutionalized a powerful model of professional training in which the pedagogy of apprenticeship, rooted in narrative through practical interaction, is overshadowed by the analytic paradigm. We saw something of the structure and import of that model in the earlier description of the positivist ideal of knowledge, which reached its apogee in the midtwentieth-century American university. Then, the "cognitive complex" centered on development of analytic intelligence, especially as embodied in scientific theory and technology, appeared to be the definition of reason and the sole generator of progress. Theoretically at least, it cut ties to the narrative understandings embodied in traditional culture. Thus a thinker of the stature of Talcott Parsons could declare the clergy, despite its ancient seat in the university, was no longer a true profession in the modern sense precisely because it fell outside the ascendant model of knowledge. By the early twenty-first century, these claims are no longer uncontested. But the historical tradition they represent is still the dominant model for teaching and learning in higher education. Renewal of professional education must begin by coming to terms with that model.

From Alma Mater to Incubator: The University as Key Institution

Harold Perkin tells us (as we saw in Chapter Two) that the university has become the axial institution of the modern world. By this Perkin means that it is the pivotal point at which social needs and economic and political imperatives meet advancing knowledge and aspiring talent. In this complex process of negotiating knowledge, learning, and their application, Perkin continues, university faculty as a group constitute the "key profession" because it is academics who train all other professionals. As the increase of knowledge through specialized research comes to define the core purpose of the modern university, the faculties of the professional schools too refashion their purposes to include generation as well as transmission of knowledge.[4] Prestige in the university world accrues far more to knowledge creation, as it is sometimes called, than to transmission.

In the American case, the new universities of the early twentieth century were able to establish themselves as prestigious training sites for the professions in significant part because of their position as a major part of the emerging network of institutions promoting scientific and technological progress. The remarkably interconnected and flexible relationships that developed between researchers in the new universities and inventors and organizers in industry and the professions formed a matrix of creative research and application. It included the new philanthropies established by Rockefeller, Carnegie, and Russell Sage, the major corporations, the government, and the universities. As Olivier Zunz puts it, "Cooperation evolved over the years as a voluntary, contractual, often unpredictable but powerful relationship among researchers both inside and outside the universities, across a wide array of institutions."[5] Out of a collaboration among several segments of this new, flexible institutional matrix came the charter for the first of the reinvented learned professions: the Flexner Report, produced by the Carnegie Foundation for the Advancement of Teaching, which the American Medical Association used to restructure the medical profession by institutionalizing a revolution in medical education.

Medicine was a field ripe for recasting, though this was not obvious at the time except perhaps to the leadership of national professional organizations such as the AMA and the Carnegie Foundation. By 1900, a gathering improvement of scientific knowledge of disease, European in origin, showed promise of developing a new medicine that would be rooted in techniques of diagnosis and that promised a new age of control over disease. The hospital, a venerable charitable institution presided over jointly by independent physicians and local men of property, now became the site for the practice of this new medicine, attracting even the wealthy and middle classes out of their homes for treatment. The hospital taught physicians and the paying public the benefits of research, cooperation, and high standards of competence. At the same time, beginning at Johns Hopkins University, medical training was standardized on a model imported from Germany and brought into line with the new advances. Abraham Flexner's widely praised report proposed this as the best system for training physicians.

Thus legitimated, the AMA led the medical profession into a new phase of consolidation. Medical students now entered with some collegiate experience, took a controlled course of basic science, and followed that with years of closely supervised clinical apprenticeship in university-affiliated teaching hospitals as clerks, interns, and then specialized residents, all the while being socialized into the professional norms of the hospital.[6] By raising the cost of medical education and practice while reducing the number of schools and entrants to the field, the reforms boosted practitioners' income and enhanced their competence and social prestige. In a still racially segregated America, the reforms also pushed African American medical schools nearly to extinction and effected a reduction in the number of women entering medical practice.

Here was the classic case of a profession capitalizing on the growing prestige of scientific research that served to bolster and consolidate its authority. By the 1920s, these developments gave medicine prestige as a collective body through the AMA and set the field on the road to becoming the recognized model of the successful professional enterprise. This prestige allowed Flexner's model of university-based professional education to become the paradigm for most professional education in the years following medicine's reforms. Flexner argued that the old apprenticeship training of medical students needed to be subordinated to a period of formal study of the relevant natural sciences, a task he thought was best carried on in a university setting. The new kind of clinical training, though unavoidably apprenticelike in certain respects, was to be conducted within the new university teaching hospitals under the supervision of academic physicians who would also be scientific researchers.

The core of Flexner's view was that formal-analytical reasoning, the kind of thinking integral to academic natural science, should hold pride of place in the intellectual training of professionals, both logically and pedagogically. This emphasis made a fine fit with the emerging research culture of the universities. The Flexner model, which established two years of scientific courses before clinical training as the canon for medical education, improved medical education at the time, but its ideas were generalized and spread far beyond medical education, often with uncritical enthusiasm. Although most of medical education in fact continued to take place in the context of clinical practice and under the tutelage of instructors who were also practitioners, fields such as law and engineering developed university programs with far less training under actual conditions of practice. The overall result was forms of professional education whose content and pedagogy emphasized theoretical knowledge formulated in general, context-free, and value-neutral terms, virtually identifying these features of analytical thinking with a rational approach to practice. The emphasis on academic science has often led to a poorly balanced professional curriculum that may deny legitimacy to the wider understanding of reasonableness that takes account of context, narrative, and the ethical implications of knowledge. More than anything else, it is this ascendancy of analytic reason that has undercut the value and importance of traditional apprenticeship.

The result of this imbalance was to open harmful conceptual schisms, and often chasms, within professional education. For example, legal education, whose subject matter is far closer than medicine's to narrative habits of mind, typically splits "substantive" law from clinical practice, demoting the latter to second-tier status. Engineering separates its core courses in "engineering science" (which are mostly taught as applied physics) from training in design. Teacher preparation places apprentice teaching after, and below, more formal "foundations." The dominant model in the theological seminary similarly emphasizes a series of university-style courses in textual criticism and historical and doctrinal analysis, relegating professional skills to secondary, "applied" status.

Thus an often uncritical emulation of the Flexner model converts useful pedagogical distinctions among types of knowing and thinking into rigid separation. Curricular separation is in turn reflected in the organization of most professional schools. Tenured, "academic" faculty are almost always teachers of the formal-analytic parts of the curriculum, while faculty who teach the clinical and practical parts of the curriculum are relegated to secondary or "adjunct" status. In most fields, the rigidity of this model weakens the coherence of professional preparation by demoting legitimate concerns for teaching the skills of practice and the arts of judgment. Its influential role makes resistance to the slide from civic professionalism into the marketing of detached expertise harder because the question can scarcely be posed within the present model of professional knowledge.

Engaging the University Model: Schooling as "Cognitive Apprenticeship"

To learn, for the beginner, means appropriating the complex abilities of an expert. Learning happens best when an expert is able to model performance in such a way that the learner can imitate the performance so as to finally make it his or her own. This describes a novice-apprentice relationship in its simplest, ideal form. Expertise, however, is always shared among members of a community who have mastered certain social practices. When such a community organizes ways of transmitting this expertise to new members, it creates apprenticeship. The insight that apprenticeship, so understood, lies at the heart of all education is the great contribution of modern cognitive psychology to understanding learning. This insight also highlights a basic problem. Much of what experts know remains tacit. It can be passed on by example, but often it cannot be fully articulated. By observation of expert performance, though, important aspects of expert practice can be made explicit. Articulation of good performance can then become an object of imitation and practice for learners. This is pedagogy: inventing articulations of performance through which novices can be brought more effectively to share the knowledge of a particular community of practice.

Traditional apprenticeship emphasizes transmission of expert knowledge through face-to-face contact. When it is employed in today's professional training, especially in a situation in which practitioners rather than pure academics do the teaching, apprenticeship may reveal these ancient roots. To cite a famous study of surgical residency in a high-technology medical center, Charles Bosck reported in *Forgive and Remember*[7] that students were rarely washed out for errors of skill alone. They were dismissed when their mentors judged that they lacked the proper character for surgery, especially "dedication, interest, and thoroughness."

But the university does not emphasize this highly particularistic kind of training or assessment of competence, preferring instead a cognitive style that stresses analytic reasoning skills. However, the recent cognitive insights about learning open up an unexpected possibility. The very tools of thinking that display and develop analytic reasoning can also play an important role in enhancing and extending the model of apprenticeship. This insight leads to conceiving pedagogy as a "cognitive apprenticeship."

A key aspect of writing and formal representation (which are features of Bruner's analytical cognitive style) is that they can be used to make thought processes visible. As trial lawyers and school debaters have long known, arguments can be written down and then rehearsed, analyzed, criticized, and in the process improved. This same iterative mode of development can be applied to performance and practical skills as well as oral argument. Features of expert performance, either of the analytical or the narrative-practical sort, can be described as rules, procedures, and protocols for approaching a situation or problem. Cued by these devices, students can then be coached through imitation and appropriation of various aspects of expert performance.

For example, medical schools use various anatomical devices, even actors, as simulated patients to train clinical skills. In such a situation, performance can be rehearsed, criticized, and improved "offline." This removal from the exigencies of actual practice permits the instructor to focus upon particular aspects of the complex ensemble of skills. The elements and sequence of skills can then be modeled and rehearsed without immediate responsibility for the welfare of others. This kind of teaching makes it more likely that most students will reach a basic level of competent practice from which expertise can be subsequently developed.

When educators study expert judgment to make its key features visible and available to novices for appropriation, they are opening access to the profession's defining practices. By giving learners the opportunity to practice approximation to expert performance, and giving these students feedback to help them improve their own performance, educators are fostering an apprenticelike experience of the mind, a cognitive apprenticeship. All this is widely disseminated through work such as that by John Bransford, Ann Brown, and Rodney Cocking in *How People Learn: Brain, Mind, Experience, and School*.[8] Seen from the perspective of cognitive apprenticeship, professional schools are complex organizations for initiating the next generation of practitioners into the several dimensions of the expertise that defines a given profession. In this way, the idea of apprenticeship is a valuable metaphor for thinking about the university model currently ascendant in professional schooling.

The Three Apprenticeships of Professional Education

All professional schools face the challenge of shaping their students' modes of thinking so as to enable their becoming contributing members of the professional context and, ultimately, the larger society. Chartered for their public mission to train professionals, these schools institutionalize a culture that is built up through pedagogical practices plus academic activities such as scholarship and research. As organizations, they aim at a goal that is in a profound sense holistic. Their mission is to educate for professional judgment and performance. They are charged to enable students to learn how to integrate specialized knowledge with a specific matrix of skills and know-how, within the professional community's characteristic disposition toward clients and society.

Effective professional education means laying the foundation for a lifelong process of mastering these complex tasks. Yet the university, the site at which this process has to be organized and begun, is built around a curricular structure, as well as research and pedagogical traditions, that are specialized, independent, and often intentionally competitive with each other. This competition drives research forward, but its educational effects are less uniformly positive. The challenge of professional education is to square this circle by bringing the disparate pieces of the student's educational experience into coherent alignment. The pieces fall roughly into three large chunks, each based in its own facets of professional expertise as the particular school teaches them, and guided by a variety of distinct pedagogical intentions.

The first apprenticeship, so to speak, could be called intellectual or cognitive. Of the three, it is most at home in the university context since it embodies the institution's great investment in quality of analytical reasoning, argument, and research. In professional schools, intellectual training is focused upon the academic knowledge base of the domain, including the habits of mind the faculty judge most important to the profession. The students' second apprenticeship is to the often tacit body of skills shared by competent practitioners. Students encounter this skills-based kind of learning through quite different pedagogies and often from faculty members other than those through which they are introduced to the first (intellectual) apprenticeship. In this second apprenticeship, students learn to take part in imagined or simulated practice situations, as in a case study, or in actual clinical experience with real clients.

As in the second apprenticeship, the third, which introduces students to the values and attitudes shared by the professional community, is ideally taught through dramatic pedagogies of participation. In some fields such efforts are primarily didactic, in others more participatory. The essential goal is to teach the skills and traits, along with the ethical comportment, social roles, and responsibilities, that mark the professional. Through learning about and beginning to practice them, the novice is introduced to the meaning of an integrated practice of all dimensions of the profession, grounded in the profession's fundamental purposes. If professional education is to introduce students to the full range of professional demands, it has to initiate learners into all three apprenticeships. But it is the third apprenticeship through which the student's professional self can be most broadly explored and developed.

These three types of apprenticeship are a metaphor or analytical lens through which to see more clearly how the business of professional training is carried on in diverse fields and schools. They represent more than three elements in the curriculum served by different pedagogies. These dimensions of apprenticeship also reflect contending emphases within all professional education, a conflict of values with deep roots in the history and organization of professional training in the university. To see this more clearly, consider today's education for the law. That is, imagine how law school is experienced by aspirants to that profession. Law schools have long been an object of study and criticism. Approaching legal education as a threefold apprenticeship, however, reveals ambiguity in the current organization of legal education. At times it enlists the three kinds of apprenticeship in support of the larger goal of training competent and committed practitioners; at other times the current system undermines that aim by failing to do justice to the full range of apprenticeship.

In the end, students apprentice to a variety of teachers, but they also apprentice to the aggregate educative effects of attending a particular professional school and program. That is, they are formed in part by the formal curriculum but also by the informal or hidden curriculum of taken-for-granted practices of interaction among faculty and students, and student life itself. Much of this socialization is tacit and operates below the level of clear awareness, but abundant studies confirm its great importance in the third apprenticeship students experience: the process of learning what it is to be a professional. Many schools and many faculty will say that all their forms of teaching and learning are oriented toward the single end of preparing practitioners to enter on the work of the profession. However, a look at an actual case of professional education, such as law school, reveals that the relation between academic life and the demands of practice may be not nearly as straightforward and logical in reality as it is imagined to be in the minds of faculty. This is especially true in the area of the third, or professional, apprenticeship.

Legal Education Seen as Three Apprenticeships

Law schools have small faculties, generally in the range of thirty to fifty full-time academics, who teach the courses considered doctrinal or substantive. These are courses concerned primarily with the content of law, rather than with legal skills or the techniques of practice. Law schools, whether university-affiliated or freestanding, conform to a common pattern by way of the accreditation standards set by the American Bar Association, working with its academic counterpart, the American Association of Law Schools. Most of the 150-plus law schools are accredited. Admission is competitive, on the basis of scores achieved on the nationally administered Law School Admissions Test, plus undergraduate grade point average. Class size is typically large, especially for mandatory first-year courses in which it is not unusual to find 75 to 125 students. This high student-faculty ratio, on a base of high tuition, has long made law schools a profitable undertaking. Legal education has had no creative moment like the Flexner Report. Instead, its history is a slow and often conflict-ridden convergence toward a version of a model first developed at Harvard University in the 1870s by Christopher Langdell.

Law schools offer a three-year course of study. At one time, most of the curriculum was required, though today only the first year and parts of the second are typically occupied by required courses such as contract law, civil procedure, tort law, and so forth. This places a considerable burden on those courses: they must move students from a variety of backgrounds and degrees of intellectual preparation into the capacity to reason legally. There is considerable evidence, including the reports of students themselves, that this first phase of legal education does indeed have a powerful effect. A series of studies of legal education by the Carnegie Foundation, extending from early in the twentieth century to the contemporary scene, documents the continuing power of the law school experience on the habits of mind characteristic of the profession that today's faculty describe as "thinking like a lawyer."

The first-year experience centers around a distinctive form of teaching, sometimes called "Socratic" or the case-dialogue method. Each day, several times a day, students gather in a lecture theater where the professor stands at the center of the class, closely questioning students chosen at random about a legal case assigned for analysis. The instructor demands: What are the facts of the case? What are the legal points at issue? How has the court reasoned in justifying its decision? What underlying principles or legal doctrines are involved? How might changing the pattern of facts have altered the judgment? What analogies can be drawn between this and other cases?

Students in these classes know that they have to present more than memorized formulas and that they face detailed questioning in a situation of intense, and public, competition with fellow students. The back-and-forth between instructor and class can be by turns electric, amusing, disquieting, and insight-producing. Amid the pressure and excitement to keep up or excel, students gradually learn to put aside their instinctive reactions and lay reasoning about cases, while trying in earnest to think like a lawyer.

These practices, though diffused in the popular imagination by films such as *The Paper Chase* and books such as *One L*, carry a profound mystique. This is cognitive or intellectual apprenticeship of a peculiarly intense and dramatic kind. In a well-performed case-dialogue class session, the instructor is able to make visible for the students the mostly invisible processes of thinking that guided the legal reasoning by judges in the case under consideration. It is emphatically a teacher-centered pedagogy, with its goal being development of very specific habits of mind: those of the jurist and practicing advocate. It is in fact a quite stylized and generally successful form of interaction between teacher and student that can be described as a kind of signature pedagogy of the law.

The material for this yearlong, multicourse cognitive apprenticeship is mostly from books of legal cases. These are redactions of Appeals Court decisions and so are far removed from the narrative of courtroom drama. Legal conflict, at this level, turns on small distinctions and fine differences in how facts are interpreted and rules and legal doctrines applied. Students are thus learning to operate within a new domain of formalized thinking, with its own definitions, rules, and principles. In this way the teaching of legal doctrine is analogous to the teaching of theory in the sciences, in which students must learn to translate everyday notions into a rigorously structured formal language (such as mathematics), operate with the abstractions, and then retranslate them into more commonly used terms at the end. Beyond the intellectual intricacy of moving back and forth between practical, value-laden narrative modes of thought and analytical precision, teaching students to think like a lawyer is valuable public work. Like many other professionals such as physicians and engineers, lawyers provide modern society with a human interface between the arcane world of technical knowledge, upon which our lives increasingly depend, and life's everyday needs and problems.

For all its strengths and power, this signature pedagogy of the first-year experience has two large limitations. First, it primarily ignores the matter of actual legal practice. Second, its emphasis upon technical argument—what is sometimes described as the law's "artificial reasoning"—can easily obscure in the minds of students (if not faculty) the myriad value-laden social and ethical roles assumed by the legal practitioner. Furthermore, the lack of attention in the typical law school curriculum to jurisprudence and the structure of the legal system sets little theoretical context in which to place concern for professional purpose and identity. The first (intellectual) apprenticeship, in other words, needs effective complement in apprenticeship to the practice of the law—sometimes called "lawyering"—and attention to the public and professional formation of the future practitioner. Unfortunately, such complementary experience typically receives all too little attention.

Thanks to decades of effort to improve the situation, generally supported by the practitioner wing of the profession, all law schools now give students some instruction in legal writing, as well as optional courses in trial advocacy skills, negotiation, and clinical experience assisting indigent clients. These courses are mostly taught by a separate, usually part-time or nontenured faculty. Few schools require such "practice" courses, and fewer still attempt to bring them into relationship with so-called substantive courses in legal theory and doctrine, either at the introductory or the capstone level. Negotiation stands out as a practice subject that has lately gained some admission into the substantive curriculum. It did this through building up its own body of theoretical literature—a successful case of raising practice to a higher level of theoretical interest, which has won for negotiation some standing in the legal academy.

By contrast, clinical legal education has never made the jump into full respectability or academic prestige. Law clinics are probably the most visible of all the efforts at the apprenticeship of practice. The clinical faculty, who are mostly practitioners themselves, have developed their own faculty networks and a professional journal. Clinical courses are typically open to students beyond their first year. The courses are generally organized in seminar style, with small groups of students working under one or more practitioner/instructors. The students are assigned real clients, and their work with the client is supervised by the instructor and discussed in a class session. The mode of instruction is classic apprenticeship: the instructor explains and models the process of working with clients in a variety of case situations.

These courses present experiences that immerse students into the narrative, practical reasoning entailed in professional judgment in the uncertain situation of frontline practice. They provide almost continuous feedback to students, and they often give students a rare and much-sought-after chance to work closely with an experienced practitioner. As such, they impart some balance to the heavily analytical training set out by most of the curriculum. They also often amount to highly motivating experiences for students. However, they remain controversial among law school faculty, who question whether they are intellectually rigorous enough to deserve inclusion in the curriculum (they are usually graded only pass-fail and so do not affect students' class standing).

The Problem of "Ethics" and the Third Apprenticeship

On the one hand, the dominating stature of the case-dialogue method within a narrow set of substantive courses has engendered a much-needed uniformity in ways of thinking among members of a dispersed and variegated profession. On the other hand, this system has made it difficult to direct faculty attention to areas outside the teaching of case law. This signature pedagogy also has powerful unintended consequences for law students' professional and ethical apprenticeship. In their all-consuming first year, students are told repeatedly to set justice aside, not to let their moral concerns or compassion for the people in the cases they discuss cloud their legal analyses. This is justified on pedagogical grounds, and the practice seems to be effective in helping students set aside misleading misconceptions about how the law works in order to hone their analytic skills. For second- and third-year students, the need to set concerns for justice aside is taken for granted, though experience in clinical courses or with electives in legal philosophy may arouse them. But such concerns are seldom reintroduced, even after students master the analytic skills for whose sake these concerns are stripped away. An analysis that takes seriously the threefold apprenticeship functions of professional education makes the negative spillover effect of the schools' too-narrow concentration upon competence in technical legal reasoning obvious.

But the narrow focus also makes it more difficult for students to understand and analyze the various roles played by lawyers, as well as the legal system's social functions. Since the Watergate scandals of the 1970s, the ABA and the American Association of Law Schools have mandated that a course in legal ethics and professional responsibility be a required part of the curriculum. However, there is wide disparity in how such courses are actually conceived and taught. Some are skillfully woven into the students' exposure to substantive topics, following what is called the "pervasive method" of teaching professional ethics. Often, however, it is in a "law of lawyering" course in which students learn how far they can go before incurring legal penalty.

To establish a meaningful grounding for practice, schools need to enable students to come to terms with the social and ethical significance of their future work as attorneys. The word *ethics* comes from the Greek, meaning "custom." It refers to the daily habits and behaviors through which the spirit of a particular community is expressed and lived out. In this broad sense, the third apprenticeship is ethical, though it is important to understand ethics in this basic, broad sense. It means far more than a code of rules or even a set of principles, though ethics can include that. Rather, ethics in a professional curriculum ought to be a way in which students and faculty alike can grasp and discuss, as well as practice, the core commitments that define the profession. For lawyers, just as for other professionals, the subject matter of ethics ranges from theory to practice. Ethics rightly includes not just individual identity and behavior but, importantly, the social contexts and cultural expectations that shape the practice and career of the legal practitioner.

Although they are not as widely employed as they should be, some law schools employ promising alternative approaches to introducing students to the complex demands of the lawyer's role, which also work to make ethical themes more important in students' experience. For example, schools have developed first-year programs which give an overview of the legal enterprise that works to counterbalance the intensive focus on legal analysis. Other efforts are much broader in conception than those that fill the typical first-year case book. Their design owes a good deal to use of cases in other professional schools, especially business and teacher preparation. The common feature of such programs, whether they use case books or the full-blown simulation experience of work in a law firm or court, is that they consciously place the student in a variety of roles within complex situations. The aim is to help students learn how to listen carefully; work collaboratively; and question their stereotypes and assumptions about clients, the nature of practice, and the role of the lawyer and the legal system. Such approaches make ethics less an add-on adjunct to serious legal thinking by moving ethical concerns inside issues. They reanimate the original meaning of the term.

The Inherent Danger of the Culture of Critical Discourse

Most critics of professional education emphasize the problems various groups and individuals encounter with getting fair access to professional credentials. Christopher Lasch, however, raised concerns about the effect that higher education, and particularly professional training, has on the habits of mind of those who succeed in meritocratic competition. His assessment of the effect of such schooling resonates with the dangers inherent in an apprenticeship to analytical thinking untempered by careful reconnection with the values of practice and citizenship. In *The Revolt of the Elites*,[9] Lasch termed the main effect of higher education an initiation into the "culture of critical discourse." He meant this as a descriptive rather than a laudatory term.

Critical discourse, for Lasch, meant something like what Bruner calls analytic-paradigmatic thinking. This is the common coin of the meritocratic elites who staff the professions and administer the key institutions of modern society. It is the distinctive form of consciousness shared among the symbolic analysts of Robert Reich and the creative class of Richard Florida. In the culture of critical discourse, innovation is valued over continuity, flexibility and variety over loyalty, technical intelligence and instrumental finesse over character and moral cultivation, iconoclasm over reverence. These are, of course, recognizably the prized qualities of many of the people and institutions Lasch was writing about.

Lasch insisted that this peculiar culture creates an invidious separation from supposedly ordinary people. Since it is the key to elevation into superior status, possession of credentials of critical discourse often breeds arrogance. It leads those who master it to see themselves as meritorious experts who deserve their status by solving complex problems in sophisticated ways. Such experts naturally see themselves and their lives in strategic terms, often consumed by maneuvering for the better deal in the status competition internal to professional occupations. In its unalloyed state, Lasch claimed, this shared consciousness is the soil of nihilism. It is hardly fertile ground, he pointedly argued, for cultivating an ethic of service and public concern such as that traditionally espoused by the professions.

To the degree that university preparation of professionals consists of an unreflective immersion in such a culture, Lasch's criticism has bite. It calls attention, albeit in a highly critical way, to the importance of what goes on in professional education itself. It is a clarion to attend to how the practices of higher education, and in particular professional schools, shape the consciousness as well as the character of those who participate in them—the students, of course, but also the faculty and leadership. It would be gratifying to find serious engagement with these questions in professional schools. In fact, there has been some stirring of interest in understanding the limitations as well as the strengths of professional education's formative effects. This concern has been propelled by changes in the occupational situation faced by various professions, shifting conditions of practice, and in some cases the changing demographics of students.

Recovering the Formative Dimension: The Example of the Seminary

Concern about shaping consciousness and character is less of a novelty in educating religious professionals than in the law or medicine. As in other fields, changes in the context of practice for clergy are forcing professional leaders and educators to ask anew how to train practitioners to be able to understand and cope with the tensions their contemporary roles entail. There are also major changes afoot in the demographics of seminary students, the implication of which is the need for a more intentional focus upon how to transmit skills and values as well as intellectual facility and ideas.

In an increasingly competitive cultural environment, religious professionals are often hard pressed to distinguish themselves from therapists, guidance counselors, or other human services personnel. More perhaps than engineers, lawyers, or physicians, the effectiveness of their professional mission depends upon being able to interpret and find their footing in a complex social and cultural environment. The clergy's task is to bring alive in novel encounters inherited traditions of meaning and value, to find and sometimes to create significance in difficult and even overwhelming situations that tax the human capacities of all involved. Since the tasks of interpretation and provision of counsel for communities and individuals entail both practical judgment and analytical intellectual skills, student formation has risen in salience within seminaries across the religious spectrum.

"In days of yore," comments an article on the changing nature of the rabbinate, "rabbis served as sometimes absolute arbiters in their communities, sitting in legal judgment, attending to adherents' spiritual needs and even assessing taxation." Today, however, the scope of the typical rabbi's activities, like that of the minister or priest, has narrowed to administration, "officiating at life-cycle events," and providing comfort and counsel. Nevertheless, though the scope has decreased the new situation places a host of new demands on the rabbi: "Because synagogues must compete for a congregant's time, rabbis are expected to be attractive, with winning personalities." One consequence, according to Rabbi Gilbert Epstein of Conservative Judaism in America, is that "some younger men and women have second thoughts about going into a pulpit rabbinate because of these tremendous demands."[10] All this has to be worked out in conditions of growing pluralism of religious communities and traditions.

Given these complexities, it is perhaps not surprising that the term *formation* has attained some prominence in theological education. The need for such a term has arisen most forcibly from changing demographics among aspirants to the ministry, priesthood, and rabbinate. Traditionally, candidates for the clergy came from families with long experience in the religious tradition for which the candidate was being trained. Such candidates possessed what is sometimes termed "tacit knowledge," or experiential knowledge of the particular religious tradition. In recent decades, however, an increasing number of men and women are coming to seminaries with much less informal exposure to traditional religious practice. They lack long familiarity with the mores and sensibility of the community that they are being prepared to lead.

To put it differently, many of the present candidates have not been formed by life experience so that they can feel the community's tradition as second nature. To address this perceived lack of intuitive engagement, some denominations are developing, as part of professional preparation, self-conscious pedagogies that attempt, by various combinations of theoretical study and practical immersion, to furnish in a short time a serious experience of the community's ethos and ways. The aim of such efforts is to shape deep engagement with the central practices and meanings thought to be necessary for anyone aspiring to religious leadership in that community. Without such understanding, clergy are not able to function effectively. These efforts sometimes take the form of curricular changes resulting in specialized programs. Other institutions attempt to make formative concerns pervasive throughout the usual range of academic and clinical studies. In all instances, however, one side effect of concern about formation is to raise an institution's practices of teaching and learning into higher prominence, for both scrutiny and conscious improvement.

Something like this sense of intuitive engagement is essential for all professionals at the moment in which judgment is at a premium, when the practitioner must be able to stand with integrity for the values of the field. It is this need to form practitioners who can perform at the high level demanded by the field that gives professional training its focal point. But thinking about how to train these capacities in students naturally calls up such words as *induction*, *modeling*, and *apprenticeship*. Seen through the lens of formation, the goals of professional education require that schools be able to integrate the several apprenticeships they offer for students around the goal of inculcating and testing deep engagement with the practices and loyalties of the profession. But this is education of a different stripe from what is often understood by the term in purely academic circles.

David Kelsey of Yale Divinity School has introduced an insightful distinction between two views of the goals of seminary education. Kelsey's opposing viewpoints derive from contrasting conceptions of knowledge, each with a long history. They also resonate with Bruner's two types of rationality. In *Between Athens and Berlin: The Theological Education Debate*[11] Kelsey calls the two approaches by the names of cities long associated with the two traditions of knowledge and education. The neglected status of formation—including apprenticeship—in professional education (and not only professional education) stems from the confusion generated by the contemporary academy's preference for analytic-paradigmatic over narrative-practical education.

Athens stands for the notion that education is what the classical Greeks called *paideia*, the same word they used for what we call "culture." When Cicero translated the term into the Roman language, he coined the word *humanitas*. The Latin word conveys something of the existential flavor of the Greek original. For "Athens," education is above all a kind of shaping of the person. Thus education is a reflexive training of insight. Its chief tools are use of narrative, cases, questioning, and dialogue.

Kelsey contrasts Athens with a more recent ideal of education and knowledge, one given material form in the modern research university. "Berlin" here refers to the University of Berlin, founded in a period of reform in early-nineteenth-century Prussia and based upon the Enlightenment's notion that genuine knowledge is *Wissenschaft*, or "science." For Berlin, reason is identified with procedures for testing—and correcting—claims to truth or meaning. Hence rational education is not about shaping the self. It consists in learning to test and criticize beliefs with the object of building up a body of well-established facts and principles, or laws of how things work. This is a kind of formation, of course, but it shapes a detached, critical mind, not an engaged one. The scholar-scientist is the ideal citizen of this Berlin.

With such a gulf in understanding, it is little wonder that proponents of each side have trouble understanding their opponents. Yet leaving aside the vexed question of the meaning of truth and knowledge that this contrast has given rise to, it ought to be clear that professional education cannot take place in a Berlin alone. The cognitive apprenticeship of Berlin forms a detached outsider rather than a member-participant standing inside the situation. The critical model focuses on explanations from without rather than engaged understanding, so forming its own distinctive ethos. There is a whiff here of the nihilistic potential Lasch finds endemic to training in analytical thinking and that gains some credence from legal education's difficulty in reconnecting analysis to social norms such as justice. For religious professionals, the connection comes through allegiance to religious tradition. For lawyers, it should come in the public function of law, a connection that Deborah Rhode has shown to be tenuous. Therefore there is a continuing, perhaps growing need to recognize and legitimate the claims of Athens in the enterprise of professional education. This means finding ways to give the formative dimension of professional education its due. But it also requires connecting this dimension to the necessary and valid claims of Berlin to scientific rigor where appropriate, both in discerning important knowledge and in forming the critical habit of mind as part of what needs to be engaged in professional education.

Broadening Habits of Mind in the Education of Engineers

Engineering emerged as a university study in a world where its mission was well understood. It was to control nonhuman nature at a time when the boundaries between the human and nonhuman environments were distinct. Engineers were often lionized as heroic figures. Yet engineering was also largely controlled by strong institutional authorities, either in private industry or the state, so that engineers never developed the guildlike power to set their collective destiny in the way law, medicine, and academe largely did. Today, however, the continuing technological revolution has placed humanity within a hybrid world that lacks a clear boundary between natural and technological processes. Moreover, the old institutional authorities of corporations and government are also losing their clear boundaries and have more trouble exerting autonomy.

As a result of these drastic changes in the context of practice, Rosalind Williams argues in *Retooling*[12] that engineering is often described today as simply a resource for technological innovation. This casts engineers as simple technical enablers. Technological innovation, formerly construed as the key to the "progress of civilization" and the "furthering of democracy," is increasingly described without reference to social ends. Success in engineering is measured accordingly by the market performance of a product or design.

Williams, a dean at MIT, has produced a compelling portrait of how these changes play out in contemporary engineering education by comparing the present to the career of her grandfather, Warren Kendall Lewis. A professor of chemical engineering, he was also principal author of the Lewis Report,[13] which, parallel to Harvard's famous Red Book, set the framework for the MIT curriculum (and many imitators) after World War II. The Lewis Report had two emphases. First, it emphasized the importance of a strong "science core" to give cognitive structure to the "technical subjects." It thereby placed analytical training higher than skills training, establishing "engineering science" as the core of the program. The idea was to develop a reliable, largely invariant base of knowledge and technique that would enable students to finish their education through on-the-job training in industrial firms or government work. This report helped establish the now-canonical pedagogical emphasis in engineering schools upon lecture courses in applied science, complemented by laboratory courses and some design studio experience.

The Lewis Report also recommended that engineering schools "broaden" their focus to include subjects in the social sciences and humanities beyond the "science core." The report described its aim as a "type of professional training that will fit engineers to assume places of leadership in modern society . . . in which science and technology can no longer be segregated from their human and social consequences."[14] Despite the soaring vision, historical forces kept the engineering curriculum concentrated upon teaching "engineering science" so that the second aspect of the Lewis Report never had the impact of the first. But today, Williams contends, social conditions, both in the world of practice and in the changing demographics of students, give increased importance to broadening the training of engineers, which the Lewis Report sought.

Williams's "Grandpa Lewis" and the other authors of the engineering science curriculum would hardly recognize today's MIT engineering students. There are far more women, more students from minority backgrounds, and also more from upper-middle-class families. The majority of MIT's engineers now say they would like to graduate with at least a minor in business administration. In fact, management has become the second largest major at the institution, ahead of biology, mechanical, and chemical engineering. Students are doing this, argues Williams, because they no longer look to the old, stable corporate career as their future. In its place, they are often told, they must prepare for a "flexible, impermanent world." In engineering, one MIT trustee explained, "the money is at the intersection of technology and the market," and Williams comments that "this is the cross-roads where MIT students are headed." In sum, students have begun to look for an education that is beyond the technical, though in a pragmatic sense. Echoing Lasch's worry about nihilism, Williams notes that although students are increasingly aware that they need to know how society works, this "is not the same thing as an education that highlights social responsibilities."[15]

What is at stake in these changes is nothing less than the identity of the engineering profession. Making engineering a profession, Williams argues, is not an end in itself but a means toward solving the real problem of how to organize a humane and sustainable technological world. The issue is how students, and the schools that educate them, confront the emerging matrix of technology and the market. The current focus of engineering education upon an almost exclusive diet of analytical thinking and technical training is simply not up to this challenge. Where, asks Williams, are students learning discretion, judgment, the kind of imagination, and the sense of responsibility necessary for assuming a role with broad social responsibility? In the absence of such education, engineering graduates are reduced to offering themselves as articulate tools for hire, for whom success is measured in simple monetary terms.

Williams proposes that the answer has to lie not in further overloading the existing four-year curriculum but in making engineering less an exclusively technological degree. Engineering education, that is, needs to be "reintegrated" with a general education addressed to what students need if they are to engage with a world that is "both technological and democratic." Engineering, in other words, needs to "rejoin" higher education in revitalizing its humanistic core to generate a new hybrid in which teaching engineering design can become a meeting point between the intellectual capacity nurtured in the technical fields and the interpretive and normative discipline of the humanities.

The proposal, then, is to rethink professional training in engineering through broadening its formative effects on habits of thought as well as character. To accomplish this, Williams wants to enhance the pedagogical profile and curricular centrality of the teaching of design. The essential definition of design problems must be broadened out to include the whole range of dimensions that the complex contemporary relations between the natural and social worlds demand. MIT students today are less lopsided in their interests and capacities than they were in Grandpa Lewis's day. More attuned to the verbal side of the SAT than before, such engineering students need and can benefit from the "motivational breeze" of learning how the exciting physical "stuff" of the engineering disciplines can take on meaning by helping solve problems that confront contemporary society.

A Life of the Mind for Professional Practice

Why, then, should the professions choose an academic setting for training practitioners? The university is chartered by the larger society to cultivate the life of the mind for the public good. The purpose of locating the beginning of professional preparation in the academy is thus to develop a life of the mind among students and faculty. But it needs to be a life of the mind suited to a vocation of practice. Professional schools attempt to do this through specific approaches to teaching and learning that are often identifiable with signature pedagogies such as the Socratic law school classroom or the clinical rounds of medical education. Woven into distinctive educational institutions, these pedagogies create an ethos whose purpose is to shape a particular professional imagination.

These ends are common to professional education, yet worked out through a history and a context that remain quite specific to each field. There is no generic professional education, but there are common themes and issues that all forms of professional preparation must address and try to resolve. As we have seen, some of these issues derive from the particular needs of an individual profession. Some arise from the peculiar character and history of the American university system. Still others result from the need to bring the demands of professional competence within the institutional constraints of the academy while forming professionals to serve public purposes. These are problems that various professional schools have attempted to resolve in distinctive ways.

Imagining these issues from the students' perspective, looking through the lens of apprenticeship to the professional school, reveals recurring problems in properly balancing and integrating the distinctive concerns of the three apprenticeships. Thinking about these issues comparatively, across the range of professional domains, can enrich each field's understanding of its particular challenges by placing them in a wider perspective. Taking a comparative approach also makes available to each domain a range of resources going beyond the experience of the particular field. The genius of scientific advance resides in creating networks of research and reflective practice through which discoveries can be communicated and ideas tested. By analogy, a wider recognition of the common issues involved in preparing professionals holds the potential for advancing general knowledge in this important area. It may also be a valuable stimulus to the renewal of professional education upon which a strong civic professionalism depends.

To enable the professional schools to serve as a rallying point for professional renewal, however, two issues need serious attention: the distinctive nature of professional knowledge, and how that knowledge can best be integrated with the moral core of the professional enterprise. It is these themes that the following chapters attempt to explore.

Chapter Seven

What Is Professional Knowledge?

Expertise and the University

The spirit of professionalism grew up in the key institutions of industrial America that made their appearance a century ago. The corporation, the hospital, the governmental administration charged with economic and social function, the educational complex, and especially the university: these have been the professions' natural homes. Today, though some of these institutions face new global competition, others are in serious dysfunction of their own or have become the object of intense public scrutiny. Through its enormous expansion during the intervening years, the university, as the common training ground for most professional occupations, has until recently been successful in resisting changes to its basic structure and organization. Now, however, the nation's universities face mounting public worry and often hostile legislative scrutiny as to their functions. Government support and involvement has become less influential, while sensitivity to market position and pressures has grown. These developments pose new and serious challenges for reconstructing civic professionalism where it may matter most: in the university.

Meritocracy, the University, and the Market

There has been a great deal of discussion of these developments within and without the academy. Yet universities are curiously slow to mobilize effective resources for either defense or reform in a way that would be consistent with their historic cultural and civic mission. Derek Bok, the former president of Harvard, has for some time been an articulate participant and observer in these momentous developments. Like Clark Kerr a generation earlier, Bok looks for insight by placing the university within the larger institutional complex in which it continues to play a dynamic and changing part. As Bok sees it, higher education is experiencing a weakening of sympathy among the shapers of opinion and public policy. This decline in support stems from a perception that universities fail to promote purposes of public value. Instead, much of academe is perceived as turning away from a public mission to concentrate narcissistically upon its members' own inner lives and advancing organizational advantages.

Even through the trials of the student revolts of the 1960s, Bok notes, universities received public support because they were seen as actively engaged in two great social tasks. One was opening up access to careers, especially in the professional fields, for newly aspiring groups, beginning with the returning GIs of World War II and extending to minorities and women. The second task was production of useful research to build prosperity and progress. He points out with pride that these genuine achievements remain unequalled anywhere. Bok has for some time maintained that universities today need new ways to serve the public but do not have them. They seem unable to repeat their remarkable postwar success in rallying around goals that enabled higher education to forge new alliances within the broad public interest. Instead, Bok now worries, in *Universities in the Marketplace*,[1] that academe's increasing embrace of the business model, with its overriding concern for profit and expansion, threatens core features of the university, such as respect for academic standards and collegial trust, upon which institutional success has been built.

The postwar university of which Derek Bok is in many ways justifiably proud functioned as the apex of what has been termed a "national personnel system." Indeed, Harvard, under Bok's predecessor James Bryant Conant, was the trendsetting model for this development.[2] The system afforded a new level of career mobility during the postwar decades and for an increasing number of Americans (including far more women and minorities than ever before in national history) college and postgraduate education formed a reliable route toward professionalized, white-collar occupations. The university thereby continued, with greatly augmented impetus, on the course it had been pursuing since the beginning of the century, toward credentialing a new class, the "meritocracy" whose claim to leadership is based upon merit, especially the talent demonstrated in academic achievement. Martin Trow first described this expansion in a paper for an international audience in 1973, as a shift from "elite" to "mass" higher education, with the participation rate of the nation's youth rising from 15 percent to 50 percent. It was a loose and decentralized system that contained vastly disparate colleges and universities, a few truly national in importance and many supplying the provincial middle class with localized occupational mobility.

At the system's core, Nicholas Lemann argues in *The Big Test: The Secret History of the American Meritocracy*,[3] Conant and his allies placed formal schooling and standardized testing. Testing functioned as the chief sorting mechanism. As Lemann sees it, the system grew during the postwar decades to channel and focus "the eternal unruly American obsession with personal ambition" into a decentralized yet increasingly homogeneous system. Spurred by the nation's success with manpower channeling through the draft in World War II, the testing system and higher education became basic to American aspirations for upward mobility. This meritocratic professional system is also heir to the utilitarian social engineers in the line of Frederick Winslow Taylor, who, as we saw in earlier chapters, sought above all to combine equality of opportunity with efficiency in managing social resources for economic growth. It also served as the major bridge institution between provincial America and the national networks of the metropolitan society, typically a one-way bridge over which talent traveled from the former to fertilize the latter. As never before, however, this whole system has come under question. The crisis of confidence in the university stems in significant part from the weakening of coherence and legitimacy in the meritocratic system.

The meritocratic ideal justifies itself on the grounds of social utility. This means that leaders who advance to power through the system of credentialism must offer proof of their merit by providing both increased opportunity for others to emulate them and, whether they are political or business leaders, show that they can spur economic prosperity. However, many of the key instruments of the meritocratic system are suspect or eroded: standardized testing and college admissions processes, public schooling as a pathway to advancement, and access to the best education regardless of wealth. At the same time, the presumed relationship between academic achievement and actual performance is being seriously challenged, not least in the professions. For many, the system is failing on its own terms.

However, as Randall Collins pointed out in *The Credential Society*,[4] American education as a whole has long been organized as a sort of protracted contest for upward mobility. By attaching themselves to the upper end of a long run through ascending levels of competitive schooling, professional schools in effect turn the credentials of successful academic competition into a ticket to good work. The longer one stays the competitive course, the more valuable the credential and the better the work. Hence the all-important professional résumé. But as American education becomes more crowded with contestants, a kind of credential inflation sets in, so that a college degree is required for jobs that once demanded only high school graduation. Colleges and universities themselves fiercely compete to become more selective, thereby boosting the prestige (and cash) value of the degree. In the end, all educational credentials are not created equal.

The result is a wildly intense competition to gain entry among those David Brooks satirically dubbed the "résumé gods," who hold degrees from the most selective institutions and then go on to the most prestigious professional programs, to jobs of the same caliber.

These critics are surely correct that this inflationary credential-into-status competition is highly expensive, often unfair, and dubiously efficient in allocating the nation's human resources into areas beneficial to the society as a whole. It also seems beyond anyone's control, absent a powerful central force such as is exerted by national governments in Europe and Japan. As we shall see, this contest system extends into the academy as well as among universities in a way that bears negatively and positively on the internal workings of the preparation of professionals.

To these criticisms, Derek Bok adds his own in *The Cost of Talent: How Executives and Professionals Are Paid and How It Affects America*.[5] Bok found that since around 1970, the end of the postwar boom, professional compensation has become more and more radically skewed toward leading figures in the private sector. In the United States, the rewards earned by elite among business executives, physicians, and lawyers are two to three times greater than those earned by their European counterparts. Their rewards are also much greater than those enjoyed by most of their colleagues in their own fields. By contrast, professionals serving the public sector, such as teachers, civil servants, and social service providers, earn significantly less and enjoy far less social prestige in America than do their peers in Europe and Japan. These tendencies, Bok argues, harm the nation's long-term interest in a balanced distribution of skilled professionals among a variety of professional fields. The disproportionate channeling of rewards into a few areas of the private sector tempts talented young people to oversubscribe those fields, to the detriment of overall social efficiency and often individual happiness.

The Threat to Formative Education

As Bok points out, the background for the crisis of the university and the meritocratic system is the uneven performance of the economy over the past two decades. Compared to the evenly spread growth of the postwar period, recent economic change has generated more inequality of wealth, raising the stakes of educational success. Where Conant sought to give the meritocracy a broad cultural base through encouragement of general education as a support for specialized study, Bok wants to make the meritocrats more socially responsible by expanding their sights outward toward areas of social need. This is why he greeted the coming of the more commercialized marketplace in higher education with judicious but unmistakable chagrin.

Bok notes that emulation of business models can have benefits for improving the academy. Universities, for example, could learn from business organizations that constantly attempt to diagnose their own shortcomings and improve their quality and adaptability. This could be especially valuable if applied to the academy's own pedagogical methods, which rarely receive the serious and rewarded inquiry granted to scientific research. On the other hand, commercialization places greater pressure on academic institutions, and individual academics, to pursue whatever competitive advantage they can find. Bok fears that this bodes ill for high standards of scholarly inquiry and the academic values of collegiality and trust among peers. Commercialization, in other words, is weakening the emphasis upon craft artistry and high collegial standards that Eliot Freidson, in *Professionalism: The Third Logic*, singles out as distinctive of the "professional model" of work. Instead, the new situation is bringing to the fore an entrepreneurial emphasis upon consumer satisfaction in which prices and profits define organizational purposes. To achieve bottom-line success within the commercially oriented university, management's logic of predictability through formal rules of performance and evaluation tends to trump professional norms.

David Kirp pushes Bok's hesitant insight into this process further. *Shakespeare, Einstein, and the Bottom Line: The Marketing of Higher Education*[6] uses case studies of a variety of academic institutional types to make a forceful claim. The decline of government support and regulation of higher education intensifies competition among universities and colleges for research funding and students and, through them, for market position. Bok worries mostly about the negative effects of commercial funding of research, but with concomitant issues such as academic patenting and secrecy, Kirp focuses on the relentless competition for students. To appeal to the most desirable students, those able to pay ever-rising tuition charges and those who bring enhanced résumés to the institution's profile, colleges increasingly engage in their own "branding."

Here is the commercial ethos at full cry, with the business model firmly in command. It is happening at the very core of the academy's pedagogical identity. Campus location and amenities, especially provision of an expensive leisure colony alongside academic facilities, are among the key competitive weapons employed by each institution in the battle to entice the most desirable student-consumers. The entire enrollment process is thus driven by the imperative to improve the institution's market position—or suffer the consequences. Admissions has been turned into a key— for most institutions *the* key—"profit center." Like collegiate athletic coaches, few academic administrators are willing to risk being judged losers in this high-stakes game.

But no matter how the competition turns out for a given institution, Kirp argues that the real loss is any serious sense that higher education can be about the formation of students. The academy's desperation to compete for consumers is undermining its cultural authority and social purpose. Kirp's conclusion is clear. Without public consensus to delimit the basis and range of this competition and effect regulation to moderate it, positional warfare in the educational marketplace will destroy the shared ideals and distinction of American higher education. Unchecked, these trends are likely to make the recovery of the formative dimension of professional education all the harder.

This commercialized competition has also been having major impact on the nature and composition of the nation's faculty. Describing the "silent academic revolution" of the past decade, researchers Mark Finkelstein and Jack H. Schuster depict an American professoriate in which barely a quarter of new faculty appointments are to full-time, tenure-track positions. Projecting the trend of the early 2000s, Finkelstein argues in "The Morphing of the American Academic Profession"[7] that as today's senior faculty retire, they will, in effect, be replaced by a different academic workforce. It will resemble the less secure and leaner workforce that has appeared in the new economy sectors of information technology and business services. A small core of full-time personnel will likely staff most academic organizations, enhanced as needed by freelance technicians, often hired on a part-time, contingent basis. As Finkelstein's statistics reveal, these developments are already well advanced among the "mass provider" and "convenience" institutions that make up the vast bulk of the nation's thirty-five hundred or so institutions of higher education.

What is afoot is a disaggregation, or unbundling, of the inherited norm of the full-time professor. This figure, which became typical of college personnel during the postwar years, combined teaching, research, and a service or governance function in one identity. Today, however, information technology makes it possible to outsource various aspects of instruction, especially remedial teaching and counseling services, to specialized personnel who serve on contingent contracts that include no research or service obligation but that also hold out no hope of tenure or a permanent career path. In the competition to hold down instructional costs, these possibilities are likely to become irresistible to all but the best-placed and best-endowed institutions. Among elite institutions, which number only about two hundred in all, the traditional model is likely to endure, though in professional schools research and clinical appointments are often made outside the tenured norm. In most of the academy, though, Finkelstein concludes that "college teaching is moving toward a contingent workforce."[8] This reverses the long postwar trend of convergence "up" toward elite norms and threatens an ever more stratified system for faculty as well as students.

The political pressure is perhaps most intense on the regional and disciplinary accrediting associations. They are the frontline guardians of academic standards. As we have seen in the case of legal education, they do more than any other part of the system to maintain or change the structure of academic life. It is there that many of these issues will be practically decided over the years to come. It is important therefore that accrediting groups, which involve a large number of academic professionals in their work as visiting evaluators, understand the dimensions of the issues they face and the long-term implications of their immediate policies.

The contrast is sharp: the market model, portending a commercialized, ever more stratified higher education, versus the academy as a civic institution. Patti Gumport[9] characterizes the university's identity historically as being the institutional steward for a broad set of social responsibilities, among them formation of citizens and expansion of knowledge for the sake of greater understanding and insight. In much the way Brint described the professions' shift away from social trusteeship toward expertise for hire, the academy's situation today places it under growing pressure to move in the same direction.

The main issue is how academe is to be connected to the larger society. Will it be predominantly through the consumer-business model, or will it lie through a reinvigoration of the academy's defining purposes, as a self-aware institutional sector within the larger civil society? The future of professionalism will be profoundly affected by how we collectively decide this issue. In turn, a revitalized professional education sensitive to its own formative dimension has much to contribute to ensuring a responsible outcome, with all the public advantages it would produce. Where the postwar university largely confined its sense of mission to promoting skills in the detached sense of techniques for acquiring or generating information, the new problems bring to fore educational themes once thought to have been relegated to the past—or at least to lower levels of formal education—themes such as the nurture of character and the purposes of knowledge. Attention to these issues breaks down the wall between theory and practice. They require the university, especially its professional schools, to broaden the meritocratic agenda to embrace concern with the purpose and social organization of knowledge. Without this, it is unlikely that the university will develop an effective response to the new conditions.

The dimensions of the challenge become clearer as we ask what stands in the way of effective response. The answer is disturbing, though manifest. Beside—or rather, behind—the inertia of entrenched interests there is also an ideal and a regime of knowledge strongly resistant to the stance of social engagement and moral inquiry demanded by today's challenges. This is the epistemic regime of positivism. It has been central to the university for a century. It helped drive Conant's idea of a national personnel system guided by a scientific elite, and despite devastating criticism it has to date successfully resisted all efforts to displace it. The continuing hold of positivistic dogma over the thinking and practice of higher education is a key problem that must be confronted by anyone who concludes that the needs of our time demand a reshaping of professional knowledge as well as how professional life is organized.

Epistemology as Destiny: The University's Residual Positivism

The ideal type of the modern university, as we saw it described during its heyday in the 1960s, sharply distinguishes facts from values as it segregates generation of knowledge from its application, the theoretic from the moral-practical. In organizing itself around these distinctions, the university embodies, more fully than most institutions of modern society, the basic ideals of the "positivist" civilization enunciated in the early nineteenth century by the "prophet of Paris," Auguste Comte. Although positivism in the technical sense as a theory of science, or in logical positivism as a philosophical theory of meaning and language, has been successfully criticized many times, its power as a kind of ideology or understanding of life retains great influence. In significant part this is because the ideology valorizes scientific and technological rationality and certifies that their application to the human world can be unproblematic.

An early graduate in the natural sciences of the elite École Polytechnique, Comte developed an intellectual movement that projected a vastly influential picture of the progress of modernity. As set out in his short primer, *Introduction to Positive Philosophy*,[10] humanity was struggling to pass beyond its early immaturity, which had led to the invention of divine protectors to explain a terrifying world, into a mature outlook that could confront and master the human as well as the physical world by the unaided power of scientific reason. In the Comtean picture, the remnants of the primitive "theological or fictitious" level of knowledge were due to pass off the historical stage, as were their motley successors, the "speculative or metaphysical" notions such as the soul, under the triumphant impact of scientific, or "positive," knowledge. In this culminating stage of human cognitive development, exact measurement and application of the principle of cause and effect were enabling modern scientists to render the world predictable. They were thereby able to extend human capacities to control the workings of physical nature and, Comte hoped, the evolution of human society as well.

Neither Comte nor his followers had use for the concern with character formation that was central to the inherited educational system centered upon the ancient classics. Rather than reshape the inheritance, Comte simply moved to abolish it. The advances in knowledge and power that Comte expected were to result from methodical intelligence working on carefully defined problems in specialized fields, an intelligence that was to be completely detached from moral or cultural understandings. The final achievement, positive knowledge, was to be a unified system of physical and social laws making good on positivism's promise of human betterment.

This optimistic program of progress through science exerted a huge influence upon the modern research university at its founding a century or more ago. Of course, the American university was never a pure type. Its immediate influence was the German university, refashioned by Wilhelm von Humboldt around a conception of scientific research in the service of advancing human culture, or *Bildung*. Humboldt's program gave centrality to the culture-shaping role of the humanities. The natural sciences later found a place, but within the separate institution of the *Hochschule*. Even within the human studies, however, during the nineteenth century the science of philology grew to overshadow the earlier formative concerns, establishing a positivistic ethos in many faculties. By contrast, the American model combined both humanities scholarship and scientific research. Often enough, the American university also incorporated the older tradition of the liberal arts college, whose emphases are at odds with positivism. The universities also respond to the demands of their contributors, their markets, and government as well. These demands are usually for more directly useful outputs rather than pure science. Still, it is the idealized Comtean program that has inspired the university's core development ever since.

Positivism's protagonists were amazingly successful in installing the basic features of Comte's new cognitive complex at the center of industrial civilization. Comte's purpose was to make the new kind of knowledge and the expertise based upon its application the central shaping force of the future. In many ways, his disciples succeeded in fulfilling their master's hopes. However, Comte also realized, as his epigones often have not, that the regime of positive knowledge would make exceptionally austere demands. Science described how things worked, but it could not answer the old religious and metaphysical questions. It could not say what the world really was, and indeed the desire for such knowledge was one of the chief renunciations demanded of humanity's new "maturity."

Positive knowledge yielded facts but carried no values. It approached the world as a set of processes to be neutrally mapped and, if possible, elucidated through generation of explanatory laws. The secret to the success of modern natural science, the positivists grasped, lay in its stance of objectivity, a deliberate distancing from the observer's interests and beliefs as well as from the world. Following a succession of early modern philosophers, the positivists identified reason exclusively with this methodically detached stance. Viewed in this way, observable processes could be comprehended and, as technology advanced, manipulated to serve human purposes. Hence the close connection between natural scientific knowledge and its instrumental application in technology, the scientific-industrial complex powering the modern political economy. But the ends for which they were to be manipulated, ends that presumably had something to do with the scientific observer's interests and beliefs, could not themselves be probed rationally.

Ends and meanings were, by definition, the products of something other than reason. In other words, according to Comte's austere picture, science could propose no larger meaning for life. Values could be studied scientifically, their forms and development mapped. But values could not be rationally assessed or debated. Humanity would henceforth have to find solace through cultivation of emotional expression, which is all positivism could make of the arts, morality, and religion. The notorious split between the two cultures of the sciences and the humanities—the one the generator of useful factual knowledge and the other the curator of emotive values—remains the enduring legacy of positivist dogma.

It is instructive that Comte thought his discovery too bleak for human consumption in its unalloyed form. He proposed balancing his austere system of knowledge with a consciously constructed religion of social morality. His "religion of humanity," complete with equivalents for most Christian rites, was to replace the inherited creeds that scientific truth had, he believed, rendered incredible. The aim of Comte's religion of humanity was to calm human anxiety in the face of a meaningless universe and to prevent moral backsliding into self-absorption by building solidarity upon shared feelings. Its moral expression was to be service to humanity. However, since all values derived from feeling, which was by definition nonrational, Comte found himself having to justify the proposed new religion on the grounds of social utility.

Comte was quite clear about who should impart direction to modern society. That role was to devolve upon the positivistically enlightened savants, engineers, and industrialists he saw as the shock troops of advancing modernity. This has certainly permitted a flattering self-portrait for university faculties, among others. The unresolved problem he bequeathed was whence this expert elite were to derive their purposes and values. Nevertheless, positivists are right in emphasizing the difference between the progress in instrumental knowledge that has come to us from the formal methodologies so prominent in the natural sciences and the interpretive activities typical of other areas of cultural life that do not seem to make "progress" at all. This distinction rests in part upon institutional differentiation between the processes of markets and technological production guided by criteria of instrumental efficiency on the one hand, and the human activities organized in civil society that aim at quite different goals, such as moral agreement or cultural consensus, on the other.

The consequences of the scientific and technological triumphalism of modern civilization were caught in the early twentieth century by Max Weber in his theory of the progressive rationalization of life. By *rationalization* Weber meant primarily the spread of instrumental means-and-ends reasoning to ever wider areas of society. However, Weber saw the ideal end point not as utopia but as an "iron cage." In a way that anticipated Jerome Bruner's distinction between formal and narrative cognitive capacities, Weber saw that the triumph of theoretic reason was being bought at the price of meaning itself. Another contemporary theorist, Ernest Gellner, related the distinction in types of reasoning to the social logic of modernity. "The idea underlying the division of labor," according to Gellner in *Plough, Sword, and Book: The Structure of Human History*,[11] "is that if you do one thing at a time you do it better; and moreover, that one 'thing' is to be defined by one criterion, for only then can you tell whether indeed it is being done better or worse." This pattern of thought is what ballistics has in common with genetic research and both have in common with inventors toiling at a better mousetrap—or business strategists trying to undersell their competitors. Once organized within the institutional settings of the market or the bureaucratic organization, means-and-ends thinking improves effectiveness by encouraging the frequent obsolescence of means in the pursuit of goals.

As Gellner notes, however, even a highly rationalized society cannot get by on instrumental automatic pilot. Rationalized organizations may try to minimize human judgment through operating by formalized rules or computer programming, but when decisions are to be made at the top they must use another kind of thinking. Where what matters is integration among several goals or kinds of activity, or where overall policy must be considered and evaluated, or where general purposes must be translated into specific judgments in particular contexts, "decisions cannot be effectively disaggregated into separate, single-aim issues." In such a situation, goals must be compromised as they are blended with other values. Such balancing has long been one of the most prized abilities in jurisprudence and statecraft, as development of capacity in holistic, practical judgment was taken as the supreme task of humanistic education. Needing to maintain orientation amid rapid storms of change, modern societies need more, rather than less, these capacities of practical as opposed to technical judgment. In this important way, the ideological triumph of positivism, especially in the university, does not serve us well.

We have seen in earlier chapters how professionalization arose as both a consequence of this enormous expansion of differentiated functions and a response to the tensions generated by the conflicts among these functions and groups over their interests and goals. Economic efficiency does not automatically produce social justice and peace; nor does military power establish political legitimacy. Modern societies must continuously engage in the complicated, ongoing effort to balance their several social processes, some technical and some moral and cultural, from whose interaction the unique freedoms and potentials of modernity arise. This is the task of civic democracy, to which professions can contribute only if they see themselves as part of an interacting public discussion of these problems. Civic democracy demands the ability to think in terms of complex balance rather than maximization of effectiveness as measured by a single objective. Unfortunately, this more complex task and vision is obscured by positivism's naïve, nineteenth-century faith in an automatically unfolding progress. This unexamined faith is the source of both the narrowness of much of the academy and its nearly invincible self-righteousness.

What, then, must happen if the limitations of the reigning dogma are to be transcended and professional knowledge is to be organically connected to the historical needs of our time? The critical step in this direction lies in rehabilitating nonformal modes of rationality that do not screen out the practical, moral, and historical standpoint of both the subjects and the objects of knowledge. This means rediscovery and expansion of the idea of practical rationality. In *Return to Reason*,[12] Stephen Toulmin argues that this rediscovery of practical rationality, a form of what cognitive scientists identify as narrative thinking, is what enables us to achieve the full promise of modernity, a promise at once less grandiose but more humane than the rationalistic conquest of nature pursued by positivists. However, taking practical reasoning seriously in the university requires major reorientation in significant areas, not least in professional education. The great gain for the professions would be a much tighter link among the three apprenticeships, not fusing them but giving a certain leading role to the third apprenticeship as a way to embrace theoretic intelligence and technical skill in the service of fostering an enlightened practice.

The Relevance of Practical Reasoning

The clearest way to grasp the insufficiency of the positivist model of professional expertise is to notice what the positivist account of knowledge leaves out but must take for granted. Its hallmark of identifying intelligence with a style of formal analytical reasoning leaves tacit the goals implicit in any given act of inquiry. It is as though one believes that the practice of driving can be exhaustively understood without ever asking about the goals of actual drivers or the contexts within which driving occurs. The pragmatist philosophers, especially C. S. Peirce and John Dewey, criticized this account of knowledge for ignoring the fact that all inquiry takes place as part of an engaged social practice. This was, they argued, preeminently true of that highly refined and stylized kind of inquiry practiced by the natural sciences.

The core of the pragmatist argument is that knowledge results from inquiry, and inquiry is always a response to a perplexity that interrupts an ongoing practice. Without an implicit interest in continuing this practice, which may be a theoretical practice such as science or a more obviously practical one such as engineering, there can be no focus for the inquiry, no problem to engage cognitive attention. That is, inquiry is always implicitly structured and guided by some end or purpose. This purpose derives in part from the character and identity of the investigator.

Particularly in the case of scientists or other practitioners of traditions of disciplined inquiry, this character of the investigator derives its focus from participation in a community sharing certain values—in the case of the scientific community, commitment to the good of argument and experiment. Thus, Peirce insisted that science's nature as an essentially social activity crucially affected what it discovered as well as how it came to discover it—a position that has come to be generally accepted only within the past decade or two, attendant upon Thomas Kuhn's famous *Structure of Scientific Revolutions*.[13] In short, the pragmatic approach directs our attention to knowing and inquiry as human activities that we are engaged in ourselves even as we ask these questions. This approach breaks out of the false detachment of the positivist position to assume a more active yet more reflective stance toward inquiry. Concretely, it means becoming more reflective about what skilled professionals, including scientists, actually do.

Professional practice, as we saw in the previous chapter, always involves cognitive movement between the detached stance of theoretic reasoning and the highly contextual understanding typical of engaged expertise. Thus the experienced physician begins the encounter from within a specific framework of meaning, as someone shaped by the profession of medicine. This is a social organization that embodies an ongoing tradition of concern with healing, including a commitment to use the best available scientific knowledge, to promote that goal. From this tradition, physicians learn to be effective agents of healing, willing and able to focus their skills and knowledge on assisting patients. They are also trained in scientific analysis and problem solving, learning the detached stance of a researcher in the biomedical sciences. Perhaps most important, they are taught, through intimate relationships of apprenticeship, habits of moving back and forth between these two cognitive positions so as to reengage more effectively with the therapeutic situation. Professional expertise, that is, embodies a threefold pattern of practical reasoning, a rhythm of moving back and forth from engagement with the concrete situation, through detached observation and analysis, and back again to more informed engagement with the person and situation.

For Dewey, understanding that all rationality was ultimately a species of practical reasoning was rooted in humanity's evolution as a learning and problem-solving species. Dewey spoke of inquiry as a three-part process of moving from perplexity through efforts to analyze the situation in hopes of resolving the perplexity and on to renewed practical functioning. His notion of inquiry included scientific thinking within the larger notion of rationality, but it placed the detached, analytical stance of scientific investigation as a "moment" within the larger process. Dewey noted how science enables our species to better understand the workings of nature, and in certain areas to control nature in support of human purposes. Even so, the reason for undertaking the investigation in the first place, as well as its potential meaning, can come only from those shared, historically rooted cultural meanings that Dewey sometimes called "experience."

Dewey claimed that it was a shared experience, though what he meant was more an inherited cultural ethos than particular individual perceptions enabling a group of researchers to perceive a situation as problematic and therefore a stimulus to investigation. Purposeful human activity, or *praxis* in the Greek sense, is thus the ground and also the goal of the scientific phase of investigation. In this pragmatist view, the point of inquiry is to restore, or reconstitute, the flow of meaningful activity. Human rationality in its full sense is, then, ultimately practical (and therefore social and historical) in nature.

The great revolution in thinking that we call modern science gradually codified and institutionalized the second analytical phase of the circuit of practical reason. Approaching nature with objectivity and distance proved enormously fruitful in producing accurate information. It also engenders new powers to control and transform the natural processes understood in this way, as the achievements of modern technology powerfully demonstrate. The neat, bounded quality of the observer's stance is one of the charms of scientific theory. Another is the sense of certainty available in theory, so welcome compared to the unsettled uncertainty and anxiety of decision that pervades the realm of practice. However, the aesthetic appeal of these qualities inherent in theorizing has produced the kind of positivist seduction of reason that has led to the delusion that scientific thinking exhausts rationality itself, that information is all of knowledge. This is a serious mistake. Fixating on the analytical phase of inquiry threatens to short out the vital circuit of practical rationality.

A more expansive sense of practical reason can help to release this fixation. A grasp of inquiry in its full, practical sense also offers a remedy for the widespread worry that we live today awash in meaningless information, overwhelmed by the production of knowledge that, in the form of weaponry and environmental degradation, threatens human survival itself. As these threats reveal, the great challenge of our era is precisely to reintegrate the analytical phase of investigation and knowledge production with those frameworks of cultural orientation and meaning (ultimately narrative in nature) upon which we depend in order to secure human flourishing in the long run. As we have seen, in all the professional schools there are examples of pedagogical practices weaving connections across these differences. Strengthening formative education in the professions, however, requires augmenting and enhancing these efforts. For this, the perspective of practical reason is an important theoretic device.

Learning from Practice: An Epistemology of Practical Reason

The constricting fixation of positivist dogma is nowhere so apparent in professional schools as in the widespread assumption that practice can simply be reduced to applied theory. The imagined transmission of knowledge is essentially one-way, from theory to practice. Practice, on the other hand, is understood to contribute little to theory except perhaps to aid in testing hypotheses. The premise here is, of course, that analytical knowledge is more or less self-sufficient. This assumption is strongly enhanced by the success of electronic data processing. There, mathematical representations can be used to solve problems by translating them into precisely defined forms that can be processed according to precisely defined procedures. Myriad tasks of calculating, organizing, storing, and manipulating data, such as record keeping, money management, and optimizing allocation and scheduling, can now be handled without the intervention of subjective judgment. The intellectual temptation is to jump to the conclusion that all skilled tasks can be treated in the same way. Indeed, in some circles in the academy as elsewhere this has become a virtual article of faith.

But there is also a persuasive body of thinking, consistent with the pragmatist understanding of practical reasoning, that argues that formal modes of thinking such as information processing not only are qualitatively different from skilled human performance but are in fact ultimately parasitic upon it. This is the argument advanced by Hubert and Stuart Dreyfus, a philosopher and an engineer, drawing on both the phenomenological philosophy and experience with artificial intelligence and systems engineering. In *Mind over*

Machine: The Power of Human Intuition and Expertise in the Era of the Computer,[14] they propose a model of expertise directly counter to the positivist dogma of applied theory. Their model has much relevance to the training of professionals; in the following section we see its use as a guide to nursing education.

The core of the Dreyfus model is an account of how expertise is actually developed in a variety of human activities, from chess playing to airplane piloting to nursing practice. In all cases, they argue, the progression is the *opposite* of the common belief that learners simply move from concrete examples toward gradually more abstract conceptions. In contrast, the work by the Dreyfuses tries to show that mature skill acquisition moves *from* a distanced manipulation of clearly delineated elements of a situation according to formal rules *toward* involved behavior based upon an accumulation of concrete experience. The evolution here works through the gradually developing ability to see analogies, to recognize new situations as similar to whole remembered patterns. Expertise means a learned ability to grasp what is important in a situation without proceeding through a long process of formal reasoning. Sometimes called expert "intuition" or "judgment," it is the goal of training for practice in the mode of apprenticeship.

The Dreyfus model proposes that learning embodied skills proceeds through five stages. In the first, the *novice* stage, there is no perceptual grasp or ability to interpret a situation as whole. Instead, the novice must learn to recognize certain well-defined elements of the situation and apply precise and formal rules to the elements, regardless of what else is happening. For example, the novice automobile driver learning to use a stick shift must memorize and practice shifting according to the speed the car has attained, regardless of traffic or anticipated stops.

Following the rules allows gradual accumulation of experience. But to progress, the student driver has to start noticing features of the context such as traffic and approaching stop lights, which occur outside the rules. The second stage, *advanced beginner,* marks the point at which the learner can start to think by analogy to past experience. So the driving student starts to learn to shift according to engine sounds, or to take account of other drivers in deciding when to apply the clutch or the brake. The advanced beginner, by contrast, is still heavily dependent upon the training wheels of formal procedures and elements defined independently of context, such as the car's speed in miles per hour.

The third transition is to a level of basic *competence*. This development is triggered when the amount of accumulated situational information starts to overwhelm carrying out the rule-governed procedures. What saves the competent performer from situational overload is discovering a goal. (The novice is often too beset with remembering and carrying out context-free rules to think about purpose at all, or in imaging a goal he or she may attempt things a competent performer knows from experience to be impractical.) Driving to save time or to avoid skidding on wet road surfaces enables the competent driver to ignore some features of the situation and attend to others, adjusting performance to achieve the desired end.

The new capacity here is the ability to judge that when a situation shows a certain pattern of elements, such as heavy traffic and a wet roadway, a certain conclusion should be drawn and a particular way of behaving put into effect. The ability to choose a goal or plan, however, is often quite difficult for the competent performer. At first, performers at this stage may need to think in a self-consciously analytical way about the situation, problem-solving by testing and eliminating options. Much of psychological theory takes this to be the norm for all deliberation, as in the influential work of Herbert Simon.[15] However, as competent learners gain experience and self-confidence, they rely *less* on conscious weighing of choices when sizing up a situation and deciding what to do. They gradually learn to draw analogies between a current situation and whole situations remembered from past experience.

The fourth stage is *proficiency*. It marks the point at which the learner is able to make holistic, so-called intuitive judgments, interpreting whole situations on analogy to past ones without having to decompose them into abstract elements for processing. This is a skill the novice utterly lacks. Although the competent performer has to consciously choose a purpose to order perception and judgment, proficiency means that this judgment seems effortless, as a kind of intuitive perception. The student driver no longer has to think out what to do when it starts to rain or snow while driving in heavy traffic.

Finally, the Dreyfuses' fifth stage of *expertise* is reached when a person is able to hit the mark dependably without either working through complex problem solving or devising an explicit plan. Since this level of performance cannot be fully reduced to rules and context-free procedures, it often appears to the novice, the layperson, as a kind of magical know-how. It is in fact the result of long training and practice in which feedback and coaching are essential. The expert driver, like the airplane pilot, no longer experiences driving a car or flying a plane so much as simply driving or flying: the expert has learned to engage the situation through the machine as an aspect of bodily deportment. Likewise for the skilled surgeon and the expert painter: their tools have become enabling parts of a smooth, skillful engagement with the world.

Experts are acting not on guesses but on perceptual grasp and the ability to make qualitative distinctions gained through experiential learning. Expert judgment is achieved through experiential learning. But this is not a cognitive either-or. Experts also need to reflect and deliberate, especially when confronting difficult or strikingly novel cases and situations. Then they typically engage in deliberative thinking, looking for other explanations or different understandings of the situation. This is similar to the second, analytical moment in Dewey's circuit of inquiry. Such reflection may employ analytic techniques precisely to try out different analogies or perspectives in a conscious process, so as to suggest new or forgotten possibilities. But the expert is not a Hamlet. The expert's knowledge is well grounded in the subtleties of experienced distinctions and analogical reasoning achieved through a long apprenticeship to more expert practitioners. In this process of learning, formal models and rules play an essential role, as the Dreyfus model stresses, but the formal models are themselves practically based. Put another way, in the teaching and learning of expertise, practice is often ahead of theory. It is expert practice that is the source of formal knowledge about practice, not the other way around. Once enacted, skilled performance can be turned into a set of rules and procedures to be put to pedagogical use, as in cognitive apprenticeship. But the opposite is not possible; the progression from competence to expertise cannot be described as simply a step-by-step buildup of the lower functions. In the world of practice, holism is real and prior to analysis. Theory can—and must—learn from practice.

A Pedagogy of Practical Reasoning: Teaching Expertise in Nursing

One of the sources of validation and extension for Hubert and Stuart Dreyfus's model of learning expertise came from the area of clinical nursing. Here, the work of Patricia Benner shows the relevance of "learning from practice" in order to improve understanding of expert practice—and to use this understanding to point a direction for improved professional training. Benner does not denigrate the pedagogical uses of teaching theory in order to guide the beginning clinician, showing the beginner what to pay attention to, for example, and what to expect under specific conditions. Rather, Benner argues for the need to place the constricted positivist conception that practice is just applied theory within a wider understanding of the nature of the clinical arts. Benner argues in *Expertise in Nursing Practice: Caring, Clinical Judgment, and Ethics*[16] that the educator's key aim ought to be to develop a sufficiently broad viewpoint to be able to coach students on negotiating the gap between scientific theory and clinical practice. With such a perspective, it becomes possible to guide students toward progress from beginner status to competence and expertise.

In Benner's view, nursing students make progress toward clinical expertise only with the help of modeling and coaching, typical of effective apprenticeship. Clinical theory, in the form of explicit rules and procedures drawn from scientific knowledge, becomes a necessary but not sufficient means for leading students beyond the beginner stage. To master a complex set of basic skills and learn the underlying biology, the proven methods of imparting subject matter and the repeated practice of discrete skills are essential. But to move beyond the fixed repertoire of the beginner stage, developing clinicians need experience. Recall that for the Dreyfus model beginners lack contextual understanding. They have to learn from experience to notice analogies between one situation and another. This requires extended development of analogical reasoning suited to clinical nursing. For this task, theory in the sense of making explicit what is important becomes highly valuable. Combined with coaching, representation of practice and practice situations through words and graphics is a major aid in developing students toward advanced beginner status, which Benner believes describes the goal of undergraduate nursing education.

Benner's idea of theory as a guide to practice explicitly includes the assumption that in clinical work theory is also learning from practice. To do so, however, clinical theory must make room alongside analytical thinking, which proceeds by algorithm, for analogical reasoning, which is based upon expert judgment. As we have noted, doing this pedagogically often runs counter to many of the entrenched beliefs dominant in the academy. Therefore, it is important to establish as clearly as possible how the two kinds of reasoning are being treated in this alternative model.

There is illumination available from anthropological research on how physical therapists teach their students to recognize the feel of normal versus pathological bodily movement. This research helps sustain Benner's position. For example, Mike Rose writes of the importance of what he calls "traditional teacherly devices" to direct and focus student attention. Clinical teachers typically move back and forth between simplified representations of body parts and their functions on the one hand, and actual manipulation of simulated or real bodies on the other.[17] Without such techniques, by which practice can be slowed down, examined, and reassembled, students would be overwhelmed by the sheer amount of detail and fine discrimination involved in expert practice. They would have a much more difficult time in grasping which distinctions to look for.

So once again, it is the use of abstraction to foster rather than replace cultivation of analogical and practical thinking that is important. This may be especially true in nursing. There, as Benner writes, a large part of the domain of nursing practice, which is concerned with not just care of the body but "care of the embodied person in context," has been historically "private and not formalized."[18] Much of the clinical expertise of nursing is therefore embodied in judgment within a context that is often highly charged emotionally as well as complex biologically. For example, nurses do essential health care work by coaching patients (and sometimes apprentice physicians) through illness and recovery. For this work, what Benner calls "skillful ethical comportment" is indispensable—but difficult to teach through the usual techniques focusing on procedures and the like out of context. Ethical comportment depends upon complex traditions of living that come alive only through apprenticeship experiences with "exemplars" of inherited judgment and skill.

Accordingly, Benner advocates developing an "interpretive phenomenology," based upon careful description and reflection by expert practitioners. This approach attempts to describe how experts modulate and adapt procedures for patients in various situations and contexts. This is indeed "embodied, situational" knowledge, the kind of wisdom of practice that is rarely made explicit. But it is also essentially informed by the biological sciences. To be effective, today's clinical nurse must also have insight into the sometimes baffling labyrinth of the system of health care delivery and the patient's place in it at a particular time. The goal cannot be clinical skill divorced from theoretical understanding or complex social contexts. Indeed, clinical skills can sometimes be improved through use of more theoretical knowledge, as in the kind of narrative reflection upon practice that Benner advocates, not in opposition to but distinguished from the kind of "reflective practice" within situations given currency by Donald Schön in his influential study, *The Reflective Practitioner: How Professionals Think in Action.*[19]

This insight converges with what we have observed in previous chapters about what is needed for competent practice in the professions. Benner's work argues that it is not useful for the professional school to imagine that it can train a master practitioner and send the person into any and all situations. Instead, the situational character of practical knowledge strongly suggests that the essential goal of the professional school must be to form practitioners who are aware of what it takes to become competent in their chosen domain and equip them with the reflective capacity and motivation to pursue genuine expertise. In the case of nursing, for example, this would mean studying and understanding the changing conditions of practice, as illuminated by history and the social sciences, alongside the study of the field's particular knowledge base in the physical sciences. Both these aspects of theoretical knowledge must in turn be brought to bear in the teaching of practice. But the increasing importance of establishing trust between professional and patient shows that identification and formation of skillful ethical comportment must be the organizer of competence and inspiration of expert work.

A pedagogy grounded in an understanding of practical reason redefines the role of theoretic knowledge and techniques of analysis. It is a role quite different from the one typically installed in professional curricula on the Flexner design. Rather than the supreme goal of all inquiry, as Comte insisted, analytic thinking can find its real, if less grandiose, function as a means of sustaining and enhancing the achievement of practical ends, as Dewey believed. All three phases of practical reasoning need to be represented in the learning process. The overall context must be a formative one that can encourage students toward entering and understanding the meaning and purposes of the particular professional community. Thus, the third apprenticeship of professional identity has to precede and interpenetrate the learning of formal analytic knowledge in the first apprenticeship and the development of skilled practice in the second. To neglect formation in the meanings of the community, and the larger public purposes for which the profession stands is to risk educating mere technicians for hire in place of genuine professionals. Therefore the goal of professional education cannot be analytic knowledge alone (or perhaps even predominantly). Neither can it be analytic knowledge plus skillful performance. Rather, the goal has to be holistic: to advance students toward genuine expertise as practitioners who can enact the profession's highest level of skill in the service of its defining meanings.

Such achievement was once called *phronesis*, or practical wisdom. It means the embodied sense of expert judgment that can do justice to the full range of the profession's complexity. It should now be clear why such judgment cannot be a component of the mind alone but must be understood as *habitus*, or a disposition of the person as a whole. Such wisdom is embodied in individuals but is the collective asset of a viable professional community, partly resident in the professional school but also distributed among expert practitioners in field. With a guiding understanding of practical reason, there is no longer a theoretical need to subordinate the latter to the former. Both wings of the profession are freed to learn from each other and, together, to learn from practice even as they work in diverse ways to enhance it.

Directions for Reform

These reflections hold startling implications for how the university typically conceives professional knowledge and attempts to teach professional competence. One implication is that to the extent students—and faculty—come to see expertise as a function of a large knowledge base and masses of inferential rules, they will fail to progress beyond a basic level of competence. This would be to put at risk the sum of social intelligence professionals can bring to an organization. Without a strong culture of reflective, expert practice, we can now say, the leap beyond competence to expertise is inhibited. More seriously yet, those who would exclude the wisdom of practice from serious educational endeavor in the name of basing professional training upon a purely formalized conception of knowledge "may ultimately discover that their wells of true human expertise and wisdom have gone dry."[20]

Reconceiving professional expertise under the guidance of an understanding of practical reason reveals the importance of experience and service to the professional enterprise. The new understanding needs to be incorporated into the system of selection and certification for professional competence, either by making service and experience prerequisites for admission to professional programs or by making these activities integral to the process of professional education itself. A professional model of work requires that specialization be integrated more by teamwork than by centralized direction. The desirable change is from a stiff organizational hierarchy bolstered by amassed credentials toward a partnership network in which demonstrated competence confers authority. A more permeable and flexible organization of the professions is the logical extension of these developments, and the university needs to be a critical participant in them.

Because real expertise is never entirely separable from a community of practice, it is never fully purified of social and moral engagement. Thus its contemporary institutional expression may well be partnership among organizations united in an effort to respond to the problems and possibilities of society. This kind of cooperative approach necessarily promotes practitioners and the affected community into a situation of dialogue with theorists in the academy. But students in professional schools, as they become involved in theoretically informed participation in these cooperative efforts, also need to appreciate both the practical nature of expertise and their own responsibility to the enterprise they join.

This reorientation requires that faculty and practitioners overcome mutual distrust so they can share jointly in reshaping their professional discipline away from fixation upon a rigid body of established knowledge into a more supple and interactive network of investigators. If they were to take such a goal seriously, ours could be a time of much-needed reshaping of the organization and rewards of disciplinary knowledge and research. The concerns of research in the academic fields would expand naturally to include more interest in both practice and pedagogy. To facilitate the transition from technical to practical understanding of expertise, however, it is especially important to articulate and strengthen informed, synthetic thinking in professional school curricula and professional continuing education.

In the positivist era, the method of the mathematical and natural sciences was the one model all inquiry sought to approximate. The university for our time is likely to be more pluralistic yet more interactive, requiring more reciprocal understanding and flexible cooperation among participants. In this context, the humanistic disciplines, cast as media and traditions of communication, reflection, and judgment, become much more important to the success of the entire enterprise. Increasing interest in the domain of professional ethics, especially around questions of public mission and responsibility, suggests that this direction may not be merely a fanciful hope. Accordingly, this is the topic to which we move next.

Chapter Eight

Confronting Moral Ambiguity

The Struggle for Professional Ethics

"One bad ethical decision," warns the ad copy for a new professional newsletter, "could destroy your career." But for the low subscription price of $148 the informed professional can "forestall costly lawsuits, avoid unnecessary conflicts with patients, and minimize the time spent with institutional review boards." Taking care to be ethically correct, from the professional's side at least, can signal simply canny self-protection. Indeed, everywhere the message to professional practitioners and aspirants is to focus on self-interest in the narrow sense. The lay public seems less and less to look to the doctor or lawyer for wise counsel. Today the concern is whether the professional's malpractice premiums are paid up.

The evident worry among physicians that ethics is somehow about self-protection seems to confirm from another angle why calls for health care reform began to gain widespread hearing during the 1990s: Americans were unhappy with their system of health care. Compared to a decade earlier, fewer people felt satisfied with the health care they were able to obtain, and a majority believed that doctors were "unfair in the prices they charge." Americans, it turns out, were considerably less happy with their health care system than are citizens of countries such as Canada and Great Britain. As *Time* magazine concluded, public hostility toward physicians was on the rise and "doctor bashing has become a blood sport."[1] These findings suggest that the rising concern with professional ethics has other sources in addition to a possible upsurge in conscience among practitioners.

Why the Concern with Professional Ethics Now?

Compared to other industrial countries, medicine in the United States has long enjoyed an extraordinary degree of autonomy. The result, until very recently, was physician-controlled health care. The record is one of impressive achievements in health care for many, but also a case of abused autonomy and failed public responsibility. It is noteworthy that, compared to Canada and the Western European countries, the United States consistently lags in the areas of public health, preventive medicine, and universal inclusion in health care benefits.[2] As recently as the 1960s, however, medicine appeared to be the model of a mature profession.

The professions once seemed to be embodiments of the American middle-class aspiration to contribute something of value to the world while achieving respectable status. As we have seen, the professional ideal gained legitimacy in the United States not just as a middle-class notion but as having value for everyone. Not that everyone was expected to become a professional. Rather, the professions' espoused values of competence, dedication, and service concretized a vision of how technical expertise could be made socially useful, leading individual ambition to serve the larger good. The spirit of professionalism was invoked to leaven the heaviness that monetary self-interest often imparts to ordinary occupations.

The economic dynamism of commercial competition typically goes together with considerable economic inequality, and nowhere more so than in the United States. This recurrently poses problems for a nation committed to democracy. An increasingly complex, technological division of labor increases the demand for specialization, with its concomitant diversification of social perspective. For reformers earlier in the century, professionalism seemed to be a way to mitigate these tensions. The merchant might for the sake of personal gain provide whatever was asked for. By contrast, the professional, guided by an understanding of public responsibility, could be trusted to render what was needed. By combining learning, skill, and public service, professionalism itself became an ethical ideal.

Since the high-water mark of confidence in professionalism during the first postwar decades, however, the ideal has come under increasing criticism and attack.[3] As we have seen in earlier chapters, conspicuous failures of public policies formulated by experts in the arenas of urban reform, social welfare, and education fueled skepticism about professional claims to superior knowledge. The abuse of privileged positions by greedy professionals without effective control by their peers or public oversight weakened the public legitimacy of professional self-regulation. In a less stable, more interrelated, yet highly competitive economic environment, bonds of reciprocal loyalty between organizations and their employees were rudely severed during a period of downsizing, or what was once known as laying off workers.

In response, many groups seem bent on creating laws, rules, or regulations to control the behavior of professionals and managers— but also elected representatives, police, teachers, airline pilots, clerical workers, all of whom no longer seem to respond to the norms of custom or conscience. We have witnessed a tremendous rise in anxiety and anger focused on controlling the performance of people, and sometimes organizations, performing public functions. That, of course, describes much of the modern workforce. At least as often as it was constructive, the result has been an enormous expansion in litigation, an escalation of mistrust, and a sense of collective impotence or even demoralization.

Historically considered, this urge to monitor and control at first seems puzzling. It goes against one of the longest observable trends of American life: the expansion and legitimation of areas of individual discretion and freedom. In fact, this new anxiety, and the tone of repression and nastiness it has engendered, points up a great historical conundrum. The problem is that the whole notion of the conscientious discharge of one's function, traditionally described as an ethic of vocation, seems to be breaking down. At the same time, the ever more Byzantine elaboration of rules fails to satisfactorily replace it. The furor over professional integrity is an expression of the great need modern societies have for professionalism as a reliable social ethic.

A vocation traditionally meant an inward calling to an ethically guided pattern of life. Through such a life, an individual's abilities acquire value for all by their systematic application to social tasks. The idea, we have seen here, is religious in derivation, as Max Weber showed in his famous study of the Protestant ethic of the calling.[4] In the Protestant tradition a vocation was thought to be the fruit of a "conversion," a socially structured yet personally experienced sense of having been given a special task and thereby having found one's place in life. The idea of a profession, though not identical to this ethic of vocation, still intersects it at many points. The idea of profession implies both a systematic cultivation of certain disciplines and a disinterested, public spirit in applying these skills.

In modern society, according to the accepted sociological wisdom established by Weber, the internalized ethic of vocation is headed for extinction. Along with the old humanistic ideal of education as moral cultivation, Weber argued that the internal spirit of occupational callings was being rendered obsolete by the expansion of technocracy.[5] Weber proved to be a good prophet, as something like this seems to have gradually occurred, though not as rapidly nor as universally as he believed. The problem about unlimited rationalization is that there are many problems that cannot be resolved simply by applying more external controls ad infinitum. Short of succumbing to comforting but wildly utopian nineteenth-century beliefs in self-regulating social mechanisms (whether the class struggle or the market), there is a problem of infinite regress. Someone, or some group, must somehow act out of conviction to make any institution function. This is obvious at the level of intimate relationships in institutions such as the family. Children, for example, need unfeigned love to develop as human beings. Oddly, the implication of this truism is still resisted when it is extended to larger, more public institutions; but they too work only when a large proportion of their participants believe in them and care for them. This is the disposition named by the traditional notions of vocation and profession.

In late modern society, it has become more difficult than ever to routinize the conditions of skilled work through application of external rules and controls. Where creative, responsive thinking and sustained cooperation are required, a successful work process comes to depend increasingly on the inner disposition of the worker. If the ethic of vocation did not exist, our society would need to invent it now. This is the positive significance of the calls for ethics in the professional fields, and indeed throughout the society. People are beginning to grasp with new intensity the objective need for responsible engagement and self-regulation. They are searching for ways to ensure professional integrity, aware that it is a public good on which the welfare of all depends, but which cannot be ordered into existence simply by manipulating sanctions or rewards. Professional integrity is the outgrowth and legacy of the ethic of vocation. It can be nurtured, given favorable institutional contexts, only among free human agents who come to find an important part of their identity and meaning in the work they undertake.

To nurture responsible professionals, the institutional professional order must itself be organized with integrity of purpose. When institutional conditions are good, the causality works both ways, as subjective responses help shape and are shaped by the shared forms of practice. If the institutional arrangements do not support the development of vocational integrity, a negative, downward spiral results, ending in promotion of an opportunism that undercuts vocational integrity, producing the cynicism and demoralization notable in troubled areas of the professional enterprise today.

In many areas of American life, arresting this downward cycle and supporting an upward spiral requires something akin to a gestalt switch. Like those drawings in which two objects can be seen depending upon which lines are perceived as the background and which the foreground, the continuous foregrounding of individual opportunity opened up by economic and technical advance reveals only half the picture. Even instrumental activity ceases to be productive when it consumes it's the necessary background of loyalties and social bonds, the institutional contexts that limit and direct various means toward their ends.

The Two Gestalts of Professional Ethics

Contemporary discussions of professional ethics are complicated today by an argument going on over how best to approach the subject. This argument surrounds two contending philosophical conceptions of the nature and subject matter of ethics: the ethics of principles or rules versus an ethic of virtue or character. These two ethical theories take their orientation from the two contending gestalts through which modern society is understood.

The first and culturally dominant gestalt is that of philosophic liberalism. Liberal ethics has a strong affinity for the familiar view of society as a realm in which individuals pursue their purposes either alone or in concert with others through activities instrumental in nature. It understands society as a field of opportunity for inventing one's own life, guided and constrained by institutional mechanisms governed by rules, among which ethical norms hold a prominent place. Accordingly, liberal ethics center attention on the value of autonomous decision making. By contrast, the focus of the second approach to ethics is upon character and mores, those shared habits of character upon which individual responsibility and virtue depend. According to the ethics of character, moral rules play at most a secondary role in ethical life; the real focus of ethics should be on delineation and development of good patterns of judgment and action.

The analytic ethics of principles derives its substance from the philosophic liberalism of Immanuel Kant and John Stuart Mill. For both Kant and Mill, ethics was properly based upon principles of reason that are universal in the sense that they apply to all moral agents. These principles were also universal in that they could be justified by each moral agent on the basis of independent reflection. Ethicists who follow Kant's "deontological" or duty ethics emphasize the rightness or wrongness of particular actions, asking whether an action could be made the general rule for all in a similar situation. Those who espouse Mill's revised utilitarian principle of universal benevolence stress the importance of consequences for judging the moral validity of a particular rule: Will adherence to it advance the welfare of persons generally? From these procedures come familiar ethical principles, such as do no harm, and tell the truth.

Despite differences in how they seek to justify their principles, adherents of rule ethics agree that the commanding focus of attention should be occupied by the autonomy of moral agents, the ability of moral agents to think and act for themselves. Choice, in the sense of autonomous decision, represents for both deontologists and utilitarians the crucial moral source. This liberal ethic, whose contemporary form is sometimes identified as analytic ethics because of its derivation from the midtwentieth-century philosophy of linguistic analysis, stresses the notion that ethics is above all about planning one's life well, which means making the right choices.

Within the ethics of principles, the applied ethicist is often cast in the role of coach. The ethicist's task is to give professionals a grasp of the whole theory of ethical norms and their justification, in order to make professionals more competent in applying these principles.[6] *Apply* is used in analytic ethics in a particular sense of "deduce." Analytic ethicists use ethical cases to develop students' ability to describe actions and situations so that they can be fitted into the general principles elucidated by theory. Of particular importance for this approach to ethics is the use of cases, known as quandaries, in which several principles seem to conflict. For example, how should a doctor respond to a heart patient whose delicate situation makes it likely that knowing the gravity of her situation will precipitate heart failure? Should avoiding harm take precedence over truth telling, or not? By using cases of increasing complexity and difficulty, the ethicist hopes to elicit from students a greater facility in applying ethical norms.

In their treatment of professional ethics, ethicists writing in this tradition emphasize the individual professional in relation to clients, with communities of practice and organization of professional work often reduced to a background. As, for example, physicians and their institutional contexts are undergoing the stresses of growing complexity and interdependence, it is not surprising that doctors would be unclear about who they are becoming and what they should do. It is just such situations that create the demand, as Robert Veatch writes, for "some ordering of that chaos we term a tradition, some systematic structuring of medical ethics."[7] The purpose of this ordering, according to Veatch, is that "physicians, other health professionals, government health planners, and consumers of medical care . . . can have some grasp of where they stand and why they may be in conflict with others with whom they interact."[8]

Veatch proceeds to argue the need for ethical theory in the special, technical sense. Such a theory aims to produce a set of universal principles "governing social relationships" in general. Only from the perspective of such a unified theory of ethical norms, which would be applicable to all social relationships, can we hope to deduce appropriate principles for guiding medical relationships. Medical ethics, in other words, would become a special case of the more general theory.[9]

Certainly part of the appeal of this conception of professional ethics derives from its use of a rhetoric borrowed from the natural sciences. A general theory is to provide the principles governing all phenomena within a specified domain, thus establishing the basis from which to deduce the special theories applicable to particular domains, such as medical relationships. The analytic split between theory and application also has obvious affinity with the familiar positivist conception of the relation of theory to technological application. In this approach to ethics, particular cases, ranging from confidentiality to abortion to euthanasia, can—so the theory goes—be resolved once they have been subsumed under appropriate rules and principles. It is a style of ethical thinking that resonates with the great concern in bureaucracies and organizational settings about rules of procedure. Like the scientist or the organizational theorist, the applied ethicist is wont to speak in terms of universal theory, thereby drawing a sharp contrast to the "chaos that we term a tradition."

The rival approach focuses not upon rules but on the notion of ethos, or character, understood as a cultivated disposition toward good values. Its starting point is the observation that every individual opportunity is also a situation of interdependence. The very existence of individual choices and rights depends upon the disposition of others to respect and facilitate individual projects. At the minimum, these dispositions to cooperate and reciprocate, to respect rights and adhere to rules, require cultivation and support. The virtue approach thereby emphasizes what the ethics of principles takes for granted: that the most precious of modern values, the sacredness of the individual life, requires conscious attention and collective support. That is, the liberal values of freedom and equality cannot be sustained without cultivating reciprocity, trust, loyalty, and public-spiritedness, the bedrock of civic culture.

This virtue ethics, or the ethics of character, is currently enjoying a revival, thanks in part to the problems and what is lacking within the ethics of principles. Deriving from the practical philosophy of Aristotle, whose conception of practical rationality we met in previous chapters, this tradition was a source upon which the pragmatists Dewey and Mead drew in developing their psychologies and moralities of engagement and responsibility. Here *theory* means something quite different from the set of formal principles prized by analytic ethics. Theory, for the virtue tradition, is not so much a body of general principles as a research for a connected view of things.

This kind of theory develops in close relation to concrete cases and experience. Its function is not primarily to reduce solutions to ethical problems or to prioritize rules in the event of a conflict among duties. Instead, theory should assist reflection and contribute to developing moral judgment.[10] Applying principles and rules requires judgment; as even Kant noted, the act of judgment whereby "the practitioner decides whether or not something is an instance of the rule" cannot always be guided by a rule, for that would create a regress of rules "that could go on indefinitely."[11]

For the virtue approach, professional moral discernment is thought to be learned and practiced together with the skills of a particular professional practice. The highest ethical achievement is understood as practical wisdom, the *phronesis* Aristotle wrote about, meaning the ability to act well in context. Practical wisdom, as we have seen in the discussion of practical rationality, demands the ability to balance the complexity of situations while maintaining consistent moral aims. An ethics of character finds its natural medium in the narrative of cases and analysis of the historical dynamics of institutional contexts. So, although the ethicist who works within this tradition is also likely to use cases to elicit ethical thinking, the aim is to develop habits of moral cultivation rather than to solve quandaries.[12] Thus one is more likely to emphasize examples and the contextual variations of life decisions than to seek the best single decision in terms of theoretical principles.[13]

Both of these approaches to ethics, the one foregrounding individual initiative and the other highlighting interdependence, hold up important aspects of social reality corresponding to two of the three key dimensions of professional life. The ethics of principles articulates the truth of liberalism, the ethical value of individual choice and dignity, which is crucial for professional life. The ethics of character, on the other hand, emphasizes the communitarian truth, that meaning arises through relationship, making individual liberty dependent upon responsibility defined through communal expectations.[14] This corresponds to the dependence of the professional's individual human capital upon the social capital of the professional community.

As in professional life, so in the broader society the tendency toward individual differentiation often pulls against the requirements of membership or integration into a social enterprise. Yet both tendencies need each other. They are parts of the complex whole of a viable society or meaningful human life. Finding the balance, however, and the institutional conditions that can sustain the balance, are not simple tasks. The necessity for the third civic perspective is precisely the need for trustworthy contexts that allow individuals and groups to better understand each other by seeing their own situations in light of the others' perspectives. Over time, and if sustained through conflict by a common loyalty to living together, these public dialogues enable a democratic society to generate consensus about ways of integrating individuals into meaningful relationships that enhance rather than erode personal freedom and dignity.

The persistence of conflict between principles and character ethics, like that between tendencies toward differentiation and integrating efforts (think of conflict over language in the public schools), illustrates the tensions generated within modern society. The conflict between opportunity and community, choice and commitment is painful and real. However, it is frequently a consequence of social transactions—either insufficiently coordinated or too skewed by unequal power to permit sustained development of mutual responsiveness among participants—that characterizes civic democracy. The resolution to the riddle of how to make interdependence work without subordinating individuals to the collective is in large part a practical matter rather than a theoretical one. The challenge is to develop publics comprehensive enough to recognize and restructure the often divided processes of interaction so that individuals can recognize themselves and their relationships as a matter for common action. Developing an ethic of responsiveness is an important step toward enabling citizens (professionals included) to better engage the actual conditions of their lives and more fully engage one another in a common effort. Such an effort at ethical reflection, in which deliberation is already an aspect of public action, takes account of the social grounding of the values prized by liberal theorists of autonomy as well as the vocational engagement central to character ethics.

The Psychology of Engagement and the Ethics of Vocation

Certain trends in psychological research permit useful insight into the conditions that can sustain vocational excellence while enhancing individual initiative. There is powerful evidence that creative engagement in activities, relationships, and social purposes is the key source of human identity and happiness. This is because attention, or the investment of psychic energy, is how human beings develop and structure their personalities. The self, that elusive Holy Grail of contemporary culture, is from this perspective a function of how human beings focus their energies. The self grows by cultivation, but self-cultivation demands, paradoxically, an outward focus. In taking care of our garden, our relationships, or our community, we are literally making ourselves. As Mihaly Csikszentmihalyi illuminated in his book *Flow*, learning to focus attention in action is the source of whatever purpose or harmony human beings achieve in life. It is the key to intrinsic motivation.[15] Engagement with the present moment in all its prosaic, unfinished character turns out to be the magic door to the richness of life.

Upon reflection this process of cultivating meaning by caring for the things, people, and practices of our world becomes less mysterious, if no less amazing. "When a person invests all her energy into an interaction," writes Csikszentmihalyi, "she in effect becomes part of a system of action greater than what the individual self had been before." This system of action is typically a structured social practice informed by implicit norms and values and containing a purpose that can be achieved poorly or well. Through learning to take part in the activities of the practice, the individual self "expands its boundaries and becomes more complex than it had been."[16] Indeed, Csikszentmihalyi notes that people so engaged typically report a series of experiences that he calls the "flow" response, the term that they themselves frequently use and that gave him the title of his book.

Engaged people report that, provided their capacities are such as to be challenged but not overwhelmed by the intrinsic demands of the activity, and if the activity is sufficiently structured to furnish clear clues to performance, their self-consciousness disappears, time seems to slow down, and "they realize that they are willing to do it for its own sake . . . even when difficult or dangerous."[17] The continued practice of any such patterned engagement does indeed cultivate certain dispositions. This can be readily observed among the practitioners of a sport, a craft, or a professional skill. Practice develops a disposition to engage in the activity for its own sake, indeed to want to continue the practice. The flow experienced in such engagement is the chief motivational force driving development of expertise.

This psychological process has ethical dimensions as well. Particularly striking is the development of the "autotelic" or self-directed personality. This kind of person in effect internalizes as a settled disposition the qualities of the engaged flow experience. Chief among them is the "nonself-conscious individualism" of autotelic people, who are "bent on doing their best in all circumstances, yet they are not concerned primarily with advancing their own interests." Or we might say that they have identified self-interest with those of the practice or community of practice with which they are engaged.

This makes possible a transcendence of the confines of one's self-image, allowing the person to grow into the larger dimensions of the art, skill, or form of life being engaged. Such self-forgetfulness is the premise of self-development. It is also the root of creativity, the capacity to respond resourcefully to the potentialities inherent in the task or situation at hand. Responsiveness, then, is presupposition of the practical wisdom engendered in the expert practitioner by attending to "the properties of the system, so that she can find a better way to adapt to a problematic situation."[18]

The development of these psychic dispositions or virtues of engagement is the essential stuff of life. By determining the limits of our concentration, success or failure in developing responsive attention determines our ability to find meaning and fulfillment not only in work but in life as a whole. But although each person is ultimately responsible for whether this psychic cultivation takes place or not, humans are intrinsically social beings. The willingness of adults to admit children into their practices of cultivation, the relative harmony or disorder of the family's practices of attention, indeed the disorder or harmony of the surrounding social institutions all powerfully affect each person's chances, and to some extent even his or her ability, to develop meaningful engagement with life. In this way, the psychology of attention must engage with ethical and social issues.

As we have seen, the self develops through cultivating attention, shaping it into intentional disposition. But as the pragmatist psychology of meaning insists, since intention is always socially formed it reaches its proper development in the stance of intelligent responsiveness. Meaning arises not simply out of activity but out of relationship with human others who already embody in their lives and characters the pattern of a meaningful life built up in community.[19] In this view, interdependence turns out once again to be basic to the human situation, even affecting the most intimate features of individual psychology. Character is therefore essentially a disposition to respond to the world in an appropriate way, determined by how the agent interprets the situations of life. That interpretation always develops through an ongoing conversation with significant others. This is to say that the formation of personality and personal decisions have strongly conversational features. A person acts within a stream of interaction. His or her own actions are thus always a response to the actions of others. Because those actions are interpreted as meaningful, as parts of a significant pattern in which the agent is engaged, even self-initiated actions are shaped in anticipation of how others will respond.

It is obvious that ideally all parties to such interaction benefit in the long run from a willingness to cooperate. This observation poses a kind of basic rationale for an ethic of cooperation and mutual trust. However, whether this is understood by a given group of individuals is heavily dependent upon the actual social conversation of which they have become part. So if the experiential context of life rewards cooperation and trust, the individual will come to accept these attitudes as normal and rational responses to reality. If, on the other hand, experience validates a social context of distrust and threat, defensive self-interest will come to seem to such people the obviously reasonable stance toward life. Such cycles of trust or distrust, rooted as they are in social relations and not just individual

psyches, tend to develop powerful momentum, making development of a social ethic of mutual trust and reciprocal aid the key
ingredient in a successful and just society—always a precarious
project.

In this expanded context, we can now state with greater clarity
the principal issue of professional ethics. Because the self is so thor-
oughly social, the important questions of life, including our most
intimate issues of identity, are questions of how best to respond to
the larger ongoing conversations that make up our social world.
Freedom means the capacity to grasp the dynamics of one's situation and respond fittingly and well. Discerning the right and fitting
response, however, is the subject of ethics as such. From this viewpoint, professional ethics emerges in important part as a struggle for
existential meaning in the public world of work.

This search for integrity, however, goes on among practices and
institutions sustaining purposes that make claims on us. The search
for personal meaning inevitably draws us into dialogue and
contention with others. It forces us to adopt a stance toward the
possibilities offered to us and those others by the social world in
which we find ourselves.[20] Professional ethics thus falls within the
subject matter of a "politics" in the classical sense of an inquiry into
the just and worthy forms of the common life. An adequate conception of professional ethics must therefore move from the
questions of individual meaning and vocation through consideration of the social and institutional contexts of these individual
decisions. It must include the rules that govern those contexts,
seeking to make sense of the dynamics of the social situations so as
to deliberate about how to respond to them.

Despite an institutional history that has made professionalism
all too likely to take a purely technical bent, insulated as much as
possible from the claims of larger purposes, American experience
also presents striking examples of professionally trained civic leaders. Examples of this type, which have played major roles at the
highest national level, help illustrate the complex nature of civic
judgment. They also reveal why the development of networks of

positive interdependence must be a preeminent goal of civic politics. George Catlett Marshall was such a figure, a citizen-soldier in the line of Washington. Chief of staff for the entire Allied war effort during World War II and then secretary of state under Harry Truman, Marshall is most famous for his plan for the postwar reconstruction of Europe, a cooperative arrangement between the United States and Western European nations that laid the basis for the European Economic Community.

Marshall was a professional soldier, educated at the Virginia Military Institute, and a decorated combat officer of World War I. But through appointments as military attaché to diplomatic missions, Marshall gained an extraordinary understanding of the interplay between politics, commerce, and military force in world affairs. According to Dean Acheson, who succeeded Marshall as secretary of state, Marshall grasped the hard fact that relations among states pose problems that are "not susceptible to an answer" but only to "an action which is less disagreeable than some other action when probably no action is altogether good."[21] Marshall, according to Acheson, excelled in the prudence of the Aristotelian *phronimos*, or person of practical wisdom. Marshall could take his bearings in a complex situation and engage with the dynamics of the situation through the medium of his specific knowledge, turning his province of expertise into a useful point of entry toward seeking a positive outcome to the larger processes in which he found himself engaged.

Those qualities came to the fore in Marshall's conception of the plan for postwar European reconstruction. In surveying the social and political problems confronting the Europeans after the war, Marshall was struck by the deleterious effects of a decade during which interconnections of all kinds, cultural and intellectual as well as commercial, had been broken by the fascist drive for national self-sufficiency. As Marshall saw it, the only lasting road to economic prosperity lay through building connections across the frontiers of the traumatized continent, thereby sowing the seeds of new forms of interdependence that could generate a new, more pacific European civilization.

It is equally noteworthy that in the speeches in which he set out the idea for the reconstruction plan, to groups at Princeton and Harvard, Marshall proclaimed the need for Americans—especially American leaders—to "renew in their minds" the "period of the Peloponnesian Wars and the Fall of Athens," a fall that Marshall stressed was due largely to the arrogance of Athenian power. Marshall intended this as a warning against the hubris of taking one's own interests—personal, group, or national—as identical to the good of others.[22] Although Marshall's warning went tragically unheeded at home, as the history of the cold war in general and Vietnam in particular would show his aim of building the basis for a stable Atlantic peace succeeded. However, his efforts to bring these matters before the American public, as well as his counsel about how to consider them, stand as a powerful reminder of the possibilities as well as the limitations of public judgment.

"Modernized Old Age" and the Question of the Good Life

Whether or not the public is ready for such complex deliberation, contemporary society is already facing challenges that call for the exercise of not only informed professional judgment but public judgment informed by professional expertise. To illustrate, consider the difficult case of health care in our increasingly aging society. Recently, Daniel Callahan has effectively shown the moral significance of health care for the most fundamental questions about our civilization, arguing that these are problems requiring collective deliberation and a response that is not only ethical but political in its classic sense. Callahan questions whether dominant liberal ethical and political understandings are adequate to guide American society as it confronts increasingly difficult choices concerning medicine and aging. We will follow Callahan's argument part of the way in order to suggest how such work may lead toward much-needed supplements for the inadequacies of the liberal model of professional ethics, and toward a wider understanding of ethics as integral to professionalism in a democracy.

In *Setting Limits*, Callahan describes how technological augmentation of the powers of medicine has encouraged an expansionary vision of life and health. This expansionary vision has strong affinities for the liberal vision of the good life. Its practical premise is the same set of institutional arrangements that undergird the growth of the consumer society; like that form of life, the expansionary vision of life and health meets any notion of limit as a threat to autonomy.

In what Callahan calls the "modernization of old age," the later years of life have come to be looked to as a time for individual self-realization beyond responsibilities to the younger generations or society at large. Long life and health are now normal expectations, not the results of good fortune. "Modernized" old age, writes Callahan, "is no longer a time of old-fashioned disengagement and preparation for death." Instead, it becomes a "continuingly active involvement in life and a persistent struggle against decay and demise."[23]

The consequences of this change are profound. "Medicine becomes not just a way of curing or controlling disease, but no less a way of trying to cure or control the problems of life."[24] Life itself seems to shake off its traditional limits and open up to an ever greater, if not indefinite, expansion of possibilities for individual self-actualization. Accordingly, modern medicine's promise of escape from suffering and early death is now so important that it is implicitly accepted, even demanded, as a right all Americans should be able to enjoy.

Unfortunately, if Callahan is correct, this whole vision is running up against major obstacles, the most intractable of which are of technological medicine's own making. The first problem is that the high-technology, acute-care medicine that has in many cases extended life is often also responsible for plunging the aged into years of prolonged suffering. Medicine has improved the situation of aging for many elderly people. This is one of its great achievements. On the other hand, medicine's single-minded concentration upon extending life at any cost often has, especially for those in their seventies and older, the debilitating effect of consigning the patient who becomes ill to a painful, dependent, and financially exhausting life that is a cruel caricature of the promise of "modern maturity."

The second problem Callahan identifies is economic, and ultimately social. Demographically, America is becoming an aging society. Both as a proportion of the population and in absolute numbers, far more people are reaching the biblical four score and ten and beyond. As the post–World War II baby boom ages, the nation's population will become progressively top-heavy as a larger and larger proportion of citizens reach old age. At the same time, the cost of aggressively extending life at its upper limits has grown enormously. Increasingly, Callahan argues, the United States will face conflict pitting the old against the young. How will the nation justify the commitment of an increasing proportion of national resources to people in the last years of life when it means that fewer resources can go to education or child care, and that the future must be mortgaged to prolong the lives of the aged with chronic illness?

The third problem is less obvious, but in the long run it is the most unsettling. Callahan claims that our technology-driven medicine, together with the individualistic understanding characteristic of a modernized old age, undercuts its own premises. A just allocation of resources among the generations requires some widely accepted and reasonably durable notion of human needs, especially the needs of the aging. But the development of new medical technologies makes it clear that what counts as need is really a conception of the good. Needs are artifacts of public deliberation, a "reflection of what we think people require for an acceptable life."[25]

A modernized conception of life sees endlessly open choices as the self-evident good, one that justifies itself by the experience of increasing happiness. Driven by technological progress, a society so guided leaves it up to individuals to work out the practical meaning of an acceptable life. This is something, however, that few people, whatever their age or situation, have sufficient resources to do by themselves. The liberal assumption that individuals are best left on their own in the realm of meaning, when acted upon, only adds to the difficulty of arriving at a consensus about what Calla-han calls "the wellsprings of moral obligation toward the elderly in general and our elderly parents in particular." This poverty of artic-ulable shared meaning hampers collective decision making and amounts to a serious "communal deficit."[26]

The lack of widely shared convictions about moral obligation afflicts the elderly in a special way. In a social climate suffused with the ethos of open choices uncomplicated by the complexities of solidarity, the point of their lives and their place and value in the world go unaffirmed. Often they are simply ignored. This too is exacerbated by the conjunction of technology-driven moderniza-tion with individualism. The elderly, particularly as their strength fails, must struggle to maintain their self-worth against a context that exalts only autonomy and expanding horizons.

Consequently, as society approximates in some areas of practice the open-horizons vision of liberal theory, the outcomes violate many of our considered moral convictions about mutual connec-tion and responsibility. Modern economics and technology have produced real gains in longevity and opportunity, which it is essen-tial to preserve. However, to be humanly meaningful, these gains must be connected to the sort of life-defining goods Callahan enu-merates. Among them he places the opportunity to do meaningful work, share human love, participate in the full range of family life, live in community, and pursue moral ideals. These goods are indeed open choices, but they are also more. They represent possibilities for a person's participation in social practices from which the indi-vidual can draw the capacity to form lasting character and sense of integrity. Only in this way, Callahan argues, is it possible to find life meaningful in itself.

The price of an unbalanced form of life in which the goods intrinsic to particular practical commitments are subordinated to continuing modernization is not borne only by the aged. Such a culture can make scant provision, Callahan notes, for coping with one of the consequences of the vast increase in the number of dependent elderly: they are increasingly being returned to their children for care. The results are often oppressive, and "our secular morality (though not perhaps our religious traditions) provides few resources for living lives of unchosen obligations."[27] The point is not to rationalize an enforced mobilization of the younger to sustain elders to a degree the collective provision cannot or will not support. Rather, it is to suggest how morally bankrupt our culture of modernized old age is when confronted with the problem of learning to live well in the face of limitation.

The conclusion Callahan draws is that if we are to deal in a just and humane way with the changing national needs for medical care, we must undertake a "major effort to reorient medicine away from its captivity by the modernizing, technology-driven, borderless 'medical need' model of care for the aged." Life-extending treatment must be given in light of a "natural life span," the borders of which vary with the individual, so that the key policy goal becomes a fuller life span rather than a longer one where the latter is bought at the price of chronic illness, suffering, and burden on others. This effort requires a "parallel reorientation of the general public," who, like physicians, will be reluctant to give up their old "captivity" to the mirage of ever-expanding horizons promised by technological medicine.[28] For the sake of a life worth living, we must freely embrace limitation.

The really difficult conclusion is that such a massive policy change "can be morally acceptable only within a context that accords meaning and significance to the lives of the individual aged and recognizes the positive virtues of the passing of the generations."[29] This is to say that a morally tolerable system for providing health care can take root only if it functions within, and lives symbiotically with, a vital culture of civic values. Achieving this reorientation of policy, Callahan concedes, requires a long process of public debate and persuasion. We may note that it also demands new emphases in educating professionals to prepare them to sustain the sort of connections and continuous dialogue that this ongoing process requires.

The process in turn requires institutional arrangements that open up space for public discussion about the ends medicine should serve and its means. For such discussion to take place, neither technological necessity nor economic pressures can be allowed to work automatically. To make such dialogue fruitful, a medical ethic concerned with more than autonomy and open choices, valuable as they are, is clearly a necessity. Physicians must be especially attentive to restoring health and alleviating human suffering yet also aware that these goods are part of a large fabric of meaning to which their work and institutions contribute. Medical problems, such as continuation of life when the biological gains can only be small and the quality of life improved even less, are also moral problems and have to be defined as such. The aim of cure at all costs must be reintegrated within the more encompassing goals of compassion and care for the aging person's life in its integrity.

The complicated situation of aging in American society is a microcosm of the many webs of interdependence that the developing technology and economy weave, often over the heads of participants. This complexity, unless it is mastered cognitively and given moral meaning through reshaping our institutions, is likely to produce a host of unintended miseries, such as those ironically generated by increasing longevity when it is accompanied by chronic illness. Professionals are often those most strategically placed to begin focusing public attention on these issues. They are also often the groups first charged with dealing with them. The moral integrity and civic capacities of professional groups is accordingly a significant public concern.

The question becomes, Can professionals in their individual and collective lives learn to think and act cooperatively with us, as both experts and citizens?[30] These are the defining questions for a professional ethics of responsibility appropriate to our times. Health care is exemplary of the larger tasks of the professional enterprise: the very economic and technological forces that induce self-seeking professional behavior are also generating problems that reveal more clearly than ever before the profoundly civic nature of the professional enterprise. The problems of health care have their analogies in education, the law, journalism, and other professional fields. Just as individual professionals must be in some degree moral philosophers, so professionals in their organizational lives must be active citizens, committed to working out a common good as new problems and possibilities arise.

Renewing the Moral Sources of Civic Professionalism

Whether professionals play their civic roles well or badly has, as we have seen, a great influence on the welfare of all members of society. But under contemporary conditions, the civic role of professionals increasingly means learning to bring their particular expertise into a larger, more complex deliberation about ends as well as means. The challenges confronting us around modern health care and old age exemplify a larger fact. Most of the really critical issues—equality for women and minorities, equity and stability in the global economy, the viability of families and communities, environmental protection—cannot be addressed without drawing upon professional expertise. On the other hand, the ability of professional groups to contribute to resolving these problems is, as we have seen, uneven. Like many of the health care providers and policy makers encountered by Callahan and Prothrow-Stith, or the educators described by Bok, other professionals also lack an understanding expansive enough to be useful in crucial public deliberations.

This is why the furtherance of civic orientation among professionals is becoming increasingly significant. The value of the current interest in professional ethics, then, is that it constitutes an opening on the agendas of professional reform and public discussion for the concerns of civic professionalism. To strengthen civic tendencies in the professions, it is important to work toward a civic public philosophy that can affirm professional concerns while giving them a larger mission. At the same time, it is necessary to press on with constructing actual social contexts in which professional groups can learn and practice the attitudes of a responsible elite, as described by John Judis.[31] But professional communities need to be in reciprocal dialogue with the publics they serve. They have to recharter their professional social contract. This is a task that cannot succeed without effective enfranchisement of a more diverse and active public of citizens.

Fortunately, there are several moral sources in contemporary American culture that can contribute to an ethos of vocational responsibility. The liberal ideals of free choice and personal dignity remain central to any conceivable good society, but their proponents benefit along with everyone else once they recognize that these ideals can only be realized through cultivation of social and personal virtues, as some liberal thinkers have come to accept.[32] But the adherents of virtue ethics can also benefit from serious engagement with the importance to their own purposes of those liberal values of self-direction and responsibility for oneself.

To these should be added the important contributions of religious ideas, especially of biblical covenant, that have been so important in American life. In covenantal morality, obligations arise for professionals from the relationships that make their practice possible, connections with the past as well as to colleagues, clients, and institutions. In this view, these benefits demand in return a loyalty on the part of recipients to handing on these goods to others.[33]

Feminism and environmentalism, among other contemporary social movements, articulate important professional values in ways that have become compelling to many. Several strands of feminist thinking emphasize the importance of struggling to balance the sometimes conflicting values of personal exploration and differentiation with the desire for connectedness and mutual loyalty.[34] Within the environmental movement, some thinkers are drawing on theories developed in modern biological research that see all ecosystems as dependent upon an evolving balance or synthesis between the two polar processes of differentiation and integration. The ecological perspective presents a powerful rationale for understanding the chief ethical imperative as devising patterns of living that can support increasingly individuated yet interrelated growth.

Articulating moral possibilities is vital for solving the problems of professional life. It is equally true, however, that articulation of meaning is likely to remain confined to the realm of ideas unless it is accompanied by development of the social bases that render ethical ideals plausible and practicable. For civic professionalism those social bases are the educational system, including its linkages with the occupational domain, and also the networks of social capital among organizations that make a particular place or sector of society able to act in concert to address its needs.

At the level of professional groups and the major organizations that train or employ professionals, there is need for leaders who understand these frequently delicate patterns of relationship on which practical intelligence and civic cooperation depend. At the other end of society, among the large populations of alienated and marginalized citizens, there is also serious need for leaders who can weave networks of mutual recognition to enable the powerless to command respect and so take effective part in democratic life.

This neglected civic role has been taken up by one national organization, the Industrial Areas Foundation. The IAF is actually a kind of support organization of professional community organizers, founded in the 1940s by Saul Alinsky. Today's IAF works toward an explicitly civic vision of democratic empowerment that, starting with the congregations of local religious organizations, works to build larger relationships over time. The aim, in the words of one organizer, the Rev. Leo Penta, a Roman Catholic priest, is to establish "islands of political community, spaces of action and freedom in the sea of bureaucrats, political image-mongers, and atomized consumers."[35]

By concentrating on developing politically effective networks, rooted in local religious loyalties, the politics of the IAF complements the aims of civic professionals in other areas. Penta is correct, even if overstating the case, that all such efforts, no matter how important for the people involved, will remain mere islands of citizenship in a hostile or indifferent sea so long as they remain alone. Like the other examples of dedicated civic professionals encountered earlier, the islands of public life created by these efforts are the basis for a larger archipelago of great potential value.

For all who come to take part in their life, these contexts afford practical experience and training in the ethical capacities necessary for resolving the harmful exclusions and painful dichotomies that beset contemporary society. Where it successfully takes hold, civic professionalism begins to make integrity a practical rather than utopian possibility for living.

Conclusion

Experts and Citizens

In the American imagination, integrity is closely associated with the world of professional life. The heroic physician, the fighting lawyer, the dedicated teacher are staples of popular culture, along with the wise judge, the healing nurse, and the crusading journalist. These figures are typically portrayed as moral exemplars whose personal dedication visibly strengthens the larger fabric of the community. Yet today there is also a widespread perception that professional integrity is breaking down or is seriously at risk of doing so. This anxiety suggests that many people feel socially vulnerable, personally threatened by loss of professional integrity. It testifies to the importance of professional functions in modern society, even when professionals hold little power over others.

Earlier chapters have unraveled this apparent contradiction by developing a critique of professionalism linking its moral dimensions to history and social situation. By viewing professionalism as an evolving social enterprise, the critique was able to highlight the complex interconnection that needs to exist between personal integration and vocational performance in modern society, for integrity is a particularly modern concern. Modern societies hold out to individuals many vocational choices and opportunities for personal satisfaction. Traditional ties and moral constraints have loosened, yet individual lives are ever more intricately tied into unseen networks of interdependence, increasing the need for forethought and large-scale cooperation. This conjunction of developments promotes both the exhilaration of personal freedom and an increasing burden of individual responsibility. Coherence and significance in modern life are of necessity highly personal achievements and yet deeply dependent upon social relationships.

Integrity mediates these tensions. It implies that one is honest and fair, that one is at home with oneself in one's desires and decisions. Integrity thus strengthens individuality by raising the quality of the individual's life beyond mere pursuit of satisfaction, giving a distinctive style to one's words and acts. But integrity also has a social dimension. It acquires content only through relationships, by caring for people and purposes and sustaining commitments. This is why integrity is so naturally bound up with the commitments and relationships involved in work and calling.

Integrity is never a given, but always a quest that must be renewed and reshaped over time. It demands considerable individual self-awareness and self-command. Yet it also depends for its realization upon the availability of actual social possibilities, since some situations clearly make it more likely that an individual can achieve integrity than others. It is therefore significant that the moral imagination so readily reaches toward professionals to exemplify integrity. In fact, the qualities of integrity and the demands of professional life are in this way remarkably congruent. Integrity of vocation demands a balanced combination of individual autonomy with integration into shared purposes. Individual talent needs to blend with the best common standards of performance; the individual must exercise personal judgment as to responsible application of these communal standards.

The complex requirements of integrity define two of the basic dimensions of professional life. Professional occupations create recognized opportunities for individuals to make something of their talents and capacities. On the other hand, this is possible only through personal commitment to the disciplines of a community of practice. At its best, professional life enables individual freedom to find fulfillment as it advances the well-being of the larger society. The person who succeeds in mastering the standards and aims of a professional discipline achieves a substantial focus for living, a purpose that relates the individual to others and the world in a significant way. As the novice learns the practices and values of a professional community through learning to trust mentor figures, the developing professional is also coming to view self and world as that community does.

Institutions are necessary to support and stabilize these achievements. Organized professional communities uphold the integrity of particular purposes, as with the values of care for health or education or technical efficiency. At the same time, however, professional organizations are interests among other interests in civil society. How they see themselves and the world is influenced not only by their internal concerns but by the kind of interaction they have with the other members of society. The quality of this interaction in turn depends heavily upon the extent to which qualities of civic cooperation prevail in the larger social environment.

This introduces an essential civic dimension to professional life. Where the level of trust, self-restraint, and degree of cooperation is high, where social interaction includes most parts of that environment on an equitable footing and is perceived as mutually beneficial, professional organizations—and individual practitioners—are more likely to behave as good citizens, taking responsible (sometimes leadership) roles in the society's life. In return the professions maintain good will, public support, and often prestige. In such circumstances, individual professionals are likely to find their efforts at integrity recognized and rewarded. These are the conditions of positive interdependence. Conversely, however, where civic cooperation is weak or sporadic, mediation between individual goals and social need is likely to break down, releasing aggressive efforts to escape social responsibility, with corrosive effects upon democratic life. A direct consequence is the worsening of possibilities for integrity in professional life. Many of the disagreeable aspects of contemporary professional activity have their root causes in this experience of negative interdependence.

From this perspective, then, the professional enterprise is an important modern civic institution. The professions have pioneered and continue to model a socially attuned way to organize work, thereby amounting to a potential democratic resource through bringing the concerns of citizenship into a variety of specialized occupations. The integrity of professional life—indeed, its whole future—is bound up in the health of civic culture in the United States. This is why discussion of professionalism is necessarily not only ethical but political. It concerns the shape of the civil society that is the basis of democracy.

In modern civil society, no group or institution enjoys permanently guaranteed status. Social relations remain open and fluid. Professions compete with other professions and other organizations, sometimes to the benefit of society and sometimes not. But what matters decisively is the prevailing climate of social interaction as a whole. In this important sense, the whole is always more than the sum of its parts. The peculiar strengths of strong civic cultures in the economic as well as social dimension derive from just this holistic effect of widespread and pervasive patterns of public cooperation. By many accounts, the United States has been suffering from a pervasive decline of social trust and a fraying of civic bonds, weakening the capacity for cooperative organization on which a vital democracy depends. This situation gives urgency and value to the renewal of the civic orientation of professionalism and its effective institutionalization. The reforms and experiments discussed in previous chapters suggest the directions in which such an approach might lead. It amounts to a new phase in the history of professionalism.

This new professional era extends into the developing global culture what Harold Perkin, in *The Rise of Professional Society*,[1] called the "historic task" of professionalism. This is "to moralize a potentially amoral competition and to set limits to the exploitation of workers, victims of adulteration and pollution in all classes, and of society at large by fraud, embezzlement, and tax evasion."[2] Perkin is describing Britain, but the attitude he presents fits well the civic purposes we have identified at the core of the professional enterprise in the United States.

In Britain today, as Perkin portrays his society, competing groups of professionals, differently linked to the corporations, government, or independent sector organizations, wrangle over the utility of economic regulation and the welfare state versus a resurrected faith in laissez-faire. But, as Perkin points out, these ideological battles presuppose the outmoded dichotomy, common to the nineteenth-century economics of both Ricardo and Marx, that industry is productive while services are parasitic. The arrival of high-technology industry and the belated discovery of human capital make that whole argument—which since the 1970s has come once again to dominate political debate—hopelessly obsolete. Or, as Perkin tellingly comments about the facile claim that public sector services are parasitic upon private sector productivity: "It is just as valid to claim that the public sector produces and maintains, through the education and health services, most of the skills on which the private sector depends." Thus, commenting on British (or American) political debate, Perkin concludes that "in a complex interdependent society such claims and counterclaims are as naïve and unhelpful as the pot calling the kettle black."[3]

It was the economic historian and theorist of the British Labor Party, R. H. Tawney, who classically linked professionalism with social function and the common good. By doing so, Tawney proposed a vision of how to humanize and more fully democratize the twentieth-century society of large-scale industry. In *The Acquisitive Society*,[4] Tawney defined a profession as "a trade which is organized, incompletely, no doubt, but genuinely, for the performance of function . . . an activity which embodies and expresses the idea of social purpose." Not abstract credentials but demonstrated expertise and effective collective responsibility were his criteria for a profession. But these criteria hung on the practical embodiment of recognized social purposes. Tawney thought the idea sounded strange because, during the era of laissez-faire enterprise in Britain, the notion of social purpose receded into a vestigial existence in certain realms of state and church.

Tawney argued that a more interdependent and complex society cannot do without recognition of common purposes and the professional solidarities that derive from recognition. "A wise system of administration," he wrote in implicit refutation of the disciples of Taylor, "would recognize that professional solidarity can do much of its work for it more effectively than it can do for itself, because the spirit of his profession is part of the individual and not a force outside him." Indeed, continued Tawney, it is only by fully developing professionalism in all occupations that "what is mechanical and obstructive in bureaucracy can be averted."[5] If Tawney's observation proved prescient for industrial bureaucracies, though largely unheeded, how much more apt is it for building the flexible, service-intensive and publicly responsive organizations needed for the next phase of modern civilization? In an age of renewed economic laissez-faire, as we have seen, the professional commitment to prudence and integrity of function becomes an even more conspicuously necessary good as it comes to appear scarce.

Writing at the same period as Tawney though in the United States, Alfred North Whitehead offered what has become a kind of leitmotif for the future now upon us. "The fixed person for fixed duties," wrote Whitehead in *Science and the Modern World*,[6] "who in older societies was such a godsend, in the future will be a public danger." But it is not often noticed that Whitehead went on to point out that one of modern philosophy's weaknesses was its failure to grasp that the great expansion of possibilities enjoyed by the fortunate modern individual was not the cause but the emergent effect of a more interdependent and cooperative social order. That is, a good life under the more flexible conditions of the emerging economy requires a deeper, and more conscious, mutual commitment between individuals and social institutions. The solidarity this demands cannot be expected to spring from the spark of natural sympathy alone. It must be cultivated and regularly replenished through the connectedness displayed and strengthened in social cooperation. Few kinds of work would seem better fitted to these needs of the new era than professions with a civic orientation.

By the emphasis upon the quality of its product or service, and upon the value of doing that work within a community committed to the enhancement of public values, professionalism speaks to one of the great needs of our time. By undertaking to learn from practice and to improve performance, active professional communities are a reminder of how application of knowledge and pursuit of learning can benefit modern life. However, today's professions face not only changing domains of knowledge but shifting fields of practice within a dynamic and often confusing society. Therefore, the horizons of the professions need to be broad. Practitioners must be able to think critically about their own situation and that of their field in relation to its defining purposes. The institutions of professional education must model this and also challenge their students to genuine involvement as experts and citizens alike.

Aspiring professionals need serious training in how to integrate a critical yet engaged standpoint into the guild's particular sense of knowledge, craft, and attitude. To preserve the professional social contract, we need to bring the perspective of the aware and critical citizen into formation of the members of the community of practitioners. The opposing pulls of specialized expertise and the broad sympathies needed for active citizenship define this crucial aspect of learning. Genuine education presents and invites participation in intellectual and moral activities so that students can progress, metaphorically if not always literally, from apprentice to fully contributing member of a specific occupation as well as the larger civic community. This is a burden professional schools cannot be expected to shoulder alone. But it is an opportunity to strengthen the commitment of both academics and practitioners in a joint effort to renew professional education throughout the professional career.

Through its inherent logic, civic professionalism proposes an ideal of self that complements today's social imperative to achieve a positive outcome to interdependence. The ideal corresponds in one important way to the aspirations of the pervasive contemporary search for self-actualization and takes it beyond itself. Positive interdependence demands of the individual a high degree of self-awareness and a major effort to developing one's powers. But it then demands more. The goal of self-actualization itself must be transcended (or perhaps better, reoriented) by integrating individual goals with those of the larger community. The logical fulfillment of this process is a kind of character for whom what happens to these larger commitments is as important as what happens to the self, or more so.

This, of course, is the outline of integrity in professional life. According to some psychologists, it is also a description of a meaningful and happy life. This is only to repeat in contemporary idiom a much more ancient view: that what makes one free and renders life worth living is finally neither satisfying one's desires nor accomplishing one's purposes, valuable as these are, but instead learning to act with the good of the whole in view, building life act by act, happy if each deed, as far as circumstances allow, contributes to the general welfare. Anyone who has been stirred and inspired by a committed teacher, an attentive health care provider, a dedicated pastor or rabbi; anyone who has experienced a well-functioning business firm or public agency, school or cultural institution has glimpsed the enlivening possibilities inherent in communities of professional purpose. There, already manifest, is the promise of professional life.

Notes

Introduction

1. The agreement, however, is at a general level. As will become clearer, students of the professions disagree about the significance for professional work of these characterizations of the "knowledge" and "postindustrial" economy. For some pioneering formulations of the idea, see John Kenneth Galbraith, *The New Industrial State* (Boston: Houghton-Mifflin, 1967) and Daniel Bell, *The Coming of Post-Industrial Society* (New York: Basic Books, 1973).

2. The term *knowledge worker* comes from Peter Drucker's *Post-Capitalist Society* (New York: HarperBusiness, 1993). The notion of the "symbolic analyst" was introduced by Robert B. Reich in *The Work of Nations: Preparing Ourselves for Twenty-First Century Capitalism* (New York: Basic Books, 1991), and the idea of the emerging "creative class" is derived from Richard Florida's *The Rise of the Creative Class: And How It's Transforming Work, Leisure, Community and Everyday Life* (New York: Basic Books, 2002).

3. This is the view popularized and given celebrity status by Bill Gates in *The Road from Here* (New York: Viking Press, 1995).

4. Bruce A. Kimball has traced the genealogy of this idea through a succession of "preeminent vocations"—the minister, the lawyer, the professor, and the physician—across American history. See his *"True Professional Ideal" in America: A History* (Cambridge, Mass.: Blackwell, 1992).

5. This is a prominent theme in Harold Perkin's study of professions in a cross-national context. See his *Third Revolution:*

Professional Elites in the Modern World (London and New York: Routledge, 1996). The idea goes back at least to Bell (1973).

6. See Robert C. Putnam, *Bowling Alone: The Collapse and Revival of American Community* (New York: Simon and Schuster, 2000). On the relation of the professions' civic claims to these trends, see Steven Brint and Charles S. Levy, "Professions and Civic Engagement: Trends in Rhetoric and Practice, 1875–1995," in Theda Skocpol and Morris P. Fiorina (eds.), *Civic Engagement in American Democracy* (Washington, D.C.: Brookings Institution, 1999).

7. For attempts to understand what has happened to law, see Anthony Kronman, *The Lost Lawyer: Failing Ideals of the Legal Profession* (Cambridge Mass.: Harvard University Press, 1993); and Deborah L. Rhode, *In the Interests of Justice: Reforming the Legal Profession* (New York: Oxford University Press, 2000).

8. Derek C. Bok, *The Cost of Talent: How Executives and Professionals Are Paid and How It Affects America* (New York: Free Press, 1993), pp. 57–58.

9. For several assessments, see Kenneth M. Ludmerer, M.D., *Time to Heal: American Medical Education from the Turn of the Century to the Era of Managed Care* (New York: Oxford University Press, 1999); Elliott A. Krause, *Death of the Guilds: Professions, States, and the Advance of Capitalism, 1930 to the Present* (New Haven, Conn.: Yale University Press, 1996); and Paul Starr's prescient analysis in *The Social Transformation of American Medicine* (New York: Basic Books, 1982).

10. Robert B. Reich, *The Future of Success: Working and Living in the New Economy* (New York: Random House, 2000). For another elaboration, see Paul Osterman, *Securing Prosperity: The American Labor Market, How It Has Changed and What to Do About It* (Princeton, N.J.: Princeton University Press, 1999, esp. pp. 20–40).

11. See Karl Polanyi, *The Great Transformation: The Political and Economic Origins of Our Time* (Boston: Beacon Press, 1967 [1944]), esp. pp. 3–20, 151–162.

12. Reich (2000), pp. 88–107.

13. See Joseph Schumpeter, *Capitalism, Socialism, and Democracy* (New York: HarperCollins, 1950 [1942]), pp. 81–86.
14. Bok (1993), pp. 65–89.
15. Steven Brint, *In an Age of Experts: The Changing Role of Professionals in Politics and Public Life* (Princeton, N.J.: Princeton University Press, 1994), pp. 202–209.
16. I have addressed these two aspects of the situation of medicine in "What Is Left of Professionalism After Managed Care?" *Hastings Center Report*, 1999, 29(2), 7–13.
17. In addition to the analyses of Derek Bok and Steven Brint already mentioned, see political scientist Andrew Hacker's assessment of these developments in *Money: Who Has How Much and Why* (New York: Scribner, 1997).
18. Terrence C. Halliday, "Knowledge Mandates: Collective Influence by Scientific, Normative, and Syncretic Professions," *British Journal of Sociology*, 1985, 36(3), 421–447.
19. Halliday (1985), pp. 423–431.
20. Steven Brint, "Knowledge Society and the Professions: Professionals and the 'Knowledge Economy': Rethinking the Theory of Postindustrial Society," *Current Sociology*, 2001, 49(4), 101–132, quote from p. 126.
21. Eliot Freidson, *Professionalism: The Third Logic* (Chicago: University of Chicago Press, 2001).
22. Freidson presents extensive documentation of these effects. See "The Centrality of Professionalism to Health Care," in his *Professionalism Reborn: Theory, Prophecy, and Policy* (Chicago: University of Chicago Press, 1994), pp. 184–198.
23. Freidson (1994), p. 210.
24. Howard Gardner, Mihali Csikszentmihalyi, and William Damon, *Good Work: When Excellence and Ethics Meet* (New York: Basic Books, 2001).
25. John W. Gardner argued for the creative potential of committed professional work in his classic account *Excellence: Can We Be Equal and Excellent Too?* rev. ed. (New York: Norton, 1995 [1961]).

26. Kimball (1992).
27. Kimball (1992), pp. 301–303.
28. For a schematic representation, see Kimball's summary and diagram (1992), p. 310.
29. As in the theory of Milton Friedman, a leading figure in the influential "Chicago School" of free market economics. See his *Capitalism and Freedom* (Chicago: University of Chicago Press, 1982 [1962]).
30. Reich (2000), p. 5.
31. Reich (2000), p. 6.
32. Lawrence Haworth, *Decadence and Objectivity* (Toronto: University of Toronto Press, 1977), p. 58.
33. Haworth (1977), pp. 54, 96, 100.
34. Haworth (1977), p. 25.
35. Haworth (1977), pp. 86 and 89.
36. Sheldon Rothblatt, "How 'Professional' Are the Professions? A Review Article," *Comparative Studies in Society and History,* 1995, *37*(1), 194–204.
37. Freidson (1994), p. 69.
38. Michael Burrage, "From Practice to School-Based Professional Education: Patterns of Conflict and Accommodation in England, France, and the United States," in Sheldon Rothblatt and Bjorn Wittrock (eds.), *The European and American University Since 1800: Historical and Sociological Essays* (Cambridge and London: Cambridge University Press, 1993), pp. 142–190.
39. Lee S. Shulman has developed these aspects or "commonplaces" of the professions, along with some implications for professional education, in "Theory, Practice, and the Education of Professionals," *Elementary School Journal,* 1998, *98*(5), 511–526.
40. Gardner, Csikszentmihalyi, and Damon (2001), p. 7.

Chapter One

1. For example, see Peter M. Blau and Otis Dudley Duncan, *The American Occupational Structure* (Hoboken, N.J.: Wiley, 1976).

2. See Harold Perkin, *The Rise of Professional Society: England Since 1880* (New York: Routledge, 1989).

3. The importance of professionals and professionalism in modern society, especially the United States, was a major theme in the sociology of Talcott Parsons, so influential at mid-century. See his *Essays in Sociological Theory* (New York: Free Press, 1954). For a sense of the scope of the issue and its complexities, see Bell (1973), an analysis updated in his "World and the United States in 2013," *Daedalus*, 1987, *116*(3). See also Magali Sarfatti Larson, *The Rise of Professionalism: A Sociological Analysis* (Berkeley and Los Angeles: University of California Press, 1977) and the discussion by Eliot Freidson in *Professional Powers: A Study in the Institutionalization of Formal Knowledge* (Chicago: University of Chicago Press, 1986), esp. pp. 48–58.

4. "The Quest for Doctors: Hospitals in a Quandary," by Lisa Belkin, *New York Times*, Dec. 16, 1991, p. A1.

5. See Burton Bledstein, *The Culture of Professionalism: The Middle Class and the Development of Higher Education in America* (New York: Norton, 1976).

6. Gardner, Csikszentmihalyi, and Damon (2001), p. 5.

7. Brint (1994).

8. Joseph Stiglitz, "The Roaring Nineties," *Atlantic Monthly*, Oct. 2002, pp. 75–89.

9. George May, quoted in Mike Brewster, *Unaccountable: How the Accounting Profession Forfeited a Public Trust* (Hoboken, N.J.: Wiley, 2003), p. 61.

10. This is a major theme of Elliott A. Krause (1996).

11. This is the emphasis in Magali Sarfatti Larson's *Rise of Professionalism: A Sociological Analysis* (1977).

12. Randall Collins, *The Credential Society: A Historical Sociology of Education and Stratification* (New York: Academic Press, 1979).

13. Brint (1994).

14. Kimball (1992).

15. See Samuel Haber, *The Quest for Authority and Honor in the American Professions: 1750–1900* (Chicago: University of Chicago Press, 1991).
16. Collins (1979), p. 58.
17. The work of Talcott Parsons articulated this view, as did in some ways that of Robert K. Merton and Everett Hughes. See Parsons, "The Professions and Social Structure," *Social Forces,* 1939, *17*(4), 457–467; Robert K. Merton, *Some Thoughts on the Professions in American Society* (Brown University Papers, no. 37, Providence, R.I.: Brown University, 1960); C. Everett Hughes, *Men and Their Work* (New York: Free Press, 1958). Some contemporary thinkers have endorsed a similar viewpoint; for example, Freidson (2001) and Perkin, *The Third Revolution* (1996).
18. Collins is typical of this approach. See also Andrew Abbott, *The System of Professions: An Essay on the Division of Expert Labor* (Chicago: University of Chicago Press, 1988); and Thomas L. Haskell (ed.), *The Authority of Experts: Studies in History and Theory* (Bloomington: Indiana University Press, 1984).
19. This is one of the major claims put forward by Eliot Freidson in *The Third Logic* and his other work.
20. Starr (1982).
21. Ludmerer (1999).
22. Starr (1982).
23. Starr (1982), p. 380.
24. Ludmerer (1999), p. 379.
25. Krause (1996), pp. 36–49.
26. Perkin, *Rise of Professional Society* (1989).
27. This is the thesis of Perkin (1989).
28. Brint and Levy (1999), p. 200.
29. Brint (1994), pp. 203–209.
30. Sir Donald Irvine, "The New Professionalism," *Lancet,* 1999, *353*, pp. 1174–1177. See also his *Doctor's Tale: Professionalism and Public Trust* (Abingdon, UK: Radcliffe Medical Press, 2003).

31. Irvine (2003), p. 205.
32. "Medical Professionalism in the New Millennium: A Physician Charter," *Annals of Internal Medicine*, 2002, *136*(3), 243–246.
33. Rhode (2000), p. 213.
34. Rhode (2000), p. 208.

Chapter Two

1. This point is made by Eliot Freidson in *Professional Powers* (1986), pp. 32–35.
2. See, for example, E. Digby Baltzell, *Puritan Boston and Quaker Philadelphia: Two Protestant Ethics and the Spirit of Class Authority and Leadership* (New York: Free Press, 1979), esp. pp. 57–106.
3. Donald Scott, *From Office to Profession: The New England Ministry, 1750–1850* (Philadelphia: University of Pennsylvania Press, 1978), p. 148.
4. The picture of American development presented in this chapter is indebted to the work of Robert H. Wiebe. See *The Segmented Society: An Introduction to the Meaning of America* (New York: Oxford University Press, 1975), and *The Opening of American Society: From the Adoption of the Constitution to the Eve of Disunion* (New York: Knopf, 1984).
5. See the discussion of these developments in Gordon S. Wood, *The Radicalism of the American Revolution* (New York: Knopf, 1992), esp. pp. 189–225.
6. Thomas Bender has called these free professionals of the early republic "civic professionals" to contrast them with the specialized "disciplinary professionals" of the twentieth century. See his "Cultures of Intellectual Life: The City and the Professions," in John Higham and Paul K. Conkin, eds., *New Directions in American Intellectual History* (Baltimore: Johns Hopkins University Press, 1979), pp. 181–195; also "The Erosion of Public Culture: Cities, Discourses, and Professional Disciplines," in Thomas L. Haskell, ed., *The Authority of Experts: Issues in History and Theory* (Bloomington: University

of Indiana Press, 1984), pp. 84–106. See also Peter Dobkin Hall, *The Organization of American Culture, 1700–1900: Private Institutions, Elites, and the Origins of National Identity* (New York: New York University Press, 1982).

7. See Alexis de Tocqueville, *Democracy in America*, J. P. Meyer, ed. (Garden City, N.Y.: Doubleday, 1969 [1835]), pp. 264–267.

8. Quoted in William G. McLoughlin, *Revivals, Awakenings, and Reform: An Essay on Religion and Social Change in America, 1607–1977* (Chicago: University of Chicago Press, 1978), p. 139.

9. Quoted in Marvin Meyer, *The Jacksonian Persuasion: Politics and Belief* (Palo Alto, Calif.: Stanford University Press, 1957), p. 21. See also Robert H. Wiebe, *The Opening of American Society* (1984), esp. pp. 234–252.

10. The independent citizen as character ideal is discussed in Robert N. Bellah, Richard Madsen, William M. Sullivan, Ann Swidler, and Steven M. Tipton, *Habits of the Heart: Individualism and Commitment in American Life* (Berkeley: University of California Press, 1985), pp. 35–41.

11. Quoted in Meyer (1957), pp. 281–282.

12. See "Author's Introduction," de Tocqueville (1969 [1835]), pp. 9–20.

13. de Tocqueville (1969 [1835]), II, part 2, chapter 5, pp. 525–527.

14. de Tocqueville (1969 [1835]), II, part 1, chapter 11, p. 465.

15. de Tocqueville (1969 [1835]), p. 465.

16. de Tocqueville (1969 [1835]), pp. 466 and 468.

17. William Appleman Williams, *The Contours of American History* (New York: Norton, 1966), p. 351.

18. See also Louis Galambos and Joseph Pratt, *The Rise of the Corporate Commonwealth: United States Business and Public Policy in the 20th Century* (New York: Basic Books, 1988). The notion of "market shelter" is a major organizing concept in Larson's *Rise of Professionalism* (1977).

19. Burton Bledstein has traced the development of these possibilities in post–Civil War America in *The Culture of Professionalism* (1976).

20. Robert H. Wiebe, *The Search for Order: 1870–1920* (New York: Hill and Wang, 1967), pp. 111–112. For a critique of Wiebe's assumption that professionals and professionalism were the moving forces in the undeniable social transformation that brought the professions new importance, see Walter P. Metzger, "A Spectre Is Haunting American Scholars: The Spectre of 'Professionalism,'" *Educational Researcher,* Aug.–Sept. 1987, pp. 71–79.

21. This is a major theme of Richard Hofstadter's *Age of Reform, From Bryan to FDR* (New York: Knopf, 1955), esp. pp. 148ff.

22. Karl Polanyi, *The Great Transformation: The Political and Economic Origins of Our Own Time* (Boston: Beacon Press, 1957), p. 52.

23. For example, see George W. Corner, *A History of the Rockefeller Institute* (New York: Rockefeller Institute Press, 1964).

24. See the discussion by Leonard Silk and Mark Silk, *The American Establishment* (New York: Basic Books, 1980).

25. On Frederick W. Taylor there is a considerable literature and considerable disagreement. See Monte Calvert, *The Mechanical Engineer in America: Structure and Aspirations, 1830–1910: Professional Cultures in Conflict* (Baltimore: Johns Hopkins University Press, 1967); and Samuel Haber, *Efficiency and Uplift* (Chicago: University of Chicago Press, 1964). For a skeptical view, see David Noble, *The Forces of Production: A Social History of Industrial Automation* (New York: Knopf, 1984).

26. Frederick Winslow Taylor, *The Principles of Scientific Management* (New York: HarperCollins, 1911), pp. 20–28.

27. See Sean Wilentz, *Chants Democratic: New York City and the Rise of the American Working Class* (New York: Oxford University Press, 1984); David Noble, *Forces of Production: A Social History of Industrial Automation* (New York: Knopf, 1984). See also David Montgomery, *The Fall of the House of Labor: The Workplace, the State, and American Labor Activism, 1865–1925* (Cambridge, Mass.: Cambridge University Press, 1987); and Alan Trachtenberg, *The Incorporation of America: American*

Culture in the Gilded Age (New York: Hill and Wang, 1982), pp. 64–69.

28. See Harold Perkin, "The Historical Perspective," in Burton R. Clark (ed.), *Perspectives on Higher Education: Eight Disciplinary Perspectives* (Berkeley and Los Angeles: University of California Press, 1984), pp. 17–55.

29. This process is described in detail by Lawrence Veysey, *The Emergence of the American University* (Chicago: University of Chicago Press, 1965). See also Bledstein (1976).

30. For the story of the efforts to establish social scientific knowledge as the basis for institutional autonomy, see Thomas Haskell, *The Emergence of Professional Science and the Nineteenth-Century Crisis of Authority* (Urbana: University of Illinois Press, 1977).

31. These developments are chronicled in Starr (1982), esp. chapters 3–6.

32. Quoted in Veysey (1965), p. 346.

33. W.E.B. Du Bois, "The Souls of Black Folk," in John Hope Franklin (ed.), *Three Negro Classics* (New York: Avon, 1962), esp. chapter 9.

34. Douglas Sloan, "The Teaching of Ethics in the American Undergraduate Curriculum, 1876–1976," in Daniel Callahan and Sissela Bok (eds.), *Ethics Teaching in Higher Education* (New York: Plenum Press, 1980), p. 4.

35. This characterization relies on Veysey (1965).

36. Max Weber, "Bureaucracy," in Hans Gerth and C. Wright Mills, *From Max Weber: Essays in Sociology* (New York: Oxford University Press, 1946), p. 243.

37. Wiebe, *Segmented Society* (1975), p. 25.

Chapter Three

1. James T. Kloppenberg, *Uncertain Victory: Social Democracy and Progressivism in European and American Thought, 1870–1920* (New York: Oxford University Press, 1986), p. 6.

2. For an overview of the issues surrounding the legal realist movement and sociological jurisprudence, see Robert Samuel Summers, *Instrumentalism and American Legal Theory* (Ithaca, N.Y.: Cornell University Press, 1982); and William Rumble, *American Legal Realism* (Ithaca, N.Y.: Cornell University Press, 1968).

3. See Samuel Haber, *Efficiency and Uplift* (1964), pp. 52–59 and 77–80.

4. Quoted in Alpheus Thomas Mason, *Brandeis: A Free Man's Life* (New York: Viking Press, 1946), p. 389.

5. See Robert L. Nelson, "Ideology, Practice and Professional Autonomy: Social Values and Client Relationships in the Large Law Firm," *Stanford Law Review*, 1985, *37*, 533ff.

6. Louis D. Brandeis, "The Opportunity in the Law," in *Business— A Profession* (Boston: Small, Maynard, 1914), pp. 315–316. This discussion of Brandeis follows David Luban, "The Noblesse Oblige Tradition in the Practice of Law" (unpublished manuscript, University of Maryland Law School, 1987).

7. Brandeis (1914), p. 317.

8. See John P. Frank, "The Legal Ethics of Louis D. Brandeis," *Stanford Law Review*, 1965, *17*, 683ff.

9. Aristotle, *Nicomachean Ethics*, Martin Ostwald trans. (Indianapolis: Bobbs-Merrill, 1965), 1141b, p. 157.

10. Perkin, *Rise of Professional Society* (1989), pp. 83–128.

11. Perkin (1989), pp. 138–139.

12. Herbert Croly, *The Promise of American Life*, Arthur R. Schlesinger, ed. (Cambridge, Mass.: Belknap Press of Harvard University Press, 1965 [1909]), p. 434.

13. John Dewey, "Democracy and Education" [1916], in *John Dewey: The Middle Works* (Carbondale: Southern Illinois University Press, 1978), vol. 9, p. 105.

14. Lawrence A. Cremin, *Traditions of American Education* (New York: Basic Books, 1977), p. 94.

15. John Dewey, *Individualism Old and New* (New York: Capricorn Books, 1962 [1929]), pp. 51 and 55.

16. Jane Addams, *Twenty Years at Hull House* (New York: New American Library, 1961), p. 297.

17. Addams (1961), p. 95.

18. Addams (1961), p. 297.

19. Addams (1961), p. 300.

20. Croly (1965 [1909]), pp. 431 and 439.

21. Quotation in Charles Forcey, *Crossroads of Liberalism: Croly, Weyl, Lippmann and the Progressive Era, 1900–1925* (New York: Oxford University Press, 1961), pp. 22–23.

22. Forcey (1961), p. 23.

23. Vincent Scully Jr., *Modern Architecture: The Architecture of Democracy*, rev. ed. (New York: Braziller, 1974), pp. 11–12.

24. Susanne K. Langer, *Feeling and Form: A Theory of Art* (New York: Scribner, 1953), quoted in Kevin Lynch, *The Image of the City* (Cambridge, Mass.: MIT Press, 1960), p. 13.

25. See John Rykwert, *The Idea of a Town* (Princeton, N.J.: Princeton University Press, 1976).

26. Scully (1974), p. 12.

27. Kenneth Frampton, *Modern Architecture: A Critical History*, rev. ed. (London: Thames and Hudson, 1985), pp. 23–25.

28. This is a major theme in John R. Stillgoe's study *The Common Landscape of America: 1580–1845* (New Haven, Conn.: Yale University Press, 1982). The long-term effects of this pattern are discussed in Richard M. Merelman, *Making Something of Ourselves: On Culture and Politics in the United States* (Berkeley: University of California Press, 1984), esp. pp. 53ff.

29. On Olmsted, see Thomas Bender, *Toward an Urban Vision* (Baltimore: Johns Hopkins University Press, 1982), chapter 7.

30. See the discussion by Bernard Michael Boyle, "Architectural Practice in America, 1865–1965: Idea and Reality," in Spiro Kostoff (ed.), *The Architect: Chapters in the History of the Profession* (New York: Oxford University Press, 1977), pp. 309–344.

31. Sullivan, quoted in Lewis Mumford, *The Brown Decades: A Study of the Arts in America, 1865–1895* (New York: Dover Books, 1971 [1931]), pp. 63 and 73.

32. Paul Boyer, *Urban Masses and Moral Order in America* (Cambridge, Mass.: Harvard University Press, 1978), p. 272.

33. Quoted in Thomas S. Hines, *Burnham of Chicago: Architect and Planner* (Chicago: University of Chicago Press, 1974), p. 174.

34. Quoted in Hines (1974), pp. 328–329.

35. Hines (1974), p. xvii.

36. For an overview of these contrasting developments, see John Friedmann and Clyde Weaver, *Territory and Function: The Evolution of Urban Planning* (Berkeley and Los Angeles: University of California Press, 1979), pp. 19–86.

37. Lewis Mumford, *The Culture of Cities* (Orlando, Fla.: Harcourt Brace, 1966 [1938]), pp. 484–485.

38. Lewis Mumford, *Sticks and Stones: A Study of American Architecture and Civilization*, 2nd rev. ed. (New York: Dover, 1954 [1924]), p. 60.

39. Mumford (1954 [1924]), p. 113.

40. Mumford (1954 [1924]), pp. 110 and 106.

41. Hannah Arendt, *The Human Condition* (Chicago: University of Chicago Press, 1958), p. 153.

42. Arendt (1958), p. 153.

43. See, for instance, Thorstein Veblen, *Engineers and the Price System* (New York: Viking, 1921).

44. See the treatment of Mumford by Casey Nelson Blake, *Beloved Community: The Cultural Criticism of Randolph Bourne, Van Wyck Brooks, Waldo Frank, and Lewis Mumford* (Chapel Hill: University of North Carolina Press, 1990), esp. pp. 290–291.

45. Walter Lippmann, *Preface to Morals* (New York: Time-Life Books, 1964 [1929]), pp. 106–107.

Chapter Four

1. John Locke, *Second Treatise of Government*, C. B. Macpherson, ed. (Indianapolis: Hackett, 1980), chap. V, 49, p. 29.

2. National Resources Planning Board, Pacific Southwest Regional Office, "After the War—New Jobs in the Pacific

Southwest," quoted by Mel Scott, *The San Francisco Bay Area: A Metropolis in Perspective,* 2nd ed. (Berkeley and Los Angeles: University of California Press, 1985), p. 258.

3. See Henry R. Luce, "The American Century," *Life,* Feb. 11, 1941, pp. 61–65.

4. See, for example, the description of the formation of American foreign policy in the early postwar era by Walter Isaacson and Evan Thomas, *The Wise Men: Six Friends and the World They Made* (New York: Simon and Schuster, 1986).

5. Bell (1973), pp. xii and 126–127.

6. Bell, "Labor in Post-Industrial Society," *Dissent,* Winter 1972, *19,* 70–78. See also the corroborating estimate by sociologist Eli Ginzburg in "The Professionalization of the U.S. Labor Force," *Scientific American,* 1979, *240*(3).

7. Bell, "Post-Industrial Society" (1972), pp. 373ff.

8. Bell (1972), p. 377.

9. Perkin (1989), pp. 3–4.

10. Perkin (1989), pp. 331ff. T. H. Marshall's notion of "social citizenship" has found new expression in the United States in the work of Michael Walzer; see the latter's *Spheres of Justice: A Defense of Pluralism and Equality* (New York: Basic Books, 1983).

11. John Kenneth Galbraith, *The New Industrial State* (Boston: Little, Brown, 1967), pp. 58–59.

12. Talcott Parsons, "Professions," vol. 12 of *International Encyclopedia of the Social Sciences,* David L. Sills, ed. (New York: Macmillan-Free Press, 1968), p. 545.

13. Parsons (1968), p. 536.

14. Parsons (1968), p. 542.

15. Parsons (1968), p. 543.

16. Parsons (1968), p. 536.

17. Cited in David Halberstam, *The Best and the Brightest* (Greenwich, Conn.: Fawcett, 1969), p. 272.

18. The reference is to Marshall's speech at Princeton in the spring of 1947, in which he exhorted his audience to take to heart the

lesson of Athens' overextension during the Peloponnesian Wars; quoted in Forrest C. Pogue, *George C. Marshall: Statesman, 1945–1959* (New York: Viking Press, 1987), p. 524.

19. See Peter Steinfels's knowledgeable tour through the neoconservative movement in its heyday: *The Neo-Conservatives: The Men Who Are Changing America's Politics* (New York: Simon and Schuster, 1979).

20. See William H. Whyte Jr., *The Organization Man* (New York: Simon and Schuster, 1956).

21. Clark Kerr, *The Uses of the University* (Cambridge, Mass.: Harvard University Press, 1972), pp. 87–88.

22. Ivan Illich, *Tools for Conviviality* (New York: HarperCollins, 1973), pp. 11–13. See also Illich's *Celebration of Awareness: A Call for Institutional Revolution* (Garden City, N.Y.: Doubleday, 1970).

23. See in this connection the work of Ronald Inglehart, *Culture Shift in Advanced Industrial Society* (Princeton, N.J.: Princeton University Press, 1990).

24. See James Davison Hunter, *Culture Wars: The Struggle to Define America* (New York: Basic Books, 1991).

25. See Lester Thurow, *The Zero-Sum Society: Distribution and the Possibilities for Economic Change* (New York: Basic Books, 1980).

26. The quoted phrase is the title of John Kenneth Galbraith's book *Culture of Contentment* (Boston: Houghton Mifflin, 1992). On the effects of recent economic changes upon distribution of income and social consequences, see Kevin Phillips, *The Politics of Rich and Poor: Wealth and the American Electorate in the Reagan Aftermath* (New York: Random House, 1990). At the same time, other observers have documented the tendency for increasing pressure in professional and managerial occupations to crowd out all other aspects of life. See Juliet B. Schor, *The Overworked American: The Unexpected Decline of Leisure* (New York: Basic Books, 1992); and Amy Saltzman, *Downshifting: Revisiting Success on a Slower Track* (New York: HarperCollins, 1991).

27. Barbara Ehrenreich, *Fear of Falling: The Inner Life of the Middle Class* (New York: Pantheon Books, 1989), p. 198.
28. See the discussion in Chapter Two, "The Free Professions and the Search for Professional Integrity."

Chapter Five

1. As in Thomas J. Kuhn, *The Structure of Scientific Revolutions* (Chicago: University of Chicago Press, 1962).
2. On this theme, see Jürgen Habermas, *The Structural Transformation of the Public Sphere: An Inquiry into a Category of Bourgeois Society* (Cambridge, Mass.: MIT Press, 1989). Habermas's perspective intersects directly with that of the pragmatist Progressives, and his later work has come to take conscious direction from Dewey in particular.
3. Croly's vision for a renewed American nation is discussed in Chapter Three; see also Croly (1965 [1909]).
4. Daniel Bell, *The Cultural Contradictions of Capitalism* (New York: Basic Books, 1976). See also the argument of Colin Campbell that modern hedonism, no less than the modern ethic of achievement, is the secularized outcome of a Protestant culture that trained individuals to attend to and control inner states, including feeling, thereby creating a technology of emotional self-manipulation that could be turned to self-gratification as well as to the service of God; Campbell, *The Romantic Ethic and the Spirit of Modern Consumerism* (Oxford and New York: Basil Blackwell, 1987).
5. David Brooks, *Bobos in Paradise: The New Upper Class and How They Got There* (New York: Simon and Schuster, 2000).
6. Florida (2002).
7. These parallel, though contrasting, logics define the "utilitarian" and "expressive" strands of American individualism. For a description and critique, see Bellah and others, *Habits of the Heart* (1985). See also Alasdair MacIntyre's contrast of "manager" and

"therapist" in *After Virtue: A Study in Moral Theory*, 2nd ed. (Notre Dame, Ind.: Notre Dame University Press, 1984), pp. 22–29.

8. Louis Auchincloss, *Diary of a Yuppie* (Boston: Houghton Mifflin, 1986), p. 26.

9. For a remarkable exploration of these issues through psychological case histories, see David Levinson, *Seasons of a Man's Life* (New York: Ballantine Books, 1978). These findings were given a more upbeat packaging by one of Levinson's collaborators, Gail Sheehy, in *Passages: Predictable Phases of Adult Life* (New York: Bantam Books, 1977).

10. The first strategy corresponds to what theorists of collective action call the "free rider" problem. The second is a version of the "prisoner's dilemma." In both cases, only cooperative activity provides an enduring solution to the problem of individual security and well-being. For an overview of these concepts and their applications, see Elinor Ostrom, *Governing the Commons: The Evolution of Institutions for Collective Action* (New York: Cambridge University Press, 1990).

11. See Cornel West, "Nihilism in Black America," *Dissent*, Spring 1991, pp. 221–226.

12. Reich, *The Work of Nations* (1991); Robert Reich, *The Future of Success: Working and Living in the New Economy* (New York: Vintage, 2000).

13. Reich (1991), p. 81.

14. Reich (1991), p. 87.

15. Reich (1991), p. 178. Compare Reich's figure with the demographic study done in the late 1970s by sociologist Ginzburg (1979), who described about one-quarter of the workforce as "professional and managerial."

16. Reich (1991), p. 230.

17. Reich (1991), p. 309.

18. Brooks (2000) and Florida (2002).

19. Reich (2000), p. 6.

20. Reich (2000), p. 6.

21. Robert Frank, *Luxury Fever: Money and Happiness in an Age of Excess* (New York: Basic Books, 1999).

22. David Callahan, *The Cheating Culture: Why More Americans Are Doing Wrong to Get Ahead* (Orlando, Fla.: Harcourt Brace, 2004).

23. For a wide-ranging effort to analyze this complex phenomenon, see Martin E. Marty and R. Scott Appleby (eds.), *Fundamentalisms Comprehended* (Chicago: University of Chicago Press, 1995).

24. Milton Friedman (1982 [1962]).

25. John Judis, *The Paradox of American Democracy: Elites, Special Interests, and the Betrayal of the Public Trust* (New York: Random House, 2000).

26. See John Dewey, *Reconstruction in Philosophy*, enlarged ed. (Boston: Beacon Press, 1957), esp. pp. 26–27 and 51ff. See also Richard J. Bernstein, *Praxis and Action* (Philadelphia: University of Pennsylvania Press, 1971), pp. 200–229; Robert C. Neville, *Reconstruction of Thinking* (Albany: State University of New York Press, 1981); Richard Rorty, *Consequences of Pragmatism* (Minneapolis: University of Minnesota Press, 1982); Cornel West, *The American Evasion of Philosophy: The Genealogy of Pragmatism* (Madison: University of Wisconsin Press, 1989); and Robert B. Westbrook, *John Dewey and American Democracy* (Ithaca, N.Y.: Cornell University Press, 1991). The discussion here also draws upon the contemporary development of Deweyan practical reasoning by Charles W. Anderson, in *Pragmatic Liberalism* (Chicago: University of Chicago Press, 1989) and *Prescribing the Life of the Mind: An Essay on the Purpose of the University and the Cultivation of Practical Reason* (Madison: University of Wisconsin Press, 1993), esp. pp. 11–23.

27. The notion of "human capital" has come to play an important role in contemporary social research in highlighting the

practical significance of shared expectations and moral ties. For an explication of the concept, see James S. Coleman, *Foundations of Social Theory* (Cambridge, Mass.: Harvard University Press, 1990), pp. 300–321.

28. For an elaboration of this "pedagogical" dimension of institutions, see Robert N. Bellah, Richard Madsen, William M. Sullivan, Ann Swidler, and Steven M. Tipton, *The Good Society* (New York: Knopf, 1991), pp. 1–18 and 287–304.

29. Philip Selznick speaks of "institutional integrity" as a quality of organizational behavior when the members of an organization have come to understand themselves as having responsibilities toward the larger interdependent processes in which they take part. See Philip Selznick, *The Moral Commonwealth: Social Theory and the Promise of Community* (Berkeley and Los Angeles: University of California Press, 1992), pp. 357ff.

30. The use of the term *public philosophy* here draws on earlier work; see my *Reconstructing Public Philosophy* (Berkeley and Los Angeles: University of California Press, 1982), esp. pp. 9–10.

31. Deborah Prothrow-Stith, *Deadly Consequences: How Violence Is Destroying Our Teenage Population and a Plan to Begin Solving the Problem* (New York: HarperCollins, 1991).

32. A number of scholars have recently taken up the issue of causes, remedies, and responsibilities for these massive problems, thereby giving rise to a new debate that forms part of the larger context for Prothrow-Stith's work. See William Julius Wilson, *The Truly Disadvantaged: The Inner City, the Underclass, and Public Policy* (Chicago: University of Chicago Press, 1987); Roger Lane, *William Dorsey's Philadelphia and Ours: On the Past and Future of the Black City in America* (New York: Oxford University Press, 1991); see also West, "Nihilism in Black America" (1991), pp. 221–226.

33. These and subsequent quotations are taken from an interview conducted by the author with Deborah Prothrow-Stith in Boston, Oct. 25, 1991.

Chapter Six

1. Michael Burrage, "From Practice to School-Based Education: Patterns of Conflict and Accommodation in England, France, and the United States," in Sheldon Rothblatt and Bjorn Wittrock (eds.), *The European and American University Since 1800: Historical and Sociological Essays* (Cambridge, UK: Cambridge University Press, 1993), pp. 142–190, quote on p. 142.

2. Jerome Bruner, *Actual Minds, Possible Worlds* (Cambridge, Mass.: Harvard University Press, 1986).

3. Freidson (1994), p. 69.

4. Perkin (1984).

5. Olivier Zunz, *Why the American Century?* (Chicago: University of Chicago Press, 1998), p. 6.

6. Kenneth M. Ludmerer, *A Time to Heal: American Medical Education from the Turn of the Century to the Eve of Managed Care* (New York: Oxford University Press, 1999), pp. 3-25.

7. Charles Bosck, *Forgive and Remember* (Chicago: University of Chicago Press, 1979).

8. John D. Bransford, Ann L. Brown, and Rodney R. Cocking (eds.), *How People Learn: Brain, Mind, Experience, and School* (Washington, D.C.: Committee on Developments in the Science of Learning, National Research Council, 1999).

9. Christopher Lasch, *The Revolt of the Elites* (New York: Norton, 1995).

10. Cited in Richard Bono, "Demands on Rabbis Are Increasing," *Jewish Exponent*, May 5, 1989, p. 3.

11. David Kelsey, *Between Athens and Berlin: The Theological Education Debate* (Grand Rapids, Mich.: Eerdmans, 1993).

12. Rosalind Williams, *Retooling* (Cambridge, Mass.: MIT Press, 2002), pp. 22–40.

13. *Report to the Faculty of the Massachusetts Institute of Technology, Committee on Educational Survey, Warren K. Lewis, chairman* (Cambridge, Mass.: Technology Press of the Massachusetts Institute of Technology, 1949).

14. *Report to the Faculty* . . . (1949), p. 67.
15. *Report to the Faculty* . . . (1949), p. 69.

Chapter Seven

1. Derek Bok, *Universities in the Marketplace: The Commercialization of Higher Education* (Princeton, N.J.: Princeton University Press, 2003).
2. See James Herschberg and James B. Conant, *From Harvard to Hiroshima and the Making of the Nuclear Age* (New York: Knopf, 1993).
3. Nicholas Lemann has argued in *The Big Test: The Secret History of the American Meritocracy* (New York: Farrar, Straus, and Giroux, 1999).
4. Randall Collins, *The Credential Society* (New York: Academic Press, 1979).
5. Derek Bok (1993).
6. David Kirp, *Shakespeare, Einstein, and the Bottom Line: The Marketing of Higher Education* (Cambridge, Mass.: Harvard University Press, 2003).
7. Mark Finkelstein, "The Morphing of the American Academic Profession," *Liberal Education*, Fall 2003, pp. 6–14.
8. Finkelstein (2003), p. 12.
9. Patti J. Gumport, "Academic Restructuring, Organizational Change and Institutional Imperatives," *Higher Education*, 2000, 39(1), 67–91.
10. Auguste Comte, *Introduction to Positive Philosophy*, Frederick Ferre, ed. (Indianapolis: Hackett, 1988).
11. Ernest Gellner, *Plough, Sword, and Book: The Structure of Human History* (Chicago: University of Chicago Press, 1988), p. 262.
12. Stephen Toulmin, *Return to Reason* (Cambridge, Mass.: Harvard University Press, 2000).
13. Thomas Kuhn, *The Structure of Scientific Revolutions*, 2nd ed. (Chicago: University of Chicago Press, 1962).

14. Hubert Dreyfus and Stuart Dreyfus, with Tom Athanasiou, *Mind over Machine: The Power of Human Intuition and Expertise in the Era of the Computer* (New York: Free Press, 1986).

15. Herbert Simon, "Studying Human Intelligence by Creating Artificial Intelligence," *American Scientist*, May-June 1981, pp. 308ff.

16. Patricia Benner, with Christine A. Tanner and Catherine A. Chesla, *Expertise in Nursing Practice: Caring, Clinical Judgment, and Ethics* (New York: Springer, 1996).

17. Mike Rose, "Our Hands Will Know: The Development of Tactile Diagnostic Skill—Teaching, Learning, and Situated Cognition in a Physical Therapy Program," *Anthropology and Education Quarterly*, 1999, 30(2), 133–160.

18. Benner (1996), p. 309.

19. Donald Schön, *The Reflective Practitioner: How Professionals Think in Action* (New York: Basic Books, 1983).

20. Dreyfus and Dreyfus (1986), p. 121.

Chapter Eight

1. Quoted in *Health Letter* [Public Citizen Health Research Group], 1989, 5(12), pp. 2–3. The *Time* data this article cites is confirmed by a Harris/Harvard School of Public Health Survey reported in the same article.

2. One explanation locates the problem in the differing professional and ethical bases of public health versus acute care approaches in the development of medicine; see Starr (1982) and Larry R. Churchill, *Rationing Health Care in America: Perceptions and Principles of Justice* (Notre Dame, Ind.: Notre Dame University Press, 1987).

3. See Ehrenreich, *Fear of Falling* (1989).

4. Max Weber, *The Protestant Ethic and the Spirit of Capitalism*, Talcott Parsons, trans. (New York: Scribner, 1958). See also Gerth and Mills, *From Max Weber* (1946).

5. Weber's general conception of rationalization, of which this is one aspect, has had an enormous impact on twentieth-century

social thought. David Riesman's famous analysis of the loss of "inner-directedness" in modern organizations could be taken as one application, as is Alasdair MacIntyre's analysis of "bureaucratic individualism." See Riesman, with Nathan Glazer and Reuel Denney, *The Lonely Crowd: A Study of the Changing American Character* (New Haven, Conn.: Yale University Press, 1950); and MacIntyre, *After Virtue* (1984).

6. The literature on professional ethics within this "applied ethics" approach is considerable and contains a variety of points of view as to how ethical principles are to be rationally grounded. The common theme among what can be characterized as deductive theories, however, is that principles can be grounded independently of the practices and contexts for which they serve as norms. Because of this independent and foundational position of ethical theory, ethical reasoning can be analyzed for its logical validity quite independently of the question of whether the principles or norms involved are judged ethically valid. Empirical facts about situations are highly relevant to ethical decision making, though, as they help identify those aspects of situations that are ethically relevant—that is, those which can be subsumed under general principles and rules. For some representative samples of this approach, see Michael D. Bayles, *Professional Ethics* (New York: Wadsworth, 1981); Alan H. Goldman, *The Moral Foundations of Professional Ethics* (Lanham, Md.: Rowman and Littlefield, 1980); and Robert M. Veatch, *A Theory of Medical Ethics* (New York: Basic Books, 1981). The major progenitor of contemporary applied ethics is John Rawls, *A Theory of Justice* (Cambridge, Mass.: Harvard University Press, 1971).

7. Veatch (1981), p. 5.

8. Veatch (1981), p. 5.

9. Veatch (1981), pp. 113ff.

10. The reference is to Aristotle's opening discussion in Book One of Nicomachean Ethics.

11. Immanuel Kant, "On the Proverb: That May Be True in Theory, But Is of No Practical Use," in *Perpetual Peace and Other*

Essays, Ted Humphrey, trans. (Indianapolis: Hackett, 1983),
p. 61.

12. Attention to ethos is usually linked to the Aristotelian tradition in moral philosophy. This tradition has received important
restatement by a number of recent thinkers. See MacIntyre
(1984). For an application of these ideas in religious ethics, see
Stanley Hauerwas, *A Community of Character: Toward a Constructive Christian Social Ethic* (Notre Dame, Ind.: University of
Notre Dame Press, 1982). For this approach in the realm of
professional ethics, see William F. May, "Professional Ethics:
Setting, Terrain, and Teacher," in Callahan and S. Bok (1980),
pp. 204–244. For the importance of ethos in the empirical
study of professional life, see Eliot Freidson, *The Profession of
Medicine: A Study of the Sociology of Applied Knowledge* (New
York: HarperCollins, 1970).

13. The virtue approach has affinities with the casuistic approach
to ethics, a tradition of reasoning that has much in common
with legal reasoning. Like the ethics of character, casuistry is
also undergoing a revival. In casuistry, the aim is to blend reasoning in its inductive form (moving from decisive cases
toward general norms), with the deductive approach (moving
from principles to cases), so that principles and cases mutually
influence each other. See Stephen Toulmin and Albert Jonsen,
The Abuse of Casuistry (Berkeley and Los Angeles: University
of California Press, 1988).

14. For an overview of the liberal-communitarian debate, see
Markate Daly, *Communitarianism: A New Public Ethics* (Bel-
mont, Calif.: Wadsworth, 1994).

15. Mihaly Csikszentmihalyi, *Flow: The Psychology of Optimal Experience* (New York: HarperCollins, 1990).

16. Csikszentmihalyi (1990), p. 65.

17. Csikszentmihalyi (1990), p. 71.

18. Csikszentmihalyi (1990), p. 205.

19. This approach was pioneered by the pragmatic thinkers
Charles Sanders Peirce, John Dewey, and George Herbert

Mead. See especially Dewey's *Human Nature and Conduct: An Introduction to Social Psychology* (New York: Random House, Modern Library, 1930 [1922]) and Mead's *Mind, Self, and Society*, George W. Morris, ed. (Chicago: University of Chicago Press, 1934). H. Richard Niebuhr developed the implications of this approach as a distinct method for theological ethics in *The Responsible Self: An Essay in Christian Moral Philosophy* (San Francisco: Harper San Francisco, 1978 [1963]). Recently, Eugene Halton has argued for the power of this approach in social theory and criticism in *Meaning and Modernity: Social Theory in the Pragmatic Attitude* (Chicago: University of Chicago Press, 1986).

20. Charles Taylor presents a detailed argument for this claim, starting from the value of personal authenticity itself, in *The Ethics of Authenticity* (Cambridge, Mass.: Harvard University Press, 1993).

21. Pogue (1987), p. 148.

22. Pogue (1987), pp. 210ff.

23. Daniel Callahan, *Setting Limits: Medical Goals in an Aging Society* (New York: Simon and Schuster, 1987), p. 26.

24. Callahan (1987), p. 19.

25. Callahan (1987), p. 135.

26. Callahan (1987), pp. 97–98.

27. Callahan (1987), p. 96.

28. Callahan (1987), pp. 157–158.

29. Callahan (1987), pp. 197–198.

30. It is noteworthy that Callahan, along with Willard Gaylin, cofounder of the Hastings Center for the Study of Society, Ethics, and Life Sciences, has for twenty years played a sustaining role in promoting ethical reflection of all three types in the health field.

31. Judis (2000).

32. See William A. Galston, *Liberal Purposes: Goods, Virtues and Diversity in the Liberal State* (Cambridge, Mass.: Cambridge University Press, 1991).

33. See William F. May, *The Physician's Covenant* (Philadelphia: Westminster Press, 1983).

34. For example, see Carol Gilligan, *In a Different Voice: Psychological Theory and Women's Development* (Cambridge, Mass.: Harvard University Press, 1982); and Mary Field Belenky, Blythe Clinchy, Nancy Goldberger, and Jill Tarule, *Women's Ways of Knowing: The Development of Self, Voice, and Mind* (New York: Basic Books, 1986). See also Jean Bethke Elshtain, *Public Man, Private Woman: Women in Social Work and Political Thought* (Princeton, N.J.: Princeton University Press, 1981). For a discussion of the implications of these issues for professional legal judgment and practice, see Rand Jack and Diana Crowley Jack, *Moral Vision and Professional Decisions: The Changing Values of Women and Men Lawyers* (Cambridge, Mass.: Cambridge University Press, 1989).

35. Quoted by William Greider, *Who Will Tell the People: The Betrayal of American Democracy* (New York: Simon and Schuster, 1992), p. 223.

Conclusion

1. Perkin (1989).

2. Perkin (1989), p. 437.

3. Perkin (1989), p. 501.

4. R. H. Tawney, *The Acquisitive Society* (Orlando, Fla.: Harcourt Brace, 1948 [1920]), pp. 92 and 98.

5. Tawney (1948), p. 150.

6. Alfred North Whitehead, *Science and the Modern World* (New York: Macmillan, 1967 [1925]), p. 196.

Index